MICK MACKEY

HURLING LEGEND IN A TROUBLED COUNTY

HENRY MARTIN, author of the widely acclaimed *Unlimited Heartbreak*, played underage with Galbally in Limerick and still plays club football. He played hurling for Garryspillane when hurling in Galbally disbanded and has been a GAA referee since 2002. A graduate of the University of Limerick and qualified teacher, he wrote a weekly GAA column in the *Limerick Leader* and now writes for *Hurling World* and the website *An Fear Rua*.

MICK MACKEY

HURLING LEGEND IN A TROUBLED COUNTY

HENRY MARTIN

The Collins Press

First published in 2011 by
The Collins Press
West Link Park
Doughcloyne
Wilton
Cork

British Library Cataloguing in Publication data

Martin, Henry, 1976 or 7-
Mick Mackey : hurling legend in a troubled county.
1. Mackey, Michael. 2. Hurling players—Ireland—
Biography. 3. Hurling (Game)—Ireland—Limerick
(County)—History—20th century.
I. Title
796.3'5'092-dc22

ISBN-13: 9781848891012

Typesetting by Carrigboy Typsetting Services
Typeset in Baskerville
Printed in Malta by Gutenberg Press Limited

Cover images: *(front)* Mackey receives the Liam McCarthy cup at the 1940 All-Ireland final; *(back)*: the famous Mackey v Ring photograph taken at the 1957 Munster final by Justin Nelson. Mick Mackey, an umpire for the game, allowed a Tipperary goal which the referee overruled. Christy Ring, leaving the pitch injured, has words with Mackey.

Dedicated to the late Ger Power (RIP) of Knocklong,
who died on 10 November 2010. Ger was a positive influence on
many people, and he managed to reawaken my enthusiasm for
English as a fifteen-year-old, when all seemed lost. Without his
inspiration, hard work, and patience, I would have struggled to
complete my secondary school education. I will forever
be indebted to him. May he rest in peace.

CONTENTS

☙

ACKNOWLEDGEMENTS

ભ

Late one night in December 2008, I received a phone call from a former Galbally GAA teammate, Dessie Hayes. He was watching a Magners League game at Herbert's Bar in Lisnagry and got talking to Turlough Herbert. Both men had been at the launch of *Unlimited Heartbreak – The Inside Story of Limerick Hurling* some weeks earlier but hadn't spoken to one another on the night and would only have known one another vaguely. Inevitably, *Unlimited Heartbreak* came up for discussion.

Desmond, as I sometimes call him, decided to ring me and put Turlough on the phone. He mentioned how intrigued he was about the impact his father's injury had on Limerick hurling and said that there were a number of people around who could provide greater depth on the Mackey era. Turlough has been a huge assistance to me, putting me in touch with the right people and encouraging them to agree to interviews.

Mick Mackey is a Limerick legend and a sporting icon, and it was an honour to be asked to write a book about him. *The Mackey Story* by Seán Murphy and Séamus Ó Ceallaigh was an excellent book. Seán Murphy has numerous publications to his name and would have seen both sides of the coin, writing with and without the benefit of technology. However, Séamus Ó Ceallaigh wrote all his material in the days when the long slog was the only method. In many ways it's easier for a 'cheeky upstart' like me to become an author when I have modern contraptions such as laptops, USB dictaphones and A3 scanners.

While *Unlimited Heartbreak* wasn't flavour of the month at local level, it received many complimentary reviews at national level. I would dedicate those solely to James Lundon. His amazing attention to detail when proofreading is phenomenal. James threw his weight behind this book too, and while we had heated discussions over the content it didn't deter him from his stated objective – to make it as presentable as possible to the readers.

The list of others I need to thank is endless and sincere apologies to anyone I have omitted. Of Mick Mackey's family, I would like to thank his son, Greg Mackey, and his granddaughter, Catherine Doyle, for their assistance. On John Mackey's side I would like to thank his daughters, Cora Moroney (nee Mackey) and Vera Mulcahy (nee Mackey). I wish to offer my sincere thanks to John Mackey's granddaughter, Niamh Mulcahy, a sporting icon in her own right, who provided valuable assistance through the duration of this project.

My brother, Johnny, put his skills as a proofreader to the test for the second time and brought James Boyce on board as well. I wish to thank them for their efforts. I would like to thank Paul Kennedy, the respected former principal of

Lisnagry National School, for his valued assistance and local knowledge. I would also like to thank the man Ollie Moran christened 'Google' on RTÉ TV. George 'Google' Lee is the only human search engine in Castleconnell and whenever I needed to find someone, I called to George at Shannon Stores for directions. Ahane GAA club were most helpful in every way they could, most especially Willie Keane, Donal Morrissey, Bernie Quirke and Louis Quirke. Thanks also to Dan Beary, the man who opened the Limerick GAA museum in 2010. Thanks to Eugene Hogan who interviewed Timmy Ryan 'Good Boy' as a youngster and has travelled quite a distance since in the PR world.

Karl Quinn maintained the Tulla contribution by enlisting his father John Quinn to help me out. Others to help were Michael Hayes, Mike Linihan, Orla O'Donovan, Pakie 'Dingle' Bourke, John Reale, Diarmuid Grace, Joe Lyons, Brother James Dormer, Barry Duggan (*Irish Independent*), Mike Meade, Noel Tobin (Newport), Derek Russell, Dick Fleming (Waterford), Tom Power (Waterford), Jim Murphy (Waterford), Gerry Corbett (Galway), Liam Cahill (*An Fear Rua*), Frank Burke, Jackie Cahill, Enda McEvoy, John Power (Mullinavat), Barry Hickey and Paul Kinsella (Kilkenny County Board), librarians at the University of Limerick, Mary Immaculate College and Limerick City libraries, Séamus Walsh, Hughie Murphy (Kilfinane), Mary White, Francis Byrnes, John Healy (Cobh), John Arnold (Bartlemy), Matt Givens, Pat Danaher (Clare), Dominic Williams (Wexford), Jamie Keaty, Ger Luby, son of the legendary Johnny Luby, Tim Horgan, Patsy Coffey, Éamonn Cosgrave and last but not least Tommy Moynihan – the award-winning servant to the Munster Council.

I would also like to thank the people associated with Galbally GAA club who have assisted me to date and have worked with me from underage up to adult level – Jack Dillon, Tommy Sheehan, Declan Hickey, John Kiely, Ger Cussen, John Scully, Tom Casey, Johnny Cummins and Johnny Wallace.

Many thanks to all those at The Collins Press who were thorough and professional at all times. Many thanks also to Aonghus Meaney for his editing skills.

Finally, I would like to thank my mother, Terri, my aunt, Milly Hanly, my uncle, Christy Murphy, and my siblings, Maria, Siobhan and Johnny. To you all I am eternally grateful.

HENRY MARTIN

LIST OF INTERVIEWEES

☙

Andy Fleming – Former Waterford hurler and Railway Cup star with Munster

Arthur Graham – Former Ahane hurler and secretary of the Ahane club

Brendan Fullam – Well-known historian and multiple author on GAA-related topics.

Catherine Doyle – Granddaughter of Mick Mackey and daughter of Ruth Doyle (nee Mackey)

Christy Murphy – Maternal uncle of the author, former selector on the Patrickswell senior hurling team and the proprietor of the well-known hurling establishment 'The Cuchulainn Lounge' in Patrickswell

Dermot Kelly – Former Limerick hurler and lifelong friend of Mick Mackey who starred at centre-forward for 'Mackey's Greyhounds' in the 1955 Munster final

Donie Nealon – Former Tipperary hurler and Railway Cup star with Munster who served as secretary to the Munster Council for many years

Fr Liam Kelly – Former Limerick and Ahane hurler and a lifelong friend of Mick Mackey

Fr Liam Ryan – Captain of 'Mackey's Greyhounds' in 1955 and the only Cappamore man to captain Limerick to a Munster senior hurling championship

Fr Séamus Ryan – Brother to Fr Liam Ryan, and centre-back on the team that won the Munster championship in 1955

Frankie Walsh – Former Waterford hurler and Railway Cup star with Munster

Gerard Cussen – Nephew of former Limerick football stalwart and long-term selector P. J. Cussen

Gerry Piggott – Life president of Ahane GAA club and a lifelong friend of Mick Mackey

Greg Mackey – Son of Mick Mackey

Jim Fitzgerald – Former Newport hurler and brother of Danno Fitzgerald who hurled for Ahane. Father of former Irish rugby player John 'Pako' Fitzgerald

Jim Hogan – Long-serving Limerick hurling goalkeeper who played championship hurling in three decades and won county senior hurling championship medals in both Limerick and Cork

Jim O'Donoghue – Former Limerick hurler who won a National Hurling League medal in 1947

Jimmy Butler Coffey – Former All-Ireland medal winner with Tipperary who subsequently declared for Cappamore, Ahane and Limerick at the end of his career.

Jimmy Smyth – Former Clare hurler, Munster Railway Cup star, inter-county referee and long-term Croke Park official

John Lenihan – Former Gaelic footballer with Anglesboro and Galtee Rovers. He is also the father of Bríd de Brún, principal of Ardscoil Rís, to whom Limerick GAA is indebted for facilitating an upsurge in hurling at her school.

John Mulcahy – Former Limerick, Cappamore and Ahane hurler

John Ryan – Former Ahane hurler

Johnny Wall – Former workmate of Mick Mackey, and a former treasurer of Clare County Board

Martin White – Former Kilkenny hurling star from the 1930s

Maurice Regan – Former Kilfinane hurler and noted Kilfinane historian, specialising in sporting history

Michael Hynes – Former Ahane hurler and a brother-in-law to Tony Herbert

Mick Rainsford – Lifetime Limerick hurling supporter and lifelong friend of John and Stephen McDonagh of the famed Bruree hurling family

Mickey 'The Rattler' Byrne – Former All-Ireland winning hurler with Tipperary

Ned Wheeler – Former All-Ireland winning hurler with Wexford

Paddy Tuohy – Noted Castleconnell historian

Pat O'Dwyer – Limerick Bord na nÓg official, former Limerick underage dual player and referee

P. J. Keane – Former Roscommon, Limerick and Ahane hurler and a member of the famed Keane dynasty

Ralph Prendergast – Former Limerick and Claughaun hurler and a lifelong friend of Mick Mackey

Séamus Power – Former Waterford hurler, Munster Railway Cup star and Munster Council delegate

Séamus Walsh – Former chairman of Ahane GAA club and an umpire to Pat O'Connor on All-Ireland hurling final days

Seán Duggan – Former Galway and Connacht goalkeeper

Seán Óg Herbert – Former Limerick and Dublin hurler and full-time GAA coach in Limerick schools

Seán Ryan (Malachy) – Former Ahane hurler

Tommy Barrett – Former Tipperary hurler and GAA official

Tim Horgan – Multiple GAA author and Cork GAA historian

Tommy Cooke – Former All-Ireland winner with Limerick from 1940

Tony Herbert – Former Railway Cup star and Dublin and Limerick hurler, winning an All-Ireland medal in 1940 and both Munster and Leinster championships

Vera Mulcahy – Daughter of John Mackey and former Limerick camogie star

Willie John Daly – Former Cork hurling centre-back

Willie Keane – Former Limerick hurler and lifelong Ahane committee member

To those who have passed to their eternal reward – Andy Fleming, Jimmy Butler Coffey, Michael Hynes – I am grateful for their contributions, and their memory will live on forever in this publication.

PLAYING ACHIEVEMENTS

ɞ

Ahane:
Senior hurling championships: 15
Senior football championships: 5
Junior hurling championships: 2
Minor hurling championships: 1

Clonlara:
Minor hurling championships: 1

Limerick:
National League titles: 5
Munster championships: 5
All-Ireland titles: 3

Munster:
Inter-provincial championships: 8

Army:
All-Army championships: 1

Mackey also won Oireachtas and Thomond Feis titles with Limerick

For the record, the following constitutes the 31-game unbeaten run:
15 October 1933 – National League vs Tipperary – Won 2-7 to 1-4
29 October 1933 – National League vs Offaly – Won 9-3 to 2-4
12 November 1933 – National League vs Galway – Won 5-6 to 2-3
10 December 1933 – National League vs Clare – Won 6-3 to 2-3
25 March 1934 – National League final vs Dublin – Won 3-6 to 3-3
29 April 1934 – Ennis Tournament vs Galway – Won 6-4 to 4-9
6 May 1934 – Fermoy Tournament vs Cork – Won 4-3 to 2-5
13 May 1934 – Thomond Feis vs Clare – Won 3-7 to 0-5
21 May 1934 – Ward Cup in London vs Kilkenny – Won 5-4 to 4-5
3 June 1934 – Hospital Trust Medals vs Dublin – Won 6-9 to 1-2
17 June 1934 – Thomond Feis final vs Cork – Won 3-6 to 3-4
24 June 1934 – Munster championship vs Clare – Won 6-4 to 3-2
8 July 1934 – Munster championship semi-final vs Cork – Won 3-4 to 2-2
22 July 1934 – Munster championship final vs Waterford – Won 4-8 to 2-2
5 August 1934 – All-Ireland semi-final vs Galway – Won 4-4 to 2-4
2 September 1934 – All-Ireland final vs Dublin – Drew 2-7 to 3-4
30 September 1934 – All-Ireland final replay vs Dublin – Won 5-2 to 2-6
21 October 1934 – National League vs Clare – Won 4-6 to 3-3
4 November 1934 – National League vs Waterford – Won 3-8 to 2-6
2 December 1934 – National League vs Tipperary – Won 5-2 to 0-2
10 February 1935 – National League vs Galway – Won 7-4 to 2-3
24 March 1935 – National League vs Cork – Drew 2-7 to 3-4
28 April 1935 – National League vs Dublin – Won 5-7 to 4-3

12 May 1935 – National League vs Kilkenny – Won 1-6 to 1-4

19 May 1935 – Thomond Feis vs Cork – Won 6-7 to 4-3

10 June 1935 – Ward Cup in London vs Dublin – Won 6-5 to 3-1

16 June 1935 – Thomond Feis final vs Tipperary – Won 4-7 to 1-5

23 June 1935 – National League vs Laois – Won 6-6 to 2-2

7 July 1935 – Newport Tournament vs Kilkenny – Won 9-7 to 6-2

28 July 1935 – Munster championship semi-final vs Cork – Won 3-12 to 2-3

11 August 1935 – Munster championship final vs Tipperary – Won 5-5 to 1-4

PROLOGUE

℘

Mick Mackey was born on 12 July 1912, the eldest son to John 'Tyler' and May Mackey (nee Carroll). His younger siblings were John, Ester, Sadie, Paddy, Maureen, James 'Todsie' and Breda. They grew up in Castleconnell village, with their original dwelling now better known as Meehan's funeral home. He attended Castleconnell National School, where he learned to play hurling. Growing up during a period when there was very little underage hurling meant that he didn't play the game very much at a young age. But Mick Mackey would become the greatest ever Limerick hurler, inspiring a 31-game unbeaten run for the county from October 1933 to August 1935.

Mackey was the first recognisable Irish celebrity, enjoying cult status wherever he went. His playing record was astonishing, and he propelled

This is the house where Mick Mackey was raised in the heart of Castleconnell village. It is now occupied by Meehan's Undertakers.

The old Castleconnell National School where Mick Mackey was educated and first learned to play hurling.

Limerick towards a domination the county can only dream about in the modern era. It was said after the county's trip to New York in 1936 that there wasn't a team in the world that could beat the Mackey-inspired Limerick, let alone any team in Ireland. Following his retirement as a player in 1947, Mackey served as a selector and trainer to Limerick teams, was a member of Limerick County Board, the Limerick delegate to the Munster Council, a selector on successful Munster Railway Cup teams, and he also refereed for a period. He was selected on both the Team of the Century and the Team of the Millennium in the centre-forward position.

Mick Mackey married Kitty Kennedy in the 1930s and they had five children: Paddy, Michael, Greg, Audrey and Ruth. Greg was the most prominent with the camán. He drifted from the game at a relatively young age, however, and while he was never destined to make the same headlines as his father, he is acknowledged as having been a talented hurler in his own right.

This is the story of Mick Mackey from his birth in 1912 to his death in 1982, but is not confined to his life only. It is also the story of Limerick

A Mackey family photo taken in the early 1920s. (*L–r*): John, Sadie, Paddy, Esther, Mick. Two other siblings, James 'Todsie' and Breda, are missing.

hurling from the very beginning of the GAA to the early 1970s, taking in Mackey's playing and managerial career and assessing how the changes to hurling during the 1960s made it more difficult for stars of Limerick's golden era to adapt as mentors.

HENRY MARTIN

ONE

ॐ

PRE-1932: HUMBLE BEGINNINGS

Prior to Mick Mackey's birth, Limerick hurling had built a tradition of success. In 1897, they won their first All-Ireland title, under the banner of Kilfinane, and added two more, in 1918 and 1921. Mick's father, John 'Tyler' Mackey, captained Limerick in defeat to Wexford in the All-Ireland final of 1910, but that side had to settle for two Munster championships. While the tradition of success seems to have long-since departed, another tradition took root during the very early days of the GAA. It would form the basis of many a debacle in Limerick hurling, and continues to the present day. Historian and GAA author Brendan Fullam outlines how this unfortunate legacy has afflicted Limerick hurling from the very beginning:

Having read *Unlimited Heartbreak* [Cork, 2009], I was intrigued by the controversies and the self-destruction that has dogged Limerick hurling for many years. It awakened me to the reality that controversy in Limerick hurling didn't start in modern times, or even in the Mackey era; it goes back to the very start. In 1887 there was an open draw for the first All-Ireland championship, and only counties who had established a county board were allowed to submit a team. Twelve counties entered the inaugural championship and, as it transpired, only five participated in the hurling. Limerick were drawn to play Kilkenny, and in the midst of disagreement sent two representatives up to play them, Murroe and Castleconnell. There are different stories about what went on, and it seems the Central Council declared that the two Limerick teams should play one another, with the winners facing Kilkenny. Neither team would agree to that and they both came home, denying Limerick the opportunity to compete in the first hurling championship. It could never be said that they would have won the All-Ireland that year, but there was a glorious opportunity for Limerick to possibly win the first championship. However, nobody can deny that all the Limerick controversies started from day one. I would feel that, along with Galway and Wexford, the contribution of Limerick to the game of hurling is not reflected in the number of All-Irelands they have won. The failure to win on occasions when the opportunity presented itself has often been self-inflicted.

The reason both Murroe and Castleconnell wanted to represent the county stemmed from the formation of two county boards within Limerick. The Irish Republican Brotherhood (IRB) were influential in those days and had a hand in the original and properly constituted county board chaired by Paddy O'Brien. But when O'Brien was elected, a breakaway group of delegates left the meeting and formed another county board, chaired by Fr Eugene Sheehy, parish priest of Bruree. Castleconnell declared their allegiance to the O'Brien board, while Murroe rowed in behind Fr Sheehy. Both teams declared themselves county champions and demanded the right to play Kilkenny without playing each other first. Ten years would pass before the aforementioned Kilfinane selection won the first All-Ireland hurling championship for Limerick. By 1910, John 'Tyler' Mackey was making a name for himself as the heroic leader of the Limerick hurlers. Many old-timers believed that he was a far superior player than his sons turned out to be, but media coverage was non-existent in those days and therefore his exploits never received their dues. Tony Herbert explains how he got his name:

When 'Tyler' was fifteen he was inside in Limerick city and came home with a big pair of impressive-looking hobnail boots. Someone asked him where he got them and he answered Tyler's, a well-known Limerick business of that time. The name 'Tyler' stuck until the day he died. Tyler's should have paid him a fortune in royalties for years of free advertising!

Castleconnell historian Paddy Tuohy was acquainted with 'Tyler':

'Tyler' Mackey had land a couple of miles from the village beside where I was reared and consequently I was very friendly with him. As captain of the 1910 Castleconnell team that represented Limerick against Castlebridge of Wexford in the All-Ireland final, he always had major regrets over that game. Limerick were red-hot favourites before the game, and 'Tyler' led by example and played a stormer. The reasons for defeat were many, and I can vividly recall 'Tyler' telling us about that game over the hedge in our land. They implemented new rules in 1910 relating to the size of the square, the uprights and the crossbar, and square-ball infringements. Limerick felt they were

The Limerick hurling team of 1910 that were beaten in the All-Ireland final. John 'Tyler' Mackey is in the centre of the front row, wearing the Captain jersey.

hard done by in terms of the interpretation of these new rules. 'Tyler' always maintained that they scored a perfectly good goal that was disallowed and that Wexford scored a questionable goal that was awarded. He blamed the interpretation of the rules for their defeat. He mentioned other rule changes, and that may also have been the first year that teams had to wear a standardised-coloured jersey.

Brendan Fullam concurs:

In 1910 they lost to Wexford by 7-0 to 6-2. The scoring area for a goal up to 1910 was a soccer-style goal, and the uprights for points were spaced wider, similar enough to the wider posts in the Australian rules. Prior to that year, there had been a much wider space to score points, so changing that rule was a factor. Allegedly an American citizen, who was a stranger to our games and didn't know anything about the game of hurling, acted as an umpire at one of the goals. At that time a rule existed that if a player went down with an injury, the game was stopped. Apparently a Limerick player went down but play was allowed to develop and a goal was scored. Naturally enough, Limerick objected to the result but were unsuccessful. That Limerick team ended up with two Munster titles but should have won more.

In 1911 the All-Ireland final was fixed for Cork. Limerick togged out and pucked around, but it started to rain heavily prior to the throw-in. The officials made the decision to call the game off, and it was generally deemed to be the correct decision. Kilkenny had nothing to do with calling the game off and it was re-fixed for Thurles. In those days people could be very stubborn and Limerick, led by 'Tyler' Mackey, said they would only play the game in Cork. The reason given was that they had beaten Tipperary earlier in the championship and felt that they mightn't get fair play in Thurles. Kilkenny were awarded the All-Ireland title. In 1912 Limerick were nominated to play Antrim in the All-Ireland semi-final because the Munster championship hadn't yet been completed. They beat Antrim comfortably and went back to play Cork in the Munster championship. Limerick were a point ahead, and a late Cork move resulted in a goal. The goalie took the puckout and before the ball had hit the ground, the game was over. Cork took their place in the All-Ireland final. I would say that there was at least one All-Ireland title that could have been won from 1910 to 1912. Moving on a few years from that, when you think of the hurlers Limerick had from 1918 to 1921, that team should have won more than the two titles they did secure. However, there were political controversies in Irish society around that time, such as the civil war, and that would have had an impact.

P. J. Keane believes Limerick were professional in those days:

My father Jack Keane often said that in his time they went to Foynes for three weeks' collective training. A boxer named Dalton was their trainer and he looked after their food, diet and laxatives and made sure they were in good form and training well. They were kept in accommodation and were in training full time for those three weeks. I used to say to him that in my playing days we would have relished being in camp for three weeks, and might have achieved a lot. Perhaps they organised that training because of the civil war, as it would have been difficult to get players together in the evenings. They were strange times and unless you lived through the troubles, you couldn't understand what it was like. Eventually the GAA banned collective training in the 1920s or '30s. Maybe they thought it was over-extravagant. But it has to be acknowledged that collective training did take place, and my father was a product of that. Can you imagine the advantage they had when they were all hurling together and training together for that three-week period, compared to our haphazard training during my time as a player in later years? My father played with Willie Hough and Denny Lanigan in the half-back line; they were known as 'The Great Hindenburg Line' and are widely acknowledged as being one the best half-back lines in hurling history. Any team should always be based on the half-back line and built upon from there, and that line was the key to Limerick's success in that era. He was the lightest member of that half-back line at 14½ stone fully trained and fit. I am led to believe that he was a good athlete, and was very fast and strong.

The troubles most certainly did have an impact in 1923, when Limerick were due to play Galway in the All-Ireland final, eventually fixed for June 1924. However, Limerick refused to play the game until the civil war prisoners were released. Galway refused to accept the title without winning it on the field, and the game was finally re-fixed for September 1924. Limerick were hot favourites and dominated the early stages but conceded seven goals and were well beaten in the end. Maurice Regan explains:

Jack Hanly was their goalie, and it was always said that he couldn't play unless he had a drink or two before a match. He was a great player and generally stopped everything, but was very nervous that day. Whatever priest was in charge wouldn't give him the drink. He couldn't cope with the pressure and conceded seven goals.

Tommy Cooke concurs:

Hanly was from Elton and was blamed for throwing away the 1923 All-Ireland final because of drink. When the team came home to Knocklong he was afraid to get out of the train in case he'd be lynched. He stayed on for another couple of miles, and as the train passed through Elton going on to Cork, he pulled the communication cord. When the train stopped he jumped off and ran across the fields. Years afterwards Mick Hickey, a publican, asked Guinness to honour the old Limerick team at a function in the city. There I met Mick King, the famous Galway hurler, and another player called Ned Power who was nearly 100. Both had played against Limerick in the 1923 game and said that Jack Hanly had stopped bullets in the semi-final. In the final he wasn't able to stop a football.

Having found it difficult to field teams during the troubles, the Castleconnell club effectively ceased to exist for a number of years. In the mid-1920s it was reformed under the name Ahane. Michael Hynes outlined the background:

The Ahane club was formed in the old schoolhouse in Richhill in 1926. In the absence of a local club, most of that original Castleconnell team transferred to play for either Claughaun or Young Irelands. The whole situation possibly arose due to the troubles, and the old Castleconnell club, like many others, was discontinued during that era. Gareth O'Meara, Bill Cummins, Jack Keane and Tommy Herbert were among those who formed the new club in 1926, and because of differences with Castleconnell it was called Ahane. The club didn't have a pitch. Young Irelands were the big team in Limerick that time. They played in the Markets Field and that would possibly have been their hurling field. There was a pitch in Croom, but apart from that very few clubs had their own pitches.

Tommy Cooke explains that the formation of the club wasn't all plain sailing:

'Tyler' Mackey ran the original Castleconnell club and the Mackeys fell in with the new club, Ahane, but wanted to change the name to the original, Castleconnell. They never did, though, due to lack of support, and eventually they all united and became a powerful team. They played tournaments all over the country, and Jackie Power once said, 'God must have a special place in heaven for us', they opened so many church tournaments.

Fr Liam Kelly explains the anecdote 'Come on Ahane, the spuds are boiling':

There's a square in Castleconnell, with a little green area, and sometimes I wonder how they played there, but they only played ground hurling and weren't allowed to rise the ball. They played out there every Sunday morning and when the dinner was ready old Mrs Mackey [Mick's mother] would shout, 'Come on Ahane, the spuds are boiling.'

Mick Mackey was only fourteen when the Ahane club was founded and was regarded as being too young to play, though he sometimes participated in training games. He made his Ahane debut in 1928 against Fedamore in the Limerick junior hurling championship at the Gaelic Grounds. He also dabbled in the ancient game across the border, as his niece Vera Mulcahy explains:

A lot of people mightn't realise that my father [John Mackey], my uncle [Mick Mackey] and Mick Hickey actually won a county minor championship with Clonlara in 1928. They knew the Moloney brothers inside in Limerick CBS and Clonlara [in County Clare]

The Ahane panel that won the county junior hurling championship of 1928 (played in 1929). *Back row (l–r):* William Francis Lee, Ned McDonagh, Stephen McDonagh, Pa Scanlan, Anthony Mackey, Mick O'Malley, Pat O'Reilly, Dan Givens. *Middle row (l–r):* Bill Coleman, Mick Hickey, Mick Mackey, Michael Quinlan, Pat Hilliard, Pat Joyce. *Front row (l–r):* Timmy Ryan, Martin Ryan, Pat O'Brien, Dave Conway, Joe Ryan, Mick Hourigan. *Seated:* Eddie O'Brien. (Non-players unnamed.)

needed a few players so they crossed the river and played for them. My sister Cora Moroney has my father's medal.

Mick Mackey's career on the right side of the border began well. He won a county junior championship in 1928 and alongside his brother John won a county minor championship in 1929. They won a county junior championship in 1930, though Mick didn't play in the final due to injury. He made the Limerick junior side beaten by Tipperary after a replay in the Munster championship of 1930, and was then selected on the senior team to face Tipperary in the opening round of the National League in November 1930. For some reason he didn't play that day, but having attended the next game against Kilkenny as a spectator, he was called into duty at the eleventh hour. By his own admission he didn't set the hurling world on fire, but Tommy Cooke disagrees:

Mick was on the sideline watching the game, and they got him to tog out, and he went in and hurled all around him. That's how he was picked for that game, accidentally. He became a great player and played non-stop in every match from start to finish. He wasn't a fast hurler, but feared no man and could rise the ball in front of three or four players and burst out through them. If they tried to stop him, he would hit two or three of them a belt of a shoulder and jump out over them.

His first senior championship appearance for Ahane came in 1930 and resulted in victory over Treaty Sarsfields. They progressed on a winning run from there and were ultimately beaten by Young Irelands at the business end of the championship. His only appearance at the Markets Field came in 1931, a senior challenge between Ahane and Claughaun. Ahane would win their first county championship against Croom that year, but the build-up to the game was shrouded in controversy over the venue, with the Gaelic Grounds eventually decided upon. Ahane fought to have the game there and got their way, while Croom and indeed west Limerick generally were united in their drive to secure the potential money-spinner for their territory. The controversy might well have been the first seed of a bitter rivalry between Ahane and Croom that culminated eighteen years later in a near fatality. A tempestuous county board meeting took place, coming to a head when a disgruntled delegate directed the following comment at the county chairman, 'Why, these are Mussolini tactics!'
Socialising after games was not an option, as Tony Herbert explains:

The 1931 Ahane senior hurling team that won their very first senior county championship. *Back row (l–r):* Jack Keane (trainer), Michael McDonagh, J. Aherne, Mick Hickey, Denis O'Malley, Pat Joyce, Paddy Scanlon, Timmy Ryan, M. Aherne. *Front row (l–r):* Pat Hilliard, Mick Quinlan, Anthony Mackey, John Moloney, James 'Todsie' Mackey (mascot), Mick Mackey, John Mackey, Martin Ryan (Black).

Money was scarce and players didn't drink a lot. Garett Howard didn't drink and the Mackeys didn't drink much. In later times, John Mackey got into the Health Board through his father 'Tyler', who was a councillor. 'Tyler' was in charge of the free beef and free milk at that time. John was also responsible for those, along with the vouchers for the pension. Because of the lack of wealth, people depended on hurling for entertainment, and Ahane grew into the greatest club team of all time in the 1930s. Tournaments were becoming important, and a famous game took place between Ahane and Newport in 1931. There was a lot of rivalry between Limerick and Tipperary around Ahane, men married to women from Newport parish and vice versa. Mick Kennedy, the Limerick corner-back, was actually a Tipperary man. Newport won the North Tipperary championship, and when they beat Ahane in the tournament final they rubbed it in with, 'Come over to Newport, Ahane, the spuds are boiling here.'

Jimmy Butler Coffey was on the Newport team:

The field at the time was in Portryan, behind where the Millbrae Lodge nursing home is located. We had more experience than they had. They were only a young team who were coming at the time. We got the local bragging rights after that game! A few years later, I was visiting a neighbour in hospital in Limerick, and he said to me, 'That man across the way is Michael Mackey, an uncle to the two boys.' I went over and started talking to him. 'Talk up,' he said, 'I'm deaf. Who are you?' I told him who I was. 'Were you in Portryan?' he asked. I said I was. 'I'll tell you a good one about that,' he replied. In those days if you were well-to-do, you always had a pony and trap, and the Mackeys would have been seen as well-to-do. Michael Mackey told me that one day, after the tournament final, he was driving along the road on a pony and trap. 'Tyler' and the wife were ahead of him on another pony and trap being driven by the hurlers Mick and John. The people of Ahane were ashamed to be seen in Newport after losing the final, and when they came to the next crossroads the boys turned for Newport. 'Stop!' shouted 'Tyler', 'Castleconnell! You aren't worth feeding.' 'Tyler' maintained that the boys weren't worth feeding if they were willing to travel to Newport after losing such an important game to them.

Jim Fitzgerald has a similar story:

When Newport beat them, the story goes that 'Tyler' made the young Mackeys walk home to Castleconnell after the game. I would have heard folklore growing up because we used to meet at the crossroads in the evenings. The older men were always there and we used to hear those stories from them. Ahane were cocky and convinced that they would win the medals, and Newport beat them. Newport had a good team at that time, and they had religion on their side because the local priest got the tournament going for the building of the church. A local fife and drum band used to play at those games and they wrote a poem about Newport beating Ahane.

It was also said that the priest wrapped the sliotar up in his garments when saying Mass that morning in Newport. Fr Liam Kelly explains the torment that Ahane might have suffered from their Tipperary neighbours:

My father Seán Kelly was a teacher, and played for Castleconnell and Limerick in the old days. He would have played with Mick Mackey later on, and was very friendly with him. My father hated Tipperary and one statement he always made was, 'Tipperary are very bad losers and they are even worse winners.' He also said, 'Cork are great sports, and won't rub it in.' I remember answering him back one time, 'Cork rarely lose, so they can afford to be good sports!'

It's difficult to disagree, because traditionally in the border areas Tipperary were never shy about rubbing it in. Consequently, in many border areas to this very day, the only thing that delights Limerick people as much as a Limerick victory is a Tipperary defeat. But Ahane were only beginning and would recover from this setback. Greater days lay ahead and much silverware would follow for both Ahane and Limerick, driven by Mick Mackey. Nevertheless, despite those countless victories, that defeat to Newport was never forgotten in Ahane. Or perhaps the gloating meant that they were never allowed to forget it!

TWO

❧

1932–5: GOLDEN YEARS

Having failed to make the Limerick championship team for 1931, Mick Mackey got another chance in February 1932, joined by his brother John. Tournaments were in vogue for intercounty teams and he played on the team that lost the Jim Riordan testimonial game at Kilmallock to Tipperary after a replay. Jim Riordan was a successful businessman who became disabled and the tournament was held as a fundraiser for him. He won an All-Ireland football title with the Commercials in 1896, and had been county chairman when 'Tyler' Mackey was the Limerick senior hurling captain. Mick Mackey won his first medal in June 1932, having beaten Tipperary in the semi-final and Clare in the final of the Thomond Feis tournament. The Thomond Feis was well regarded at the time, as Jimmy Butler Coffey explained:

It was a great tournament. It was played a few weeks before the Munster championship, and Limerick, Clare, Cork and Tipperary used to play in it. The League was played in the winter, but the Thomond Feis was played in better conditions when the weather was picking up. It was still running up to the 1950s. If you went well in the Thomond Feis, you knew you had a great chance in the Munster championship.

Most people wouldn't normally associate the word 'Feis' with hurling. Vera Mulcahy is no different:

My father [John Mackey] used to speak highly of the tournament. I used to think that the Thomond Feis related to something like traditional music or Irish dancing, but he told me it was the dress rehearsal for the Munster championship, and was regarded even more highly than the League.

Winning the Thomond Feis proved that Limerick were on the rise and were about to embark on the greatest voyage the county had ever seen. Mick Mackey

11

*scored two goals on his Munster championship debut to inspire them to victory
over Tipperary by 4-2 to 1-5. Cork would stop their march in the semi-final,
winning by 5-4 to 3-5 in a game where John Mackey made his debut as
substitute. Limerick may have been beaten but expectations were rising. Tony
Herbert recalls the 1932 campaign:*

In the Munster semi-final, Cork's Gah Aherne, a great centre-
forward, struck a ball from about 40 yards out and it went all the way
to the net. Paddy Scanlon [Limerick goalkeeper] didn't see it. That
was the decisive score. However, Cork were beaten by Clare in the
Munster final, but Limerick were coming.

*Ahane were dethroned as county champions by Young Irelands, but in
retrospect that was a mere blip and it turned out to be the only Limerick hurling
championship match Ahane lost between 1931 and '41. Limerick continued
their march towards greatness and took another step by reaching the 1933
National League final against Kilkenny. Martin White missed the League final
through injury, but the Kilkenny players were aware of the Limerick threat:*

We beat Limerick in the 1933 League final. That was the first year
we were involved in serious hurling against Limerick. We were an
experienced team by then, far more so than Limerick. We had played
the three All-Ireland finals against Cork in 1931, and had beaten
Clare in the 1932 All-Ireland final. Our 1931 conquerors, Cork, were
beaten in the Munster championship in 1932 by Clare and dropped
out of contention for a few years. When Clare came in 1932 we would
have expected them to be back again the following year. However, we
had also taken note that the Limerick team started coming in 1932
and while they lost to Cork that year, they had beaten Tipperary and
were very young and very keen. Because Limerick hadn't won an
All-Ireland for some time, they were very keen on winning another
and were building towards that. They had great players, such as the
Mackeys and Paddy Clohessy. Paddy's brother Dave was an excellent
player too. I thought at the time that they would eventually win more
than they did.

*Mick Mackey was marked by the great Paddy Phelan and didn't star in the
League final. The game turned after Mickey Fitzgibbon had to leave the field
with an injury. Nevertheless, the defeat proved to be an important learning curve.
Limerick retained the Thomond Feis Cup, beating Clare, and then Tipperary
in the final. In the Munster championship, Limerick went head to head with the*

A word in his ear: Mick Mackey takes advice from an ardent supporter.

reigning Munster champions, Clare. Mick Mackey was on fire, scoring 2-1 in a comfortable victory, but all was not well in the Clare camp, as Tony Herbert explains:

Limerick beat Clare by a cricket score. Canon Hamilton was in charge of the Clare team and was also the chairman of the Clare County Board. A famous man and a Canon Punch-type character. He ran the whole Clare team and he destroyed them in 1932 and '33 because he got his own way and made a bad job of the team. A few years later for a Munster championship game he dropped John Joe 'Goggles' Doyle, an outstanding half-back, and Larry Blake, a centre-back who Mackey always struggled to get the better of.

Three points from Mick Mackey helped Limerick to victory over Cork in the Munster semi-final, but he believed there was room for improvement after the Cork game:

A right hard match it proved, with a high standard of hurling maintained throughout the hour. The general opinion was that Limerick were the better team but our forwards were slow to avail of their chances and many fine openings went for nought. (Seán Murphy and Séamus Ó Ceallaigh, *The Mackey Story*, p. 67)

Mackey went on to score a personal tally of 2-1 in the 3-7 to 1-2 Munster final victory over Waterford, winning his first Munster championship medal in the process. With eight minutes remaining, a brawl on the field led to a pitch invasion by spectators. The Limerick players tried in vain to clear the pitch and the match was abandoned. Subsequently, the Munster Council decided that Limerick were far enough ahead on the scoreboard to be deemed champions without the necessity of a replay. Limerick were in the All-Ireland final, where they continued their rivalry with Kilkenny. Mick Mackey recalled the occasion, decided by 'Lovely' Johnny Dunne's great goal:

All Limerick was in a ferment as we trained for our first All-Ireland final [since the early 1920s]. Our team travelled by train the previous evening, and were met at Kingsbridge by representatives of the Limerick people resident in Dublin who gave us a very enthusiastic welcome.

Huge throngs journeyed by every mode of conveyance to the metropolis and it was no surprise to see all Irish sporting records broken – 45,176 people paying to see the game. It was reckoned that another 5,000 were disappointed when all gates had to be closed twenty minutes before play commenced.

Croke Park on All-Ireland final day is an unnerving experience for the newcomer. The packed stands and terraces, the batter of photographers, the march around behind the bands, the tense moments of waiting, all combine to produce what could be a terrifying introduction for a temperamental player.

As the Boherbuoy Band who had travelled from Limerick with the team played 'Faith of our Fathers', Most Rev. Dr Collier, Bishop of Ossory, stepped on the pitch accompanied by President de Valera, with the then chairman of the Central Council, Seán McCarthy of Cork, who introduced them to the referee – Stephen Jordan, TD [Athenry], and to both captains. Another moment and the big game was on. I was playing on Paddy Byrne, against whom I also played in the 1935 and 1936 finals.

It turned out to be a wonderful struggle with plenty of grand hurling. Kilkenny's defence was superb, our shooting was bad. We got plenty of the ball thanks to the sound work of our midfield pair. The sides were neck and neck during the greater part of an hour of real hurling thrill. We were level – four points each – at half time.

It was still anybody's game nearing the end of the hour when Johnny Dunne's wonder goal – the only major score of the day – gave victory to Kilkenny. We fought back determinedly in a last effort to prevent defeat but could not master the Noreside backs. (Murphy and Ó Ceallaigh, *The Mackey Story*, pp. 68–9)

Michael Hynes believed that the lack of experience was a factor:

Prior to that final, Timmy Ryan and a couple of others had experienced playing in Croke Park with the Railway Cup team, but it was the first time playing in Croke Park for the team in general. In later years they knew what it was like to win an All-Ireland and therefore would have had a greater chance of victory. The lack of big-game experience at Croke Park definitely cost them in 1933.

Jimmy Butler Coffey was unsure if the title 'Lovely' Johnny Dunne was deserved:

He was a good hurler but he wasn't a great hurler. That time, producing flashes of hurling in one big game could give you a great name, even though you might never do it again. The Kilkenny men planned a move at half time where someone would get the ball and drive it into the corner. The full-forward would dash out from the square, leaving the space wide open in front of goal. The opposite corner-forward would then drift into the space when the ball was sent across.

Martin White continues:

After playing Limerick in the 1933 League final, we knew we would need to produce something special to beat them in the All-Ireland final. At the same time, we knew we were as good as anyone in 1933, and had more experience than them that year. Matty Power, the corner-forward, was a very elusive player and it wasn't easy to mark him. In my opinion, he was one of the best corner-forwards ever. He was great to score, and was a great distributor of the ball. He was also very intelligent. If he got loose, a defender had to go to him, but he was very difficult to follow and used to always put himself in a position where there was another forward nearby. Sometimes he would be able to slip away loose himself waiting for the ball. Give him a ball anywhere and he could score a point, the angle didn't matter. In the second half Matty got the ball, beat his own man and drew out Tom McCarthy who was a great full-back. Matty laid off the ball to Johnny and all he had to do was put it into the net.

Tommy Cooke believes McCarthy should have been more ruthless:

I remember Johnny Dunne's goal, and nearly cried that day. Tom McCarthy was a great full-back but was too honest and should have taken out Johnny Dunne. When Dunne got the ball he sidestepped McCarthy and scored. Sure Scanlan hadn't a hope of stopping it. That goal won the match and if they prevented that goal they would have won the match. Limerick were just short a score to win.

Tony Herbert believes the better team won:

Limerick weren't good enough in 1933, they had too many weak men and bad forwards. Mick Mackey struck a ball for goal at one stage and Pat Ryan 'Shake Hands' of Cregane [a Limerick team-mate] blocked it with his backside. There were good backs but the forward line was poor. They were up against a great Kilkenny team who had tough backs to get through such as Peter Blanchfield and Peter Reilly. Ned Cregan wasn't a classy hurler but he was a good tough man like Tommy Cooke who played with us in later years. There was no great craft in him but it took a great man to get the better of him. Garett Howard, Paddy Clohessy and Mickey Cross were great hurlers and formed a great half-back line.

Ahane Hurling Club county senior championship winners 1933. *Back row (l–r):* Dave Conway, Pat O'Reilly, Paddy Joyce, Michael Hayes, Mick Hickey, Paddy Scanlon, Jim Byrnes, Jack Scanlan, Liam Cummins, Davy Power. *Middle row (l–r):* John Doyle, John Mackey, Anthony Mackey, Timmy Ryan, Mick Quinlan, Jack Roche, Tommy Byrnes. *Front row (l–r):* P. Power, Jimmy Close, Mick Mackey, Mick McDonagh. *Missing:* Denis O'Malley, Joe Ryan, Martin Ryan

Ahane won back their county title on 26 October 1933 after a 1-7 to 1-1 victory over Croom. Having failed in two bids to lift national titles in 1933, Limerick targeted victory in the first round of the League against Tipperary. They won the match, for their seventh consecutive victory over Tipperary, but there was food for thought, as Mackey explained:

Limerick's big weakness was in the top line of the attack, as was very evident in the All-Ireland final, and in this respect it was interesting to study the tactics of Tipperary's full-forward Martin Kennedy, long regarded as a past master in the art of decoy. He was the ideal spearhead to any attack, a master strategist. To watch him play was a treat in itself. (Murphy and Ó Ceallaigh, *The Mackey Story*, p. 70)

He remembers winning his first Railway Cup medal in 1934:

I was playing on Eddie Byrne, who was in fine fettle, but I managed to give him the slip on two occasions to take passes from Larry Blake that reached the back of the Leinster net. We won 6-3 to 3-2 and for all but Mickey Cross it was the first Railway Cup medal. I figured in eight further inter-provincial finals and was on the losing side on only one occasion – in 1936 when I captained the team and we lost to Leinster by a solitary point. (Murphy and Ó Ceallaigh, *The Mackey Story*, p. 70)

Eight days later, Limerick, inspired by John Mackey, paved the way for Mick Kennedy to lift the National League title, having beaten Dublin 3-6 to 3-3 at the Gaelic Grounds. The papers had high regard for the role of the lesser-known younger brother:

Clearly Mackey [John] won the match for Limerick and had he been absent Limerick would not be now holders of League honours. (Murphy and Ó Ceallaigh, *The Mackey Story*, p. 72)

They retained their Thomond Feis Cup with a 3-6 to 3-4 win over Cork. The next target was to retain their Munster title and to enable them to have another crack at regaining the McCarthy Cup for the first time since 1921. There was no such thing as a handy Munster title in those days, and Limerick had to beat Clare, Cork and Waterford before Timmy Ryan 'Good Boy' got his hands on the Munster Cup. The forwards were beginning to click and Mick Mackey scored three goals in the first round against Clare, while Jackie Connell scored three in the Munster semi-final against Cork. Mick Mackey scored 1-7 in the Munster final victory over Waterford, with Dave Clohessy adding 2-0. Jimmy Butler Coffey had high regard for Jackie Connell:

Action from the 1934 Munster senior hurling final at the old Cork Athletic Grounds.

As a hurler, the best Limerick player of that golden era was Jackie Connell who played in the early 1930s. He was a beautiful hurler but he had very bad legs, and if he turned sharply he would fall. Mackey was a much better man overall, and if he went out and gathered a ball and got it into his hand, nothing would stop him. But purely in terms of hurling ability and as an out-and-out stickman Jackie Connell was definitely the best Limerick hurler.

Mick Mackey acknowledged that you have to walk before you can run:

Of course everyone likes to win an All-Ireland medal but still, you have to win in Munster first which is a fact and was a very hard job in our time. Because when we started out on the campaign any of the five counties could beat each other. You could be beaten in the first round just as easily as you could be beaten in a final. ('A Celebration of Munster Hurling', RTÉ Television, 1976)

However, things were far from harmonious in the Limerick camp. Jimmy Close of Newport transferred to Ahane and threw in his lot with Limerick. Christy O'Brien had been a regular in 1933 and played the first round against Clare in 1934. Ultimately he was the man to make way as Close cemented his place on the team. Jimmy Butler Coffey explained the scenario:

I was as good as being outside the county of Tipperary because I was in Newport, on the border with Limerick. That meant it was generally very difficult to get picked on Tipperary teams, but they picked both Jim Close, who was also from Newport, and myself. Close won two Munster championships at minor with Tipperary, 1930 and '31, and an All-Ireland minor in 1930. He left Newport and went to live in Castleconnell and began to play with Limerick. It was controversial at that time because of the man who was dropped from the Limerick team to make way for an outside man, Jimmy Close. If a player was hurling with Ahane at that time, it more or less meant that he was an automatic contender for a place on the Limerick team. If you were good enough for Ahane, you were deemed to be good enough for Limerick. A chap called Christy O'Brien from Cappamore had been on the Limerick team and was ousted. It wasn't Jim Close who dropped him. He had nothing to do with it apart from the fact that he happened to be playing for Ahane and was selected on the Limerick team. O'Brien never really got his place back and missed out on the great days. He was taken on the trip to America with the Limerick team a few years later but wasn't ever happy about being dropped for an outsider. Nobody would be. But Christy O'Brien was a good hurler.

With the Munster title on board, Limerick set about finishing the job. They won a physical All-Ireland semi-final against Galway at Roscrea by 4-4 to 2-4. They were now in the All-Ireland final against a Dublin team containing many country folk, and beat them after a replay. Tommy Cooke recalls the games:

In 1934 they were very lucky to draw with Dublin and Dave Clohessy scored four goals to beat them in the replay. Bob McConkey was playing full-forward the first day against Dublin and he was sick for the second game, so Dave Clohessy was moved in from corner-forward, and he liked being closer to the goals. He used to boast a lot about the four goals in later years! He spent a few years in America afterwards and did plenty of talking about the four goals over there too!

A major factor in the preparations for the replay was the recruitment of legendary Cork trainer Jim 'Tough' Barry. Paddy Scanlon missed the replay because of a poisoned finger, so the vastly experienced Tom Shinney of Fedamore received a late call-up. Timmy Ryan 'Good Boy' raised the McCarthy Cup and Mick Mackey, as he explains, was jubilant:

Timmy Ryan kisses the bishop's ring prior to the 1934 All-Ireland final.

The greatest thrill I got really was beating Dublin in a replay in 1934 when I collected an All-Ireland medal. After being beaten in 1933, we went up for the All-Ireland and we looked a certainty but we were lucky, we were very lucky to come out of it with a draw. We went back a second time I think it was late October/early November and we won, and when we won it was my greatest thrill. When the whistle blew I said I got an All-Ireland medal anyhow. ('A Celebration of Munster Hurling', RTÉ Television, 1976)

The golden era was well underway and Limerick were in the midst of a record-breaking 31-match unbeaten run. They retained their League title in 1935 in a system without a final. Jimmy Butler Coffey saw them beat Kilkenny along the way:

Limerick were approaching greatness at the time, and they had to play Kilkenny in the second last round of the League which was effectively a semi-final. Limerick won by 1-6 to 1-4 and the hurling was the last word. The ball was travelling like lightning. It was without doubt the best match I ever saw. But you could never compare teams

The Limerick panel that beat Dublin in the 1934 All-Ireland final. *Back row (l–r):* Dave Conway, Jack Keane, Paddy Mackey, Pat O'Reilly, Mick Ryan, Jim Roche, Jackie O'Connell, Paddy Scanlon, Anthony Mackey, Garrett Howard, Timmy Ryan, Pat Ryan, Tommy McCarthy, Willie Hannon, Ned Cregan, Christy O'Brien, Mick Mackey, Paddy Clohessy, W. P. Clifford. *Middle row (l–r):* Mick Neville, Denny Lanigan, Mickey Cross, John Mackey, Bob McConkey, Mick Kennedy, Jimmy Close, Dave Clohessy, Liam Scanlon. *Front row (l–r):* Mick Hickey, Mickey Condon, Dan Flanagan, Peter Browne (trainer).

from different eras. You couldn't compare a team in the 1930s to a team in the 1960s.

They beat Cork comprehensively by 3-12 to 2-3 in the Munster semi-final, a game in which there was a near fatality. Jimmy Butler Coffey explained:

Mick Ryan of Cregane was a Murroe man and there was no team in Murroe at the time, so he hurled with Newport. He won a North Tipperary championship with Newport in 1924 when he was still only seventeen. He was involved in an incident in the 1935 Munster semi-final between Cork and Limerick. Limerick were growing into a great side at that time and there was terrible tension in the match. After Paddy Clohessy was sent off Mick Ryan from Cregane went to centre-back from midfield and Mick Mackey moved out to centre field. Even with fourteen men, they still beat Cork comfortably. A ball dropped between Tadhg Kelly of Cork and Mick Ryan and they were both trying to pull on it overhead. I wasn't at the match so I can't describe

Mick (*left*) and John Mackey pose for a photograph before a Limerick game in the early 1930s.

exactly what happened apart from what I was told, but it seems Mick Ryan drew on the ball a split second faster than Kelly and connected with him right on the forehead.

Kelly fell to the ground and was reported dead. He was administered the last rites on the field and was then removed to hospital in Thurles. All the players knelt down on the field and there was total silence as everyone in the ground said a decade of the rosary. There may have been terrible tension in the match but it was always said that the belt was totally accidental. The match started again and they played on to the end. Kelly woke up in the hospital afterwards and went back to Cork the following night with the team. He was fine afterwards and went back hurling again. There was never any trouble for Mick Ryan, he wasn't sent off or anything.

Tony Herbert was introduced to Tommy Kelly at a later stage:

Tommy Kelly was a Blackrock man and at that time the Blackrock men were tough. They were a powerful club and provided ten or twelve players to the Cork team that day. I met him afterwards down in Cork and the man that was with me said, 'There's Tommy Kelly, the fella who died and came back to life on the field in Thurles.'

Limerick advanced to the Munster final and retained their title. The Irish Independent *of Monday 29 July 1935 credited one man with the victory: 'The match was a personal triumph for Mick Mackey of Limerick who gave one of the most brilliant and spectacular individual displays of hurling ever seen.' Mackey was beginning to achieve greatness and was clearly the thorn in Tipperary's side in a 5-5 to 1-4 victory. That set up a meeting with Kilkenny, but Limerick were controversially beaten in difficult, wet conditions. Limerick were awarded a close-in free at the very end to level the game. Jack Keane issued an instruction from the sideline that Timmy Ryan, the captain, was to take the free and put the ball over the bar. As he lined up to take it, Mick Mackey pushed him away and took the free instead, striking it below the crossbar. The ball was caught by the Kilkenny goalkeeper and cleared. Kilkenny were victorious by 2-5 to 2-4. When the conspiracy theories started, some were adamant that Mackey went for glory, mindful of the newspaper headlines he was beginning to attract. He had a profile greater than the team and it's acknowledged that he was conscious of that. He was beginning to hold a stronger role in terms of decision-making on and off the field. To this day, many refuse to believe the truth – that Mackey would risk the result by going for goal – and hold that his reluctance to speak of it throughout his life supports their claim. Sadly, they are wrong. At the moment of reckoning, a disgusted Timmy Ryan confronted Mackey and asked him why he went for goal. Mackey replied, 'What good was a draw to us?'*

Michael Hynes, however, gave Mackey the benefit of the doubt:

The big question in that final was, 'Did Mick Mackey go for a point or did he go for a goal?' I don't think he went for a goal but nobody knows. He took that to the grave with him. The ball that time was completely different to what they use now. The wet day isn't as big a disadvantage now, but that day in 1935 was the worst wet day we ever got and it was known as the 'Wet Day' All-Ireland. The 1939 All-Ireland final, known as the 'Thunder and Lightning' final, was played in similar conditions. The 1992 All-Ireland final would have been something similar, though not as bad. When Limerick played Tipperary in the 1971 Munster final at Killarney, the conditions would have been similar. So the weather conditions had a massive bearing on the game. I would say that Mick Mackey went for a point and because of the conditions missed it. Jimmy O'Connell was in goals for Kilkenny, and he caught it in his hand and cleared it. It was the last puck of the match.

Jimmy Butler Coffey had similar thoughts:

At that time, the Limerick team in my estimation were the best team of all time. If they had won in 1935 there would have been no stopping them. Timmy Ryan was captain and he was taking the free. Timmy would have tapped it over for the replay, but just as he was about to take it, Mackey came over and pushed him away. I'd say he was going for a point but nobody knows what was in his mind that day only himself.

Martin White gives a Kilkenny tactical viewpoint:

I thought Mackey went for goal. He should have known better because Peter Reilly the full-back and Paddy Larkin the right-corner-back were on the line and they were deadly in the goals. Jimmy O'Connell the goalkeeper had a great eye because he was a handballer. There wasn't much of a chance of getting a goal on Jimmy O'Connell when he was on his own in the goals, not to mind when he had Paddy Larkin and Peter Reilly on either side of him. Our Kilkenny team didn't crowd the goals back then like they do now when defending a close-in free. It was felt by crowding one another they were only blinding each other, so they generally only put three on the goal line. I am of the opinion that when Mick Mackey saw only three on the line he thought he'd get it in past them. But it just didn't happen that way. He mightn't have connected right, but he was going for goal. Everyone in the ground knew that the goal had been missed because all the shouting from the crowd came from the Kilkenny supporters when the shot was missed.

Tony Herbert has no doubts, but acknowledges Mackey's greatness:

Mackey was a law unto himself and nobody could agree with him. He was over-ambitious, wanted the full limelight and wanted to burst the back of the net with that free. The papers generally gave Mackey the credit for everything, the headlines in the papers were all about him, but Limerick weren't just about one man, they were a great team. I don't think other players were jealous or annoyed and it certainly didn't bother me when I was playing with him a few years later. But for all his failings he was a great man. He had great physique, great control of the ball and could run up and down on a solo run, keeping that ball on his stick.

Martin White believes Mackey earned the right to his opinions:

Mick Mackey showed the way in terms of his hurling when he was on the field. When you played with him you had to play well, or else you weren't going to be there. He did it himself on the field, and the other players had to be able to do it with him. If a player wasn't able to go along with him, play with him and think with him, he wasn't going to be there. Some players of that time weren't able to think with Mick Mackey. It was the same with Eddie Keher playing with Kilkenny in later years, Eddie was a very intelligent player and you had to be able to think quickly to keep up with what he was going to do. Mick Mackey would think quickly like Keher. As a hurler he was different to Keher in style but he had strength, and no matter where he was, he went straight towards goal for a score.

When interviewed later in life, Mackey didn't carry any major regrets:

I got two more afterwards [two more All-Ireland medals after 1934] and was beaten a point in one [the 1935 final]. They always say I lost the 1935 one by missing a free but that never worried me really. (Mick Mackey interviewed by Val Dorgan, RTÉ Television, 1969)

Timmy Ryan, on the other hand, took it to his grave:

What really annoyed me was that I knew we would beat them in the replay. It still rankles with me. (Brendan Fullam, *Captains of the Ash*, p. 139)

Martin White analyses the game:

Paddy McMahon was a great hurler on that Limerick team. He died fully convinced that they should have beaten us in 1935. He always said, 'We left one behind us there.' I would say Limerick were the better team on the day, and they were the younger team. Peter Reilly and Paddy Larkin were playing [for Kilkenny] as far back as 1926. Neddy Doyle, Matty Power and a couple of others were playing in 1922. That Kilkenny team was getting old, even though most of them won yet another All-Ireland a few years later. I would say our experience won it for us. We knew how to keep with them, and weren't going to lose it if there was a chance. We were definitely the better team when we met two years earlier in 1933, but I think we beat a better team than ourselves in 1935.

I don't know if the wet day was a factor but there were two trains of thought at the time. It's very questionable, because some people said that the wet day didn't suit the Kilkenny style of hurling. They said Kilkenny wanted a dry ball on the top of the ground. The other way of looking at it is that if a good hurler meets a wet day, his superior hurling will get him through the game. His skill levels will ensure he can hurl in all conditions. Other people say the rain slows down good players, and that it would suit Limerick because it would slow down the good hurlers on the opposition team.

I started the 1935 final at left-half-forward, playing on Mickey Cross. Johnny Dunne got knocked out after a belt on the head and went off. He was playing right-corner-forward on Mick Kennedy, a great player and very tight marker. I was moved onto Kennedy, a great friend of mine in later years, when Johnny Dunne went off. On the stroke of half time, Jack Duggan's wrist got broken and he had to go off altogether. Johnny Dunne came back on to the field with a big bandage on his head so I was moved out to centre-forward onto Paddy Clohessy. It meant that I played on three men who were all recognised as great backs. I often played on Garett Howard as well who was also recognised as a great half-back. Being a utility man is not to your advantage though because normally players get their place and hold down a place. As a utility man you can be moved around, and one bad day could cost you your place.

And so the 31-game unbeaten run came to an end, and how fitting it was that the games they lost either side of the run were both to Kilkenny in All-Ireland finals. Limerick began the rehabilitation process against Tipperary in a League game before Christmas. It was not for the faint hearted. As explained below:

The game ended in the draw. The referee was Tommy Daly, a Clare man based in Dublin, a great referee. Limerick took the lead with about four minutes to go, but Tipperary came back. This ball went into Paddy McMahon and it was cleared out and driven way down the field, and Tipperary got a goal from it. Limerick went back up the field on the attack and the ball went into McMahon. If he was still there now, Dinny McLoughlin wouldn't let him hit it. Eventually the referee gave a free to Limerick and they scored to equalise. The referee blew the whistle and the match ended in a draw, 3-3 apiece. There was a priest from Tipperary in the crowd and he went into the referee after the match and said, 'Well Tommy, only for that [the collar], I would give you that [the fist].'

☙

1936–9: STEADY DESCENT

By 1936, the Limerick team and particularly Mick Mackey had become a major attraction, for hurling people and non-supporters alike. The publicity surrounding their unbeaten run led to an invitation to visit the US, and they travelled there along with the Cavan footballers in May 1936. Prior to their departure, Ahane beat Kildimo 6-8 to 2-3 in a delayed 1935 county final, and a Munster selection containing nine Limerick players surrendered their Railway Cup crown to Leinster by 2-8 to 3-4 on St Patrick's Day. However, there was consolation in the form of a third successive League title a couple of weeks later following a 7-2 to 4-4 victory over Dublin at Croke Park.

The US trip got off to a tragic start, however, as Fr Liam Ryan explains:

The match programme for the double header between Limerick and New York in hurling, and Cavan and New York in football at the Yankee Stadium, New York, in 1936. Mick Mackey is incorrectly named as Mike Mahoney.

In later years at a golf outing in Castletroy, Mick Mackey told us a story about the 1936 trip to America. Limerick got a bye into that year's Munster final because they were going on the trip. They travelled from Cobh, and a huge crowd waved them off. Two days after leaving Cobh, Michael McKnight, a county board official, dropped dead, leaving a wife and four small kids at home. I don't know what they did with the body.

The team came back a month or so later and they all called in to the family to sympathise over the next few days. Mackey told Mrs McKnight that her husband had had a lovely death, 'died in my arms'. Timmy Ryan called two days later and told the same story, as did Paddy Scanlon and Jackie Power: 'a lovely death, died in my arms'. Mackey said that at the end of the week the mother turned to the children and said, 'I declare to God, your father didn't die at all, I think they smothered him.'

The Limerick senior hurlers on the boat to the US in 1936. This Limerick side were unbeaten in 31 games over a 22-month period from October 1933 to August 1935. This included six games against both Cork and Dublin and four each against Clare, Galway and Tipperary. This amazing record has never been equalled in the history of hurling.

Mick Mackey (*right*) watches the toss with the Cork captain at a game in the late 1930s. The identity of the Cork captain is unknown.

Jackie O'Connell and Dave Clohessy were unable to make the trip for Limerick, who beat New York by 3-7 to 2-3 in the first game before 40,000 at Yankee Stadium. It was part of a double header where Cavan beat New York by 1-7 to 0-5. The low scores would suggest competitive games, which could be due to a combination of travel tiredness and the fact that New York had a number of ex-pats in their teams. The Mackey brothers were on fire, with Mick scoring 1-3 and John 0-3. In the second game of the series Limerick beat New York by 6-3 to 0-8, and rounded off the tour by defeating the Massachusetts All-Stars by 9-4 to 2-2 at Russell Field, Cambridge. The players were wined and dined like royalty and their iconic status attracted female attention. Some old-timers have suggested tongue in cheek that there may well have been the makings of a fine New York hurling team in the 1950s! Limerick showed no sign of tiredness on their return, demolishing Tipperary by 8-5 to 4-6 in the Munster final to win their fourth successive crown, with Mick Mackey setting a record that may never be equalled, scoring 5-3. Jimmy Butler Coffey explained:

Flanagan was in goals that day, and wasn't a bad goalkeeper, and normally he would never let a ball in past him. Mackey had a great day, and it's still a marvellous record. He often played as well and even better afterwards but he never put up as high a score. Mackey himself reckoned that some of the goals were very soft. I felt sorry for Flanagan because he was from north Tipperary too and would have experienced the same difficulties being picked for the county team that I would have. In general we wouldn't have been afraid of Mackey in Tipperary. We would have been thinking of the overall team rather than just Mackey. We wouldn't be worried about one man simply because Limerick overall were a great team. They went out and hurled every Sunday and were nearly always at full strength.

Prior to the Munster final, Clare had demolished Cork after a replay, and Tipperary had then beaten Clare comfortably in the semi-final, so Tipperary were in fine fettle entering the Munster final. Mick Mackey was captain of Limerick for the first time in the Munster championship, while Timmy Ryan had been captain for the League success. For some reason, a system seemed to prevail at the time whereby the championship captain didn't relinquish the armband until the following year's championship. That was also the case two years earlier when the captain for the 1933 championship, Mick Kennedy, captained them to League success and Timmy Ryan then took over and captained them to Munster championship and All-Ireland success. There is also a local tale told whereby in a game where Timmy Ryan was still captain, during the parade Mick Mackey jumped into the line ahead of Ryan and led the team around. It may well have been the moment when Mackey took over as captain. In any event Mick Mackey lifted the Munster trophy and, according to the Irish Independent *of Monday 3 August 1936, led by example:*

If one man more than another is deserving of credit for bringing victory to Limerick it was Mick Mackey, who was here, there, and everywhere, and contributed no less than five goals and three points to the winners' total score.

It is widely said that Mick Mackey was very boisterous when celebrating scores and wasn't too worried about rubbing salt into the opposition players. This could sometimes extend to antics that modern-day soccer players involve themselves in. Patrick M. O'Sullivan's review of David Smyth's The Unconquerable Keane *includes the following:*

Mackey, the playboy of the 1930s, was ebullient, electric in a world of paraffin lamps, unstoppable. He had scored 5-3 in the 1936 Munster final, a game during which he supposedly bared his buttocks to the crowd as a provocation to the Tipperary supporters.

Mick Mackey (*third from left*) and the Galway captain check the toss before the 1936 All-Ireland semi-final.

Clearly Mackey took great satisfaction in putting one over on Tipperary in such dynamic fashion. Perhaps motivated by the defeat to Newport in 1931 as an Ahane player, he felt the need to show his Tipperary neighbours that the tables had now turned. Limerick marched on and with fifteen minutes remaining led a fiery and incident-fraught All-Ireland semi-final against Galway at Roscrea by 4-9 to 2-4. However, the game was stalled following an alleged deliberate injury to a Galway player. Supporters invaded the pitch, and when the referee refused to send the perpetrator off the Galway players walked off the field. Limerick were awarded the match by the Central Council and Galway were suspended for six months. In the final Limerick faced their old adversaries Kilkenny, demolishing them by 5-6 to 1-5. The Kilkenny mindset before the game was similar to that of Tipperary before the Munster final. There was no specific plan to stop Mick Mackey. Martin White explains:

I never heard anyone in Kilkenny saying to watch Mick Mackey in particular, but whatever man was going out to stop him knew what Mackey was capable of. There were a few players that would have been able to beat him around that time and in later years. John Keane in Waterford was always master of Mackey. In Kilkenny we had Podge

Byrne, a big strong man who wasn't really fast but had the knack of always being where the ball was. Podge had a couple of fellas around him that were very good and if Podge wasn't getting the better of Mackey, there was always someone to give a hand.

People used to say that Mick Mackey was a dirty hurler but I disagree with that. I believe he took more punishment than he gave, because people who had a chance to have a go at him, and there were many, took their chance to do him. He had to dish it out on his own. He didn't lie down, but I can't remember him doing anything of note. He was so strong and domineering that the opposition didn't like him. He played hard but fair and didn't do anything dirty. John Mackey, on the other hand, would hit you a sneaky one and nobody would see him doing it, but anything that Mick did was really above board for everybody to see. Mick had a name for blackguarding, but that was only because opposition players didn't like him because he was so good.

I remember Paddy Phelan was playing on John in a League game at Kilkenny one day. He was beating John. Mick, who was centre-forward, couldn't bear to see John being beaten and he left Podge Byrne all on his own and went out to help John. Paddy Phelan beat the two Mackeys for the rest of the match. When the match was over they went over and shook his hand and took him by an arm each into the dressing room. It was great to see it.

Limerick had peaked as a hurling force, and were rated far and wide both collectively and as individuals. Here are some tributes to some of the main players who played with Mackey, as told by those who saw them in the flesh either in the 1930s or in later years:

John Mackey:

John Mackey was a much better hurler than Mick, he was a lot faster to play the ball. Mick was a great man, but you couldn't put him down as a great hurler. He didn't have the real instinct of what to do if he didn't get the ball in his hand. However, if he got the ball in his hand he would push you to one side and he was gone through. (*Jimmy Butler Coffey*)

John Mackey never got the credit he deserved. When Mick Mackey was there he got all the credit but John was a better hurler than Mick. He was also a better team man, and never got credit for what he was able to do. He was a great hurler, but Mick stole the limelight from him. When John played on Paddy Phelan the hurling between them used to be great. Two complete hurlers. (*Martin White*)

John wasn't as good a hurler as Mick, but he was a very robust hurler in around the square, especially if he was in at full-forward in later years. You couldn't really compare them because they were different types of hurlers. (*Mickey 'The Rattler' Byrne*)

John was a great hurler but an awful rogue. He would hit you the lousiest belt of an elbow. I played with him and against him several times in both the football and hurling. When I was playing against him I would always hit him a belt of a shoulder and I would hurl away. But he would watch his opportunity to get you back. I remember one day playing with Knockane against Ahane in Caherconlish in the football. A ball hopped between us, but he made no attempt to jump for it. As I was passing him to jump, he hit me a belt of an elbow and he knocked stars out of me but luckily enough I wasn't knocked out. He would hit you in the jaw or the side of the head, or anywhere he could, just to get a belt at you. (*Tommy Cooke*)

John Mackey was a great hurler, but I don't think he was a better hurler than Mick or had better hurling in him. He was a vicious kind of player. Mick was a genuine player and would go through you but he wouldn't be vicious. (*Andy Fleming*)

Paddy Scanlon:

Scanlon was the king of the goalkeepers. He won a couple of county championships with Liam Mellows. He played in Galway because he used to work with McMahon's the timber yard and they sent him up to work in a place they had in Galway. (*Gerry Piggott*)

Paddy Scanlon had few equals that time, he was one of the best goalkeepers of all time. One day, the Cork fellas went to kill him when they couldn't score on him. They hit him badly that day. Scanlon was one of the best goalies that there ever was down through the years and there were a lot of good goalkeepers. (*Martin White*)

Tom McCarthy:

Tom McCarthy was a great full-back and kept Mick Hickey off the Limerick team for years. It was only when Tom McCarthy went to America that Hickey became the full-back on the team. He went out to America with the Limerick team and came back for a couple of years before emigrating again. (*Gerry Piggott*)

I remember Tom McCarthy above in the moat field in Kilfinane pucking the ball. He could strike it from one field out into the next. He was able to drive it 90 or 100 yards, which was unheard of that time. Whoever would be pucking it back to him wouldn't be able to reach him, and I might be 50 yards closer to Tom and would have to hit it back the rest of the way. He was a serious loss to Limerick when he went off to America. Richard McCarthy who plays for Blackrock and Limerick these days is a grand-nephew of Tom McCarthy and you can see the old McCarthy blood in him. (*Maurice Regan*)

Timmy Ryan 'Good Boy' was famous for scoring points directly from puck-outs by doubling on the ball overhead. He once did it on the greatest stage of all, a Munster final against Cork:

Timmy Ryan 'Good Boy' was a great centre field man, a great worker but wouldn't have been as good as Mick Mackey. Mackey was the best man of the whole lot. (*Jimmy Butler Coffey*)

Timmy Ryan covered a lot of ground in games and would be best described as a box-to-box player. One of my earliest memories of him was at a Thomond Feis game, because he used to have a fresh complexion and he used to sweat a lot. As young lads we were always admiring his gear. His brother Pak went to America after school, a big loss to Ahane and a better hurler than Timmy. (*Willie Keane*)

Whether it was on the ground or in the air, Timmy Ryan would pull on it, and the ball moved on quickly. (*Maurice Regan*)

Timmy Ryan 'Good Boy' was a great centre field man, but a different type of hurler. At that time Scanlon would puck out the ball, Timmy Ryan would double on it centre field and the ball would be driven into the forwards in about two strokes; now it takes six. You would never see an overhead pull now. (*Gerry Piggott*)

Timmy Ryan was a great player, a complete hurler, there wasn't a wrong stroke in his body. Lory Meagher was the same way, Lory hadn't a wrong stroke in him either, and the hurling used to be great between them. Timmy Ryan had Mick Ryan playing centre field with him. Mick wasn't a great hurler but he was a great man, and he did all the work for Timmy, if you like, and left Timmy do all the hurling. (*Martin White*)

Timmy was a great player but he wasn't a classy hurler. He was a great man on an overhead ball, on a dropping ball. He could take it in the air, no trouble to him. He was bony and strong because he was a farmer and spent a lot of time ploughing. He ran the whole farm because his brother was gone to America and his two sisters were at home and he had to look after them. I often heard him saying when we were training, 'I am very tired, I was ploughing and harrowing all day, and have about ten miles of ploughing and harrowing done. That should be enough training for me.' I wasn't ever too sympathetic and I said, 'Ah sure, you are well able for it Timmy.' (*Tony Herbert*)

William Francis Lee, the former teacher in Ahane, used to write a column for the *Limerick Leader* at the time called 'Gaels and their Games' under the pen name Thomond. He did an awful lot for hurling here in Ahane. Timmy Ryan used to go down to the creamery in Annacotty with milk. On a Monday morning we would know he was coming back by the sound of the horse and car. We would say, 'Mr Lee, Timmy Ryan is coming.' Mr Lee would go out and chat to Timmy Ryan for half an hour, and it was one handy way of getting out of doing our schoolwork. The *Irish Independent* that time ran a competition to find out who was the best hurler in Ireland. Pierse McGee and his brother from Lisnagry railway station wrote to the *Independent* and said, 'Timmy Ryan was faithfully known in his native parish as Timmy 'Good Boy', and not only was he a good boy but he was the greatest boy of them all.' He was a good one. (*Michael Hynes*)

Paddy McMahon:

McMahon was a great hurler, a powerfully strong man, he had a great habit of doubling on balls overhead and on the ground, and he scored a lot of goals from that. (*Jimmy Butler Coffey*)

Paddy McMahon was a product of different times. It's very hard to compare him with the full-forwards of today because the game has changed so much. (*Maurice Regan*)

Paddy McMahon could play corner as well, but full-forward was his place. He was a great full-forward. (*Martin White*)

Paddy McMahon was from Kildimo. Mick Hickey was a fishery inspector and he got him a job as bailiff on the local rivers such as the Mulcair and the Shannon on condition that he hurled with Ahane. He made the Limerick team and won the two All-Irelands in 1936 and 1940. He was a good full-forward and had a great pair of shoulders on him. He never lifted a ball up. As the ball dropped he usually met it on the drop and drove into the back of the net. McMahon was a great full-forward but I think Bob McConkey of Young Irelands was the best full-forward Limerick had. (*Tony Herbert*)

Mick Ryan:

Mick Ryan of Cregane played with Newport. I can't remember if he ever hurled with Ahane at any stage. A tough man. He was a brother of Pat Ryan the councillor, known as 'the golden handshake' or 'shake hands'. He used have the hand up before he would meet you. (*Gerry Piggott*)

Paddy Clohessy:

I would have been playing at centre-forward on Paddy Clohessy when I was playing against Limerick. He was an outstanding hurler. Whether striking the ball on the ground or out of his hand, it didn't matter. (*Martin White*)

Jackie Power:

Anybody could talk about Jackie Power. The best all-round man of all. He could play in any position. (*Jimmy Butler Coffey*)

There were several more heroes for Limerick in that golden era. Garett Howard, originally from Croom, won All-Irelands with Limerick in 1921, 1934 and 1936 and with Dublin in 1924 and 1927. He formed the half-back line with Paddy Clohessy and Mickey Cross. Cross was from St Patrick's and was widely respected as a great hurler. Dave Clohessy, a brother of Paddy's, played a very important part for Limerick, scoring 24-4 in his championship career. Another noted goalscorer was Jackie Connell, who would subsequently become a high-profile county board secretary and chairman. Bob McConkey captained Limerick to the 1921 All-Ireland title and provided valuable experience as a full-forward in 1934 when they regained it. Paddy Carroll played in 1936 and was an important part of what was arguably the greatest Limerick team of all time.

Ahane retained their county championship when beating Croom by 7-8 to 0-3 to collect the 1936 crown, which was played on 25 April 1937. Mick Mackey captained Munster to the 1937 Railway Cup title, beating Leinster by 1-9 to 3-1. He also captained Limerick to win their fourth successive National League title. In the Munster championship, he had his first major encounter with John Keane, as Séamus Power explains:

The first match I saw Mick Mackey playing in was in 1937 and he was at his peak at the time. I was eight years old and my father took me to the championship match against Limerick at Clonmel. John Keane, who I regard as our greatest ever hurler in Waterford, was only a young strapping boy at the time. He played on Mick Mackey and as Waterford men we thought Keane got the better of Mackey on the day. The Mackey versus John Keane rivalry was probably exaggerated. There was no man who could be at his very best every day, whether he was Mackey, John Keane or Christy Ring, who was the greatest hurler I ever saw. I would rate Ring as being better, I think he had that little bit more. I was young when Mackey was in his heyday but my father used to think he was outstanding.

Andy Fleming gave his view:

I would have played with John Keane a lot because he was my club-mate. I remember one day we played Limerick here up in the Sportsfield in Waterford. John Keane was marking Mick Mackey. The ball came down, Mick Mackey dummied John Keane and turned around and let go a piledriver of a shot that was saved. I was playing beside Keane at right-half-back, and I said to myself, 'Mick, you won't get away with that any more.' About ten minutes later the same kind of ball came down, and he did the same thing again and he turned around, and he never saw me coming in. He threw up the ball to hit it, and t'was I who hit it, man, ball and all. Mick Mackey was a big man and he dropped onto one knee. I was looking at him and he was also glancing at me every now and then. He didn't hit a ball for about five minutes. About ten minutes from the end, the ball came into the back line and I came out to around the 14-yard line, put my hand down and caught it. As I was handling it, I got a most ferocious belt on the hand. I cleared the ball, looked down at my hand and saw that my four knuckles were skinned. Mick Mackey saw me and he said in less than polite language, 'Tit for tat, you black-haired . . .' I said to myself, I must have really sickened him in the first half.

If Mick Mackey was alive today, got the ball in his hand and turned towards the goal, not alone would he walk on half the backs of the present-day teams, he would trample them into the ground. It's not that he was a hard man, it's more that he was a strong hurler, and backs are softer today. He was able to double on balls coming down from overhead, and on the ground. Now players have a light ball, and are like a pack of youngsters out on a green when they are playing matches. They can't double on it on the ground, left, right, or in the sky. You never see them doubling on a sky ball. They have to pick it up, and when they pick it, they can't hit it, they have to handpass it. In my time we doubled on a ball, left, right and in the air, and Mick Mackey was a genius at it. I think Mackey was better than Ring or John Keane. He was stronger than the two of them. John Keane was a great player, and a nicer hurler.

As far as Munster championship aspirations were concerned, the glorious golden era for Limerick hurling ended when Tipperary denied them their fifth successive Munster title. Jimmy Butler Coffey had fond memories:

In 1937 we knew we had a good chance against Limerick in the Munster final. We had drawn with them in the League in Thurles in December 1935, and it looked like we were the only team that would beat them. They were the best team around, unbeaten for two years, and seemed invincible, yet we had drawn with them. We should have won that match, but we went one better and did beat them in November 1936 in the League in Thurles, their first defeat in the League for a few years. That set us up to beat them in the 1937 Munster final. In that final, every man marked his own man, and left John Maher to mark Mick Mackey that day which he did

Mick Mackey leads the Limerick team (*back row*) in the parade before the 1937 Munster senior hurling final. Jimmy Butler Coffey is sixth from the front on the Tipperary team, with his left hand to his face.

fairly well. Johnny Ryan was a great right-half-back and he also hurled well on the day. Limerick were slipping at the time, but still it was a great game. It was 1-2 apiece at half time, and it finished 6-3 to 4-3. I was playing at right-half-forward, being marked by Jackie Power. Some time afterwards, there was a funeral in Limerick that the missus and myself were at. Mick Mackey and Power were across the road talking, and Power came over to me and said, 'I am just after saying to Mackey, I must go across the road now and talk to the man who gave me a right pasting in the Munster final in Cork.'

Martin White was at the game:

I don't think there was a lot between Limerick and Tipperary in 1937. I was at the game in Cork and I believe that Limerick could have won the All-Ireland if they had pulled through and beaten Tipperary, because they were good enough. They were unlucky that there were other teams starting to come at that time. When they were ar their best, other teams were coming. If the other teams in Munster weren't as strong, they could have won more. They were unlucky the whole way up along through the 1930s because Kilkenny were there and won a few All-Irelands that Limerick would definitely have won if we weren't around.

Limerick won their fifth League title in a row in 1938 beating Tipperary by 5-2 to 1-1 with Mick Mackey as captain. Jimmy Butler Coffey explained that he was a target for punishment after his display in the 1937 Munster final:

When we met in the League final in 1938 they crucified me in the first half. They hit me from everywhere because they blamed me for beating them in 1937. Jackie Power was a foreman in Nelligan's workshop in Newport at the time. I called in on the morning after the match, and Mick Nelligan said to Power, 'Jackie, you had the best of it yesterday.' 'Only for having another man [Butler Coffey] playing with me,' said Jackie, 'I wouldn't have had such a good game.' I got an awful doing from them that morning. There was no mercy shown that time. Limerick might have beaten us in the 1938 League final, but in 1937 we had beaten them on our way to winning the All-Ireland. We were as good as Limerick on both days but they were in decline after 1936 and the great team was beginning to break up. The older players were putting miles on the clock and Tipperary and Cork were beginning to come good.

Things didn't go to plan in the 1938 Munster championship as Limerick were beaten by Cork. In 1939 they were also beaten by Cork in the Munster final. It was a barren spell for a team that was so dominant in Munster only a couple of years earlier. Martin White was a keen observer from outside, and assesses the situation in Munster at the time:

Limerick were still a relatively young team but had got a bit of experience by the late 1930s, even though great players like Mickey Cross and Garett Howard departed. I think Limerick should have won more. Ironically, Tipperary should also have won more at the time, but they went out of it because of the Jimmy Cooney case. Cooney was attending UCD and served two suspensions, one for attending a rugby game and another arising out of a delayed paperwork declaration relating to his residence in Dublin, outside his native county.

Tipperary were notified that he was suspended for the Munster championship. Clare also told them that if they played Cooney, an objection would follow. Tipperary took their chances playing him under suspension and won, thinking Clare wouldn't object, but they did object and Tipperary were thrown out. That was the end of that Tipperary team and they didn't come back after that for a good few years. Waterford were coming strong as well at the time and had fourteen Erin's Own men on the team back in 1938. A guy called Coffey was the fifteenth man and he was playing for a country club. He then decided to join Erin's Own, so they then had fifteen Erin's Own men on the county team.

Limerick found it hard to win the Munster championship after 1936. It was very difficult to win Munster that time because the teams were nearly all equal. The proof of that is that Limerick won the Munster championship in 1936, Tipperary in 1937, Waterford in 1938 and Cork in 1939. Limerick eventually came again in 1940.

Brendan Fullam gives his assessment of Limerick's failure to win more:

Mickey Cross's horses were burned in a fire the night before the 1937 Munster final and he should never have played because he couldn't possibly have been in the right frame of mind. Tommy Doyle was on him and was flying that day, which contributed to the defeat. In 1939, Limerick shaved the post against Cork in the Munster final, and had they won that, I think they would have beaten Kilkenny in the All-Ireland final. In those days there was nothing between Limerick and Kilkenny. When you think of the calibre of men Limerick had

The Limerick team which won the Oireachtas in 1939. *Back row (l–r):* [first two players are unknown], Paddy Scanlon, Mick Mackey, Johnsie Donoghue, Dan Givens, John Mackey, Timmy Ryan, Willie Lee (Willie was there to take notes for the newspaper). *Front row (l–r):* Tommy Cooke, John Foley, Mick McCarthy, Paddy Mackey, Peter Cregan, Jackie Power, Tony Herbert.

in the 1930s, they definitely underachieved. They won five National League titles in a row, four Munster finals in a row and made four All-Ireland final appearances in a row. Tipperary eventually beat them unexpectedly by 6-3 to 4-3 in 1937.

In that game we had ten goals, the reason being that the ball was flying first time and being pulled on first time, meaning that the goalie hadn't the chance to see that final flick. Nowadays they would be trying to rise that ball, but that gives the goalie time to settle, and by the time the forward has the ball in his hand there are three defenders converging around him. The one big change from the Mackey era is that they can't ground hurl any more.

The game has evolved, but hasn't improved itself as a spectacle from the Mackey days because of the loss of the ground stroke. To say the game is faster is not accurate; they are lifting the ball, but they are not running faster. In later years such as the 1940s, Joe Kelly of Cork was a champion runner, as was Ralph Prendergast from the 1955 Limerick team, while Prendergast's team-mate Vivian Cobbe was also a flyer. There were equally fast players in the 1930s. It is a

Jackie Power (Limerick) tries to hook Jimmy Butler Coffey (Tipperary) in the 1937 Munster final, as Paddy Scanlon (Limerick) advances from his line.

myth to say that the game is faster, because it is not. The game in the past was fiercely thrilling.

Mick Mackey also dabbled in football and won a Munster junior champion-ship in 1939, as Tommy Cooke explains:

I won two Munster junior championships in 1939, hurling and football. They wanted us to play the two All-Ireland semi-finals on the same Sunday. We were due to play Kilkenny in the hurling and Roscommon in the football. We elected to play against Roscommon and Waterford took our place in the hurling semi-final and lost to Kilkenny by a point. If they had beaten them, we would have been in the All-Ireland final. We were robbed against Roscommon in the football. We had a great junior football team, and the Mackeys were playing together at midfield. Dan Givens was playing at full-forward and scored two goals. The referee gave frees instead of allowing the goals. A close-in free in football was no good that time because there were four or five players lined up in the goals.

I also won the county championship with Knockane and we played against Ahane that year. We had a fellow called Mick Higgins from

Dublin. The Ahane fellas knew he was a stranger and they hit him with everything they had. We stuck into them and shouldered them and kicked the football the first chance we got. They got no score and we won the match, and we won the final afterwards against Abbeyfcale with an illegal team. There was a Din Beary from Knockane in the army in the Curragh and he brought three fellas down to play the match. They were collected at Limerick Junction on the Saturday evening and were brought to people's houses in horses and traps. The game against Abbeyfeale was a replay in Limerick, as we had drawn with them in Ballingarry the first day. These army players were jumping up into the clouds for the ball. I knew the Abbeyfeale players because we played with them on the Limerick junior team. One Abbeyfeale player said to me, 'Who is that fella?', and I said, 'It's one of the Ryans, but I couldn't tell you which one he is.' The army men had been given false names and we called them Ryans because over around Knockane on the Tipperary border the place was full of Ryans. It was a great ruse.

While there was always conflict in Limerick during the golden era, it stayed below the surface and didn't really emerge until the less successful days returned. Mackey was by now famous for the solo run, but Tony Herbert wasn't a fan:

Mackey controlled the game himself and he dictated on and off the field. John was a better hurler than him. Mick was always at clown antics and solo runs and things like that. He never played the ball and didn't have the great craft that John had, or Dick Stokes who came later. He depended on this strength. He had good players around him but never passed the ball until he was tackled himself. Against Kilkenny one day, Mick got a right haymaker. He got the ball and John shouted to pass it, that Mick was going to get upended, but Mick wouldn't pass. A guy called Billy Burke of Kilkenny came in and hit him a belt and put him sitting on his backside.

Mackey didn't deny that the solo run was unconventional:

I think the solo run happened by accident more than anything else. I think it was in a Railway Cup match in 1935 or 1936 that I happened to break through with a clear field and just took the run. I think that's how it happened. It's not something that I had practised, though I was always prick acting with the ball and playing around with it but it wasn't something that I practised. I don't believe that I had ever seen anyone doing a solo run before. (Mick Mackey interviewd by Val Dorgan, RTÉ Television, 1969)

Paddy Clohessy was forever in the wars, as Tony Herbert explains:

Clohessy and Mick Mackey used to mark one another in club games and Mackey got no change out of Clohessy because there was very little between them. Jim Roche refereed a game involving Ahane and Fedamore and put off three Fedamore men. As a result, Clohessy refused to play for Limerick in 1939 because Jim Roche was on the team. Clohessy was wrong when he wouldn't play and he let down the Limerick team and let down his entire county by not playing.

There was a row after that club match, and we went in to help Jim Roche. I was beside Paddy Clohessy and I saw him hit Jim Roche with a steel bicycle pump on the head. Roche got five or six belts of hurleys but he flattened every fella who came towards him. Jim Roche was a tough man, a great scrapper and a great boxer.

Tommy Cooke elaborates:

Roche was a bad referee and if you didn't accept his decision, he fancied himself as a boxer and he would hit you a belt of a fist during the match. Roche wasn't a great forward either, he was more or less a ground hurler. Clohessy was always at loggerheads with Jim Roche but he was a massive loss because Cork beat Limerick in the Munster final. That's an All-Ireland that Limerick left behind them.

That Limerick team were a contrary team and if a row started, they all waded in and slated all around them. There was a big row with Galway in 1937 in Gort or somewhere, when Galway played a great game against them and they fought. Paddy Clohessy was a great friend of mine and at the start of a match he would hit his man a tip to let him know who was the boss, and if his man retaliated he would get more of it.

Cooke believes that if the referee was strict, the players played the ball:

I refereed a match in Bruree in 1940 between Fedamore and Croom for a set of hurleys. The curate in Croom asked me to referee the game. I was reluctant at first but eventually agreed. I lined them up and warned them that the first player that hit his man would go to the sideline. There wasn't a word in the match and Fedamore beat Croom for a fine set of hurleys.

Martin White says the internal conflict was no secret outside the county:

Fedamore and Ahane were two of the big noises at the time in the Limerick club championship and it was widely known that the Mackeys and the Clohessys didn't get on. Fedamore and Ahane never agreed. It was widely known outside Limerick that there were daggers thrown between them in club games. However, when they went out to play for Limerick you wouldn't notice that there was any problem between them. I was in Waterford one day with Locky Byrne, and we had nothing to do because there was no match on. At that time, there was always a mystery tour from Waterford to an unknown destination. You got onto a bus and didn't know where you would end up. We decided to get on the mystery tour and we ended up in Limerick. We got off the bus and as we were walking up along the back of the hurling grounds the players were on the way out from a match between Fedamore and Ahane. The two Mackeys were there, and there was a bit of blood spilt and there was blood streaming from them onto the ground. Next thing I met Paddy Clohessy and he had blood on him too. I said to him, 'Paddy, you must have been in a bit of a skirmish.' 'I was,' he replied 'but if you think I am in a bad state, you should take a look at the two Mackeys. I can guarantee you they are a lot worse than me.'

Politics were also rife, particularly at minor level, as Tony Herbert explains:

There was terrible misjudgement on the selection of minors to play for Limerick. If you were on the county board and you were from Askeaton, one or two players from Askeaton would be on the team. They weren't any good, but you got them on the team at the expense of better players. And that happened with a lot of west Limerick players. They got on the teams but they weren't worth their place. They played with us on the minor team in 1938, and we would have won the All-Ireland that year only for them. Too many weak players were picked on that team by selectors from their own clubs. Players who wouldn't even get their place on the Ahane minor team were being picked on the Limerick minor team. The rest of us who were good enough were saddled with that. I was captain of the team that year; we had some good players, Dick McCarthy and Seán Foley, but we had too many passengers.

Ahane won five consecutive county football championships but many games were embroiled in turmoil. Michael Hynes remembered one particular row:

There were rows in those days and it was the usual thing that time. Everyone hated Ahane because they were winning so much. They were tough too. The biggest row I saw was outside in Askeaton when Ahane played Glin in the final of the county football championship. There was an invasion that day and the players had to leave the field and take shelter. That was the worst I ever saw. The players had to rush out and the crowd were waiting for them outside on the road. Mick and John Mackey were good to fight. John was a terror altogether, had a great pair of hands . . . for boxing!

Tony Herbert played in the game:

Any time Ahane played football the game ended up in a row. Glin had a big crowd there because it was only ten or fifteen miles from the venue but we had nobody with us, except a few truck drivers or a few who had cars. A ball came into our square like a rocket and it bounced out but hit a Glin man and came back into the square. I touched it on the ground and there was a penalty given against me. Glin had a good footballer taking the penalty, but he was a bit of a fancy boy and was always doing his hair up.

Before the whistle was blown to take the penalty, John Mackey came out and kicked the ball away from the spot. He did the same thing a second time. The referee said to him, 'You will go to the line the next time you do that.' John didn't have to do it a third time because he kicked the penalty wide. So there was a big row and Glin went for the referee. We went in and stood there and blocked their supporters from getting at the referee, to save him from getting killed. I can't remember what happened afterwards but we were eventually awarded the match by the county board.

Willie Keane recalls a conversation about the encounter:

I remember talking to Mick Hickey about the game with Glin when the spectators laid siege to their dressing room. They had to get what implements they could to defend themselves and stand shoulder to shoulder until they got out of town. A local man, Jimmy Ryan, used to take Ahane supporters on a bus to some games. You wouldn't be left on the bus unless you were a fighting man. That was the kind of hostile territory you were going into.

Mick Mackey dabbled in the 'big ball' code and is photographed here with the Ahane senior football team in 1936. *Back row (l–r):* Bill Cummins, Davy Conway, Mickey Walsh, Jim Griffin, John Mackey, Billy Moloney, Dick Edmonds, Pa Healy, John Byrnes, Mick Mackey, Willie McCormack, Martin Phillips, Jim Murray (Garda), Tommy Herbert, Jimmy Hassett, Denny Minihan, Tom Moore, Pat Joyce, Rick Condon, Floss Byrnes, Martin Ryan. *Front row (l–r):* Jimmy Walsh, Jackie Power, Timmy Ryan, Bill Sheehan (non-player), Jimmy Moloney (Capt), Stan Hollis, Dan Givens, Jim Close, William Francis Lee (non-player). *Seated:* Mick Hickey.

John Lenihan played club football against Mick Mackey:

Galtee Rovers, now known as Galtee Gaels, played against Ahane in a county senior football semi-final in the 1930s. Busloads of people from Kilbenny and Anglesboro were taken to the village of Hospital for the game. The reason so many went was because Ahane had a number of high-profile players on the Limerick hurling team at the time. It would have been their first time seeing Mick Mackey and there was a poster in Anglesboro in advance of the game saying, 'Come to see the Mackeys playing'. Consequently, people who wouldn't normally go to a Gaelic football match went to see Mick Mackey. Because of the lack of transport at the time, it was difficult to get to see them playing for Limerick and they weren't going to spurn the opportunity to see them locally when it arose.

Jimmy Hassett was the best player Ahane had that day, but the bigger names weren't as noticeable. John Mackey looked to be very fast, but others such as Mick Mackey and Timmy Ryan didn't make much of an impact. Ahane won by a goal in controversial circumstances. At one stage I went down to pick up the ball near the sideline. The referee blew the whistle and stopped play, having deemed it to be a line ball. But the linesman shouted that it wasn't out, so Ahane played on, while our boys stood up thinking that play would be called back for a throw-in. However, Sergeant McKenna who was refereeing left things play on, and then awarded Ahane a 50, which should have been a wide ball.

Ahane took the 50 and it dropped short, Mick Mullins of Galtee Rovers went to catch the ball and Mick Mackey jumped up on his back and flattened him. But instead of giving a free out to Galtee Rovers, the referee gave a penalty to Ahane. We were level at the time and the penalty went in off the post to win the game for them. To this day we believe we were hard done by. The Ahane players were giving the referee verbal abuse throughout the game. We felt that the pressure coming from the big Ahane names influenced him. One incident I recall involved Mick Mackey. He was loose and calling for the ball, but his team-mate chose not to give it to him. He wasn't impressed and he shouted out in frustration, 'I am one pitied man.' He would have been used to getting the ball when he demanded it at intercounty hurling, but his local team-mates weren't as forthcoming.

In the midst of the glorious run for Limerick hurling, a talented player who should have been involved, Mick Russell from the city, was the victim of bureaucracy and politics. An old-timer outlines the story:

Mick Russell was as good an all-round sports man as existed in Limerick at the time. He was a founder member of Pike Rovers soccer club and played with the Munster schools in rugby, winning junior and senior cups with Richmond and Garryowen. He also hurled with Claughaun and this is where the story with Limerick starts. He had been playing with Claughaun but objected to the club's decision to re-grade themselves to junior in the early 1930s. Along with the two Condon brothers, he left Claughaun and joined Fedamore, who would have been one of the better teams in the county. At this stage he wasn't giving a firm commitment to GAA. He was playing rugby and was always getting caught.

He was on the Limerick hurling panel in 1935 but was suspended for playing rugby and missed the 1936 All-Ireland win. The only two players that were dropped were himself and another player called

Morrissey, but they weren't the only ones playing foreign codes. At this stage he was sick of the GAA, so decided to play rugby only and even gave up club hurling. While he was away from the game there was a procession up and down to his house in Mulgrave Street to get him back playing. They convinced him to give hurling a full-time shot in 1937; he joined Young Irelands and soon after the county board lifted his suspension. The next morning while cycling up Mulgrave Street he was shouted at by a man on the street, 'Off you go back to the GAA. See if we care.' He cycled on another 100 yards and a county board official also shouted at him less than politely, 'Off you go back to rugby.'

Limerick got to the Munster final against Tipperary and Russell was told by a selector to warm up. With that Mick Mackey went over to the sideline. 'No change will be made,' he said. 'No rugby player will play hurling with Limerick.' And so he wasn't brought on. It seems very strange given the association Mick Mackey had with rugby in later years but Russell gave up on hurling at that stage because he felt it wasn't worth the hassle.

And so the decade ended as most decades end in Limerick, with controversy overshadowing the glint of silverware. However, it must not be forgotten that the 1930s was the most glorious decade ever in Limerick GAA history.

FOUR

Cß

1940: INDIAN SUMMER

In 1940 Limerick claimed important silverware for the eighth year in a row, completing a set of fourteen major trophies since 1933. Only Paddy Clohessy, Timmy Ryan, John Mackey, Mick Mackey and Jim Roche remained from that 1933 team. Limerick played Waterford in the first round of the championship, drawing 4-2 to 3-5. Unusually, the game was played in Killarney, with Limerick winning the replay in Clonmel by 3-5 to 3-3.

Séamus Power explains:

Mick Mackey was a household name at the time, but I was still only a schoolboy so I was too young to appreciate him. In 1940 there was a great draw in Killarney and a replay in Clonmel. I often wondered why those games weren't played at Thurles. The home and away agreements weren't part of the psyche at the time. I presume the Munster Council fiddled the venue because it was neither in Limerick's nor Waterford's interests to be going to Killarney a second day. I suspect there was a stroke pulled to have that match in Killarney. There was definitely some little fiddle that took place. And choosing Clonmel for the replay as opposed to Thurles may have been a little sop or a help out to Waterford. Even though we had a good team around that time, we were only emerging and probably would be regarded as the weakest county in Munster. That said, in my opinion, we were never weaker than Clare.

I was at the replay in Clonmel, but I didn't make it to Killarney. Those were the days where the bicycle was the main form of transport. The war had started in 1939 and we couldn't get tyres because of it. A group of us young lads, aged thirteen or fourteen, got together with a few older lads and decided to cycle to Killarney to follow Waterford. I got a puncture three or four miles outside Waterford city and couldn't get a tube or a replacement valve because of the war and had to walk back.

I would agree with the assertion that John Keane was the only man to hold Mick Mackey. But it wasn't just a case of holding Mackey. Keane was an outstanding hurler in his own right and was physical. He was a great man as a young fellow, very fit, and Keane was a man you could depend on to hold anyone, not just Mick Mackey. However, Mackey was the kingpin at the time, and if you held Mackey you knew you were in with a great chance of winning the game.

Andy Fleming agreed:

In 1940 we held Mick Mackey, or should I say John Keane held him. He didn't ever score much off John Keane. It's not like now, when players are running around the field and they don't know who they are playing with. That time you held your position and you marked your man. John was a big strong man but Mick Mackey wasn't as good in the 1940s as he was in the '30s. I never played against Mackey at his peak because his career was coming to its end when I was starting. There was a period from the 1930s and into the 1940s which was the best ever era for hurling in Munster. Limerick had great players such as Mick Mackey, John Mackey, Dr Dick Stokes, Jackie Power, Tony Herbert and Seán Herbert. In Cork you had the likes of Batt Thornhill, Con Murphy, Bill Murphy, Christy Ring, Jack Lynch and all those. Waterford had a great team too, and Tipperary were strong.

The encounters between Mick Mackey and John Keane were much talked about, and Con Murphy believed that their individual clashes were worth the admission fee alone:

There was a lot of comment at that time about individual encounters on the field, say Mick Mackey versus John Keane, or John Quirke, one of our best hurlers at the time, versus Mick Mackey. Encounters like that attracted the people to the games as much as the games themselves. My first real sharp look at Mick Mackey was in the replay in Clonmel in 1940 between Waterford and Limerick. We knew about that during the week because the papers were writing it up, what would happen between John Keane and Mick Mackey, who won that encounter, and so on and so forth. I was going to see Mick Mackey and John Keane. It was a wonderful encounter between the two of them. I saw Mick Mackey throw up a ball that day and John Keane hit it. That took some doing. (Colm Keane, *Hurling's Top 20*)

A Limerick source at the game says that Keane and Mackey spent more time pulling across one another and clattering one another off the ball than they did playing the ball. Tony Herbert made his championship debut in Killarney:

I was doing the Leaving Cert and Mick Hickey from Portlaw, a hardy player, said, 'How are you getting on, young fellow?' 'All right,' I said, 'but don't try any dirty tricks, I'm sitting an exam in the morning.' I put my hand up for the first ball and the next thing I got a belt in the ribs. That was his style. Mackey poleaxed him soon afterwards with a shoulder.

Mackey acknowledged that they weren't firing on all cylinders:

When we did start out in the [1940 championship] campaign we were a shook bunch. We went to Killarney and were leading Waterford by five points and they drew level with us. A fortnight later we had to go to Clonmel [for the replay] and we survived there against a very good Waterford team. They were a good side actually, and then we had to go to Thurles [for the Munster final] and of course nobody gave us a chance against Cork. (Mick Mackey interviewd by Val Dorgan, RTÉ Television, 1969)

Tony Herbert continued his hurling education in Clonmel:

Every man stood for himself on that Limerick team. There was a big row during the replay in Clonmel and Tommy Cooke went to help Paddy Clohessy and Paddy Scanlon because Clohessy was fighting with his back to some of the Waterford players. Jackie Power said to me, 'Do you see that fella passing up there, he is after hitting Tommy Cooke the belt on the back of the head.' I then said to Power, 'I saw another guy striking you from behind earlier in the game. Bluett is his name. I shouted at you when it happened but you didn't hear me.' Power replied, 'Keep your mouth shut or else they will get you if they hear you shouting.' I was only a young fella at the time and was learning my trade and didn't see the danger. About ten minutes afterwards Bluett fell and Power saw his chance, and pulled as hard as he could and nearly cut the head off him.

As with the Waterford games, Limerick endured a thrilling double encounter with Cork. They scored 4-3 to Cork's 3-6 in the drawn game, and edged the replay 3-3 to 2-4, despite failing to score in the first half. The games had everything: fast, furious hurling, titanic clashes and, above all, a little bit of

Mick Mackey contests the throw-in by Séamus Gardiner, chairman of the Munster Council, for the 1940 Munster final in Thurles.

controversy. Paddy McMahon was the hero, scoring three goals in the drawn game and two in the replay.

Séamus Ó Ceallaigh was impressed:

They were two great games in Thurles in 1940, two really memorable games. Limerick won and then went on to win the All-Ireland. It was a kind of a resurrection for Limerick, because they had been out of it since 1936 and they had come back to win that championship. ('A Celebration of Munster Hurling', RTÉ Television, 1976)

Tommy Cooke recalls that Mick Mackey carried baggage into these games:

We met Cork in the semi-final of a tournament at Emly that year. The final was played in Tipperary, for the opening of the Seán Treacy Memorial Park. During the course of the game in Emly, Mick Mackey hit Johnny Quirke down on top of the head and he had to be taken off. It was a lousy belt, and I don't know why he hit him. Mick Hickey was full-back and while he wasn't our best hurler he was very big and strong. He was marking Ted Sullivan on both days in Thurles against Cork and got the better of him. Derry Beckett played full-forward for Cork in Emly, and troubled Hickey. Cork didn't realise Beckett was a better player until it was too late. He used to wear a scrumcap because of a bad injury.

Tony Herbert and Mick Mackey had a major disagreement:

Mackey blamed me for not winning the drawn Munster final in 1940. I was playing at midfield with Timmy Ryan, and he said to me, 'You take Jack Barrett [Cork captain] and I'll take Connie Buckley.' I got the tougher opponent. Jack Barrett was awkward to play against, a big, strong man. I hit him a belt of a shoulder, knocked him over, rose the ball and put it over the bar. About ten minutes later Connie Buckley [Timmy Ryan's man] got a loose ball in the middle of the field and put it over the bar.

Mackey blamed me and said, 'He was your man.' I replied using less than polite language, 'He wasn't my man, I am playing on Jack Barrett. That's Timmy Ryan's man, so go and tell Timmy Ryan that.' Mackey drew a belt on me and I hit him a full force lash of the hurley across the back. And the next thing I heard someone saying, 'The Limerick fellas are fighting among themselves.' They all thought it was John Mackey that was after hitting Mick!

It was very difficult to play with Mackey because he would always call your name and make a show of you on the pitch. 'Hi Herbert, get stuck in, what are you looking at?' He had a habit of getting onto a few fellas like that. Paddy Clohessy and the experienced players wouldn't take it from him and Mackey knew that himself. But still, he would get onto anyone, he didn't care who they were, he would chance his arm.

The Munster final replay is best known for a mass pitch invasion after an altercation between Micka Brennan and Paddy Scanlon. The legend goes that when Cork couldn't score on Scanlan they tried to take him out by other means but Scanlan got his retaliation in first. The incident sparked the invasion, and it took some time before order was restored. Tony Herbert begins the story:

About 3,000 or 4,000 Cork supporters rushed [invaded] the field. Dan Ryan from Kerry was the referee, a football man, who knew nothing at all about hurling and wasn't able to control the game. He was the driver of the Kerry team around that time and then he started refereeing a few matches and climbed the ladder. Paddy Leahy of Tipperary who was doing umpire for him got a belt of a fist and the hat flew off him. Leahy followed the man who hit him and nailed him before giving him an awful beating.

The supporters all came in from the Killinan end having broken the fencing. I wasn't involved at all because I was at the other end of the field. My attitude was, let them fight away among themselves. The supporters hit as many players as they could. I couldn't see much of the row because there were so many on the field. The referee kept the match going most of the time the row was taking place. The supporters were firing sticks, stones and coats at Scanlon in the goals, and the players were going in hitting the crossbar, and he was blocking balls while it was all going on. I remember that well.

Tommy Cooke explains the background:

I was marking Dr Jim Young that day and we became great friends afterwards. We in the half-backs were hurling well the whole time and driving the ball away. However, any time the ball went in over our heads the full-back line and full-forward line were fighting for it and that eventually led to the row. The full-back line were in front of the goals fighting like hell and clearing the ball, and the forwards weren't getting a puck.

Micka Brennan, the Cork corner-forward, used to wear a black cap and black togs when he was playing. Brennan went in to try and score a goal, and Scanlan thought he was coming in to hit him and decided to strike the first blow. One of the Cork fellas always said years afterwards in his distinguished Cork accent, 'Scanlan hit him and he split him like an oyster.' The Cork supporters assembled behind the goals and were firing all sorts of missiles at Scanlan, hoping to unsettle him so he would concede a few goals. When they invaded the pitch Dan Ryan kept the play going, thinking the crowd would clear off the field, but he had to stop it eventually. The crowd more or less stayed off the field, behind the endline, for the last few minutes.

Gerry Piggott was at the game:

That day there was great pulling and hell for leather. They pelted bottles at Scanlan. He stopped haws that day. Micka Brennan used to wear black tights on his legs because he had very hairy legs and when Scanlan floored him there wasn't much sympathy. Ted Sullivan was full-forward and Mick Hickey frightened the life out of him. He broke his hurley off his back. Hickey was a tough man. He was slow but he was tough. Sullivan would run a mile from him even though he was a big man too.

Jimmy Butler Coffey believed Limerick's experience stood to them:

Limerick were a very seasoned team by then, and that made all the difference. Cork went on to win the four in a row from 1941 to '44 and proved that they were a great team in their own right. They were still a very young team in 1940 and that lack of experience meant they found it difficult against a physical Limerick side.

Gerry Piggott has fond post-match memories:

Mick Mackey often brought me in under his arm to big matches in Thurles and Limerick. I brought the Munster Cup out of Thurles in 1940. I was coming in with him in the crowd and I was glued to him. He was walking in his bare feet. He took off the boots and he had the cup in one hand and his gear in the other. 'Here,' says he, 'carry that cup', and handed me the cup and he brought me in and got me a bottle of lemonade in Maher's, the pub on the right as you go into the square. Sure I was like a king.

Tommy Cooke recalls that the Mackey brothers were in no rush home:

When the match was over we went straight from the pitch to the pub to tog off and eat the dinner. The Cork crowd used to always follow the Mackeys in after matches, and they used to enjoy talking to them. It was always late when they came to their dinner. The rest of us would have the dinner eaten and we would come back out to the pub fully dressed and the Mackeys would be still in their togs.

Limerick went on to beat Galway by 3-6 to 0-5 at Ennis in the All-Ireland semi-final, a game that's almost forgotten. Tony Herbert, however, has a clear recollection of one Galway player:

Inky Flaherty was playing for them. He went on to be a referee and also a selector with Galway. He was a Connacht champion heavyweight boxer and he hit me a belt of a fist on another day I was playing against Galway. I was walking past him in that match and he flattened me!

The 1940 All-Ireland final brought Limerick face to face with their adversaries from the 1930s, Kilkenny. They came from behind to win by 3-7 to 1-7 but Jimmy Butler Coffey said they had to restructure the team drastically to save the game:

An action shot from the 1940 All-Ireland final. Pictured are No. 12 Dick Stokes, No. 14 Paddy McMahon (with cap), Jackie Power beside him partially hidden, John Mackey in front of goal, Ned Chawke under crossbar and Jim Roche outfield behind John Mackey on 21-yard line. Timmy Ryan (with 3 marked on togs) and Mick Mackey (just in front of him) are also in the picture.

It was the greatest luck ever to win that All-Ireland in 1940, because Limerick weren't a great team by then. They were going off. Kilkenny had that match won and looked like they were going to take Limerick apart until an incident in the match forced Limerick to change the team around. Paddy Clohessy went off injured and they switched Mick Mackey to midfield and John Mackey to centre-forward. Tony Herbert went on as a sub and Jackie Power went back centre-back. It was Power who won that match for them. A ball went in to the forwards from Jackie Power and Jimmy Connell of Kilkenny was waiting for it inside. Dick Stokes came in from left-half-forward and Connell, who was after driving a few great balls down the field before that, dropped this one. Stokes reacted quickly and flicked it over his shoulder into the net. Match over. That turned the game; Limerick took complete control and won by six points.

The Limerick panel that beat Kilkenny in the 1940 All-Ireland final. *Back row (l–r):* Mick Hickey, Jim McCarthy, Tommy Cooke, Paddy Scanlon, Tony Herbert, Jim Roche, Paddy McMahon, John Mackey, Paddy Mackey, Timmy Ryan, Dave Hurley, Jackie Power, Martin 'Robbie' Lawlor, (unknown). *Front row (l–r):* Paddy Clohessy, Mick Mackey, Mick Kennedy, Ned Chawke, Dick Stokes, Peter Cregan.

Martin White offers a slightly different perspective:

Kilkenny were All-Ireland champions in 1939 and would have expected to win again in 1940. Whatever happened them in the 1940 final, Kilkenny didn't play well at all. Whether it was a case of Limerick being too good for them and not letting them play or Kilkenny just having an off day, I don't know which. I know that Kilkenny didn't play well at all that day. You could see Limerick were fairly confident from the beginning of the match. They hadn't been in an All-Ireland final since 1936, and when they got their chance in 1940 they took it.

Tony Herbert enjoyed his experience on final day:

In the previous year's Oireachtas final I was playing centre field on Jimmy Kelly of Carrickshock. Timmy Ryan was on Jimmy Walsh, another Carrickshock man. That was a great Kilkenny team and we beat them by three or four points. We were coming back in the car and Timmy Ryan said, 'I bet ye lads we'll win the All-Ireland next year [1940],' and we did. He was right.

Mick Mackey receives the Liam McCarthy Cup from GAA president Pádraig McNamee on the day of the 1940 All-Ireland final.

They brought Ned Chawke onto the team instead of me for that final and the poor fella wasn't great on the day. Paddy Clohessy went off before half time and he called my name that I should go in to replace him. I went in wearing number 17 and went over to Paddy Phelan and Jackie Power went back centre-back. I beat him easily to the first ball. Power was a great back and he played very well centre-back.

I roomed with Scanlan the night before the All-Ireland final. He was at the dogs that night and made a good few quid on Robbie Lawlor's greyhound, Erin's Hope, who won the 600-yard sprint in Shelbourne Park. Everyone had him backed and they made a fortune, but Scanlan had him backed very heavily. If you made ten quid that time you were doing well. Scanlan was a gas man. He came in late and Fr Punch was looking for him. He told Fr Punch where to go in a less than polite manner.

Dick Stokes believed that moving Mackey to midfield was the key switch:

In 1940 we were two points behind at half time against Kilkenny. Positional changes were made, the principal one being that Mick went out centre field with Timmy Ryan and scored two points from outside. Then we got a goal and the whole thing began to come. Limerick just started moving – sorry, Mick started moving. He went out at centre field, he'd go anywhere, he would go back to the backs or go into the forwards, wherever there was something to be won. (Colm Keane, *Hurling's Top 20*)

Tommy Cooke explains why all was not well in the camp:

Paddy McMahon played a big part for us that year. He was a great hurler and if a ball arrived in about 2 foot off the ground he would double on it into the net, but he had bad knees and was injured a lot. The Mackeys never played that kind of a ball to him. They were always going for their own score. It was Dick Stokes or Jackie Power who would give the right kind of ball to McMahon. A lot of the players didn't get on with each other at the time. Paddy Clohessy and the Mackeys didn't get on at all because of the aggravation at club matches between Ahane and Fedamore. After the All-Ireland final, I spent the night trying to keep Paddy Clohessy away from Jim Roche. After the incident a couple of years earlier, Clohessy couldn't bear to see Roche without having a go at him. But it wouldn't be right to have a brawl in Dublin between two players who were after winning an All-Ireland.

Maurice Regan expands further:

Tommy Cooke told me at a function one night that the Limerick players were forever fighting at that time. He said to me that after milking the cows he went up to Dublin for the All-Ireland final. The team had been up since the day before, and when he went into the hotel room they weren't there. He went into another room and could only find one player there on his own. They were all after fighting the week before and half the players weren't talking at all. Yet they went out and won an All-Ireland.

Gerry Piggott explains the four-year famine:

The reason Limerick weren't successful in the championship between 1936 and 1940 was because Ahane played too many tournaments and got burned out. There wasn't a team to touch that Ahane side in Limerick. They were the greatest bunch of hurlers to come out of any parish, in any era. They were in huge demand and travelled all over the country for tournaments, Sunday after Sunday. They were at the age where they should have been at their best between 1936 and '40. It definitely cost the county team, who were good enough to win more, but the players were burned out. They were an old team in 1940 and they won that final as an old team on the way down. You had Tony Herbert, Dick Stokes and Ned Chawke who were younger than the rest, and the other newcomer Tommy Cooke was in his mid-twenties. They had a tough competition that year compared to 1936 when they demolished all before them. In 1940 they scraped past everyone, they drew with Waterford and beat them in the replay by two points. They drew with Cork and beat them by two points in the replay. They beat Galway and they beat a Kilkenny team in the final that were expecting to win. They were all tough games.

Tommy Cooke outlines the team's deficiencies:

The 1940 team was a more balanced team because in earlier years the Mackeys used to pull them along a lot. Jimmy Close wasn't a great player but they used to keep him on the team. They were always short a forward or two as well. I was only a junior hurler but at the same time I would have hurled well and kept our opponents from scoring.

Michael Hynes agreed:

Limerick were always lacking one or two really good hurlers and they were carrying different players on the team during the 1930s when they were really going well. The 1940 team was a very good, even team in all positions because newcomers like Tommy Cooke, Tony Herbert and Dick Stokes had come through.

Dick Stokes felt he didn't realise the significance of the 1940 win:

It was great, I suppose. We didn't appreciate what it meant. I remember resting with Paddy McMahon before we went out to play the 1940 final. Paddy had been in two or three of them and he appreciated it. I was a young fellow. I didn't appreciate it as much as I should. But it was a great era. (Colm Keane, *Hurling's Top 20*)

So Limerick, with Mick Mackey as captain, raised the McCarthy Cup and continued their success into the new decade. The foundations were firmly in place to dominate hurling for some time. In eight years the Limerick senior team had won three All-Irelands, five Munster championships, five National Leagues and the very first Oireachtas final. Michael Hynes, however, believed they should have done even better:

That Limerick team were way better than any team from any era. The big question is why they didn't win more All-Irelands. They won five National Leagues in succession and three All-Irelands. I often ask myself why they didn't win more, but Kilkenny were always a stumbling block to any team that went into Croke Park. Ironically Mayo were the dominant team in the Football League at that time winning a number of titles in a row but they never won much in the championship. Both counties seem to have a lot in common these days.

John Ryan regrets not catching a glimpse of the McCarthy Cup:

I used to go down to Ryan's shop beside Mackey's house for ice cream and I said to my aunt that I'd love to see the McCarthy Cup. My aunt said to stop at Mackey's next time I was passing and old Mrs Mackey would show it to me. I was only eight at the time and was a shy young lad, so I never knocked. I had to wait thirty-three years to get another chance to see the cup when Éamon Grimes brought it back to Limerick.

Mick Mackey's celebrity status was legendary, as Tommy Cooke explains:

The Cork fellas used to make out that he used to put the sliotar under his jersey when he was on a solo run! Then, when he got tired in the second half he would take off his boots and seemed to get renewed energy. I took off my boots a few times in fine weather but I used to get found out on the hard ground and it didn't suit me. However, it suited him and he used to be flying in his bare feet. The girls at home in the shops used often ask us, 'Did Mick Mackey take off his boots?' They used to be looking out for him doing that and got a real thrill from seeing him do it. I remember he played one game in Thurles, and had received eleven or twelve stitches in his head in the previous game. He got a loan of a scrum cap from a rugby club in Limerick to play the match, which was unusual that time. They made him head of the vigilantes because he used to go to all the rugby matches. He used to go when he was still hurling so there was a big risk he might be suspended.

Since the GAA was founded, Limerick were never in a stronger position than on the first Sunday in September 1940. Mick Mackey was only twenty-eight, his brother John a year younger. Tony Herbert, Tommy Cooke, Dick Stokes and Ned Chawke were only beginning their inter-county careers, while Jackie

Power wasn't much older. Power's near neighbour Seán Crotty was part of the Limerick minor team, captained by Paddy McCarthy, that won the All-Ireland minor title in 1940. The conveyor belt of talent was clicking into top gear, as Limerick had won a Munster junior hurling title a year earlier. Surely nothing could go wrong over the course of the next decade. But go wrong it did, horribly wrong in fact, in typical Limerick fashion.

FIVE

ぴ

1941–4: EMERGENCY YEARS

In early 1941, a Munster side featuring six Limerick players including both Mackey brothers demolished Connacht in the Railway Cup semi-final. It is said that the Mackey brothers were in excellent form, tormenting Connacht at every opportunity. But it would be the last game they played until late that year. Three days later, on 19 February, their brother Paddy lost his life and they withdrew from hurling in his memory.

Michael Hynes explained that there was strife in Ahane prior to Paddy's death:

There was a dispute in the Ahane club at that stage. Twenty-one medals were handed out for winning the All-Ireland in 1940, fifteen for the starting players and six for the subs. Paddy Mackey was a sub on the 1940 team and didn't play, but got a medal. Dan Givens in Mountshannon, father of Don [distinguished Irish international soccer player], was also a sub but got no medal. Paddy wasn't good enough to be starting on the Limerick team and probably wasn't good enough to be on the panel either. He was there by virtue of being Mick Mackey's brother. It caused a split in the club and as a result they started up a club in Limerick called St John's. They actually played against Ahane. Eventually it was all sorted out in some way.

Gerry Piggott explains further:

Paddy Mackey was only coming as a hurler then. He was very young, about the same age as Tony Herbert. He was in the army at the time, and they were doing exercises which involved crossing the River Blackwater near Fermoy. He got wet and developed pneumonia and had to spend time in hospital. He died eventually in Mallow hospital. He is buried with his brother John and his father 'Tyler' in Castleconnell. He would probably have made it onto the Limerick team in time, but wouldn't have been anywhere near as good as his

A Mackey family photo taken in the early 1940s. *(L–r):* Mick, Ruth, Pat, Kitty.

brothers John and Mick. It wasn't really the done thing at the time to stop playing hurling for a year after a bereavement. However, as a family the Mackeys decided not to play. They didn't play club or county.

Tony Herbert has his own views:

John and Mick Mackey didn't play in 1941, which I strongly disagreed with. It wouldn't have been the done thing at the time to take a full year out of hurling due to a family bereavement. Paddy Mackey was a commissioned officer in the army. He had wanted me to join the army with him a couple of years earlier but my father wouldn't let me, even though I could have been commissioned within a short space of time.

On 8 June 1941, Ahane, without the Mackey brothers, were dethroned by Croom on a scoreline of 4-2 to 3-1 in the 1940 Limerick senior hurling championship final. Croom took over the selection of the Limerick team for the Munster championship match against Clare a fortnight later, meaning that had they been available, the Mackey brothers were no longer in power in terms of team selection. It's widely acknowledged that Mick, in particular, called the shots and had a major say in who did and didn't play, as Tony Herbert explains:

We lost to Croom in the 1940 championship and lost to them again in 1941. For those two years, they controlled the selection of the Limerick teams. Jim Roche and the other Croom players were in control of who was on the team. The fact that Croom were county champions meant that Mick Mackey no longer controlled the team. Limerick might have been more successful in 1941 and 1942 if Ahane were picking the team. Prior to that, Mick had a big say and there were seven or eight Ahane players on the team.

Michael Hynes did not dispute this:

I would agree that when Mick Mackey was captain from 1936 on he would have called the shots on the field as regards team selection and switches. The captain would have had a big say that time anyway. The Mackeys didn't play club or county in 1941 and their absence finished Limerick for '41. The split over the distribution of medals was hanging over Ahane as well, which might not have helped the spirit of the team when the Ahane players were playing for Limerick.

Tony Herbert explains how Limerick beat Clare in June 1941:

For that game Clare were so sure of beating Limerick without the Mackeys that they dropped two players who used to play rugby with me in Mungret College, Chubby Flynn and his brother from Sixmilebridge. They had a woollen mills factory in Sixmilebridge. Sure the Limerick fellas went through them like faecal material through a goose. That's how Limerick beat Clare in 1941. It's difficult to assess if Limerick would have won the All-Ireland again that year if the Mackeys had played. The younger Limerick players were getting better but a lot of the experienced players were getting older and were entering decline.

The remainder of the Munster championship was delayed until September because of the foot and mouth outbreak. Twelve months after winning the minor and senior double, the Limerick hurlers hit rock bottom when they were humiliated by Cork in the old Cork Athletic Grounds by 10-8 to 3-2. Along with the Mackey brothers, Limerick were also without Tony Herbert, Mick Kennedy and Paddy Clohessy. Paddy Scanlan, the hero of the Munster final replay against Cork in 1940, was there in body but not in mind, as Tommy Cooke explains:

We went up to Cork in 1941 an they beat us all the way home. Paddy Scanlon had a job in a timber merchant's yard in Galway. The

Galway races were on that week and he wanted to enjoy himself at the races. He had almost reached the stage where he was an alcoholic. The reason he played so well in 1940 was that Robbie Lawlor, the trainer, had a bottle with a lot of things mixed into it. When a player would lie down that time with an injury the match would stop. Lawlor would run in and the first man he would give a swig of the bottle to would be Scanlon, then Mick Hickey the full-back, and up along to Clohessy and onto Mackey and all those. The very minute the match would start again they would hurl like fair hell. Cork used to be raging any time a Limerick man went down. In 1941 Scanlan played in Cork and he wouldn't stop a football because he wasn't getting his swig during the game. They brought him down from Galway on the Saturday and kept him in Limerick overnight, and wouldn't give him a drink. He went up to Cork in cold blood. I was marking Jim Young who said to me, 'For God's sake wouldn't he stop the ball.' They were apologising for scoring the goals. Scanlan didn't want to be there.

The Mackey brothers cut short their self-imposed exile in November 1941 to play the county final. Croom retained their title and held the selection of the Limerick senior hurling team for 1942. Limerick beat Waterford in Cork but lost the Munster semi-final at home to Cork. The Mackey brothers were back in the fold, but it was the end of the road for Paddy Clohessy and Tommy Cooke, as the latter explains:

I was sick the week of the Waterford game in 1942. I contacted Jackie O'Connell, the secretary, to tell him I wouldn't be able to play that day. He said to travel to Cork anyway, that the car would call for me. I went to Cork with my gear, and when I got there they were short of players. I was told to tog out, to be there as a sub on the sideline. Paddy Clohessy wasn't picked at all for the game, but on the day they wanted him to play. He said he wouldn't play, but if they beat Waterford that day he would be available to face Cork in Limerick a couple of weeks later. They didn't pick him for the Cork game either. Two of the Cregans had played well against Waterford and held their places. I didn't play with them any more as I was anxious to concentrate more on the horses.

With the Mackey brothers back in full fettle Ahane regained their county title in 1942, beating Rathkeale by 7-8 to 1-0. It meant they were back in power, but Canon Punch was emerging and his influence had taken root when Ahane weren't in charge. This led to a power struggle in the following years in relation to picking the team. Mick Mackey was now serving in the army because of the Emergency, winning at least one All-Army championship. There was an interesting encounter between the 7th Brigade and Ahane at Castleconnell, as Gerry Piggott explains:

A cup was presented for the winners and Ahane beat them by two points. Mick Mackey was captain of the army team, and there was skin and hair flying. John went on Mick for a while, then Jackie Power went on him, then Timmy Ryan went on him. The pulling between them all was unbelievable but especially when himself and John were marking one another.

Willie Keane recalls the game:

Jimmy Hassett, an Ahane stalwart, was at the game because his father played that day. A row took place, and Kevin Hartigan of St Patrick's and the army who had a pub at the top of William Street was involved. It was fairly hard going in the game and the row was a full melee. We were young lads looking at what was going on. I always remember Jimmy standing outside smiling with his arms folded watching them belting one another. Everyone was looking forward to the clash between the Mackey brothers, but despite the pulling I don't think there was any blood spilt between them.

The Cork GAA historian Tim Horgan spoke to Din Joe Buckley about Mick Mackey:

During the Emergency, he told me that Mick Mackey and himself joined the army and had some great tussles during their army matches. Din Joe recalled with regret being sent off with Mackey during an army match played as a curtain raiser to a major inter-county game at the Cork Athletic Grounds. 'We were both sent off for some silly thing and it was terrible walking to the line in front of such a big crowd. We were disgraced.' There was another story told (which Din Joe couldn't remember) during an army game where Mick approached him and said, 'Din Joe, I'm all sunburn. I was out all day yesterday in the sun and I'm burning alive. Don't come too close to me today.' 'I won't, Mick,' Din Joe promised, but the moment the first ball came towards them, Din Joe gave Mick a mighty whack on the back with his hand and shouted gleefully, 'How's the aul sunburn, Mick.'

Arthur Graham saw Mackey win the All-Army championship:

He won an All-Ireland with the 7th Brigade. My father took me to Dublin for that match because he was part of the same brigade himself. Mick was a driver for the army, he was a celebrity and because of that he had what would be termed a 'cushy job' driving the top brass around the place!

Tony Herbert believes Mackey's time in the army was motivated by self-interest:

Mick went into the army from the ESB at the time of the Emergency. He was a corporal, but all he wanted was to control the hurling in the army.

Paddy Tuohy, however, offers a different perspective:

Mackey was a very unassuming man and when he was in the army there was a lot of activity around Limerick at the time. One day, the army were on a mission in an army vehicle. One of the generals in the back said to the driver of the vehicle, 'What's your name, soldier?' 'Mackey, sir,' came the reply. 'Are you anything to Mackey the hurler?' asked the general. 'I am he sir,' was the reply. The general was really rolled over by the humility of one of the all-time greats. Mackey was great and he hadn't to prove to anyone that he was great.

Gerry Piggott recalls Ahane training:

Usually when Ahane weren't playing on a Sunday they would have a training game over in Reilly's paddock. The two Mackeys wouldn't play in the games at the same time or there would be blood spilt between them. Reilly's paddock was only a small paddock and the wall around the field would be lined with people watching. All the parish would be watching them on a Sunday.

Tony Herbert also remembers the great days in Reilly's field:

Reilly's field was only a small pitch. There were times when there used to be about 4,000–5,000 people watching training. They used to come out from the city and there used to be lines of buses and cars. There were eight or ten of the Ahane team playing on the Limerick team that time. That Ahane team commanded a lot of respect from people that were interested in hurling, from Claughaun, Young Irelands, especially old-timers. This was a new horizon in Limerick, for a club to command such respect and have such a say.

The Munster Railway Cup team of 1943. *Back row (l–r):* John Keane (Waterford), Dick Stokes (Limerick), Batt Thornhill (Cork), Bill O'Donnell (Tipperary), Jack Lynch (Capt) (Cork), Andy Fleming (Waterford), Mick Mackey (Limerick), Willie 'Long Puck' Murphy (Cork), Jim 'Tough' Barry (Trainer) (Cork). *Front row (l–r):* John Quirke (Cork), Jim Young (Cork), Tommy Doyle (Tipperary), Christy Ring (Cork), Jackie Power (Limerick), Peter Cregan (Limerick), John Maher (Tipperary). *Inset (l–r):* Mick Kennefick (Cork), John Mackey (Limerick).

Michael Hynes believed it reflected the times:

We would all sit out on the wall along the road at Reilly's field to watch the team training. It was a very small field, but times were different and there weren't any facilities. That's where they did all their training when they won all the county titles so it proved that you didn't need to have a perfect field at the time to be successful.

Limerick approached the 1943 season with great confidence, and beat Clare by 6-4 to 3-3 in the championship. However, they made a meek exit, losing to Waterford by 3-7 to 4-3. The heroes of 1940 were drifting away. Paddy McMahon, Tony Herbert, Mick Hickey and Ned Chawke played championship hurling for the very last time in that Waterford game. Ahane retained their county title in 1943 by demolishing Croom on a wet day. John Mulcahy recalls an interesting encounter with John Mackey around that time:

John Mackey was playing wing-back for Ahane and I was playing wing-forward for Young Irelands. I didn't even know who John Mackey was. I was after skinning him a few times and had scored 0-3 from play. After I scored one of the points, he was standing up beside me and stamped with his cogs on my instep. He nearly broke my leg. I turned around when he was walking away and hit him on the backside as hard as I could. He didn't turn around and never even flinched. It was as if he felt nothing. After that match, he ran over to me and I thought he was coming over to hit me. 'Would you play with Ahane?' he asked. 'I heard you are after being put out of the city.' I had been working in the city and he knew I had to stop that week because the unions had objected to a country tradesman working in there. I replied, 'I can't play for Ahane because I have no job.' He replied, 'We can get you a job with J.J. Murphy the builder on Monday morning.' I said, 'If I you get me a job I will play for Ahane,' so I went to Ahane and I was still able to hurl junior with Cappamore. It's amusing that it was John Mackey who picked me to play for Ahane, after I hitting him a flog of the hurley along the backside. As a man said to me afterwards, Mackey was only testing you that time.

I was standing up one day in a game for Ahane against Treaty Sarsfields and a row started. I stayed standing looking at the row. Five or six Treaty men came for me and the next thing I got a slap of a fist into the side of the jaw. Once you had an Ahane jersey on you, you were an enemy. I wasn't interfering in the rows at all because I was from Cappamore, but I still took the punishment!

The best medals we won in those days were free suits of clothes. Both club and inter-county teams played for them. They were the war years, and people didn't have much. We hurled harder for the suit lengths than we did for the medals with the backside worn out of our britches.

Tony Herbert was starting a new life in Dublin:

I played a match in Dublin for Ahane against Eoin Ruas from the northside at Croke Park and I gave an exhibition of hurling there. I was marking Jim Byrne who was on the Leinster team and I beat him easily and was offered a job in Dublin with New Ireland Assurance. I played with New Irelands for twelve months but I used to drink in Tommy Moore's and met all the Faughs players so they asked me to transfer to them. I looked for a transfer but New Irelands objected because they had paid a month's rent for me and I owed them that money. The county board turned me down and it meant I had to stay out of hurling for twelve months to secure the transfer.

In my estimation, I left an Ahane club that were very strong, a good hurling club. They were very loyal to one another. When I came to Dublin I got involved in another great hurling club, the Faughs. You didn't have anyone out of work, you would be only one day idle and they rallied around you. Publicans had a lot of contacts and a lot of people in the club worked in bars, but they were great workers and would do anything that was asked of them. Publicans had the influence in the Guinness factory and places like that. Even up to the present day Faughs can get jobs for people. I had influence in Aer Lingus and I got three Faughs players jobs there. We used our contacts wisely. I got called to the civil service and left New Irelands to begin working there. Back in Limerick work was scarce. They were all going to England or joining the army.

The older players had good jobs though. Paddy McMahon was on the river, Mick Mackey was in the ESB and the army. John Mackey was in the Board of Health, Timmy Ryan was a farmer. Mick Ryan was a farmer. Mick Hickey was a water inspector. Hickey always carried a revolver. The day we played Eoin Rua's we stayed in a hotel, and he said to me, 'Put that [the revolver] under your pillow, you might need it during the night.' Around that time, water bailiffs and inspectors were being shot at regularly. They were being targeted because they were preventing people from fishing illegally.

John Mulcahy was also playing football with Ahane:

Ahane were playing Ballyhahill in a football match at Adare one Sunday and the referee didn't turn up. We were all sitting down in the middle of the field waiting for the ref to come and no sign of him. Ahane proposed Paddy O'Shea from Tipperary who was at that match. Paddy O'Shea was playing under a false name with Ahane at the time. They very nearly got their way until someone said, 'He's in the army, he's stationed below in Castleconnell.' One word followed another and the row started without the match ever taking place and the Mackeys were involved. Ahane had little or no following there, and we nearly got killed. You would need a following of supporters there to protect you when a row broke out but we had nobody.

And the Ballyhahill crowd were shouting, 'Remember Glin' in reference to the game with Glin where the big row took place a few years earlier. The Mackey brothers were after injuring a player by the name of Culhane from Glin, the neighbouring club to Ballyhahill. He was a great footballer, and he was the only footballer Limerick had playing for Munster in the Railway cup at the time. I only found out after the game in Adare that they had injured Culhane in the previous game. We had to retreat back out the road. The Ballyhahill supporters had flags and everything and we managed to get into a pub for safety and the doors were locked from inside. But the Ahane players didn't have enough, they went out the back of the premises and threw pots out onto the street at the Ballyhahill crowd. They were still looking for a fight. At this stage the Ahane players were armed with all sorts of implements from the back of the pub, and were shouting out at the Ballyhahill crowd, 'Come on, come on you yellowbellies' and stuff like that. John Mackey was good to fight, and the Herberts were good to fight, though Mick Herbert didn't ever much use the fist but he was deadly with the hurley. I wouldn't get involved. I had enough, I had a swollen jaw at that stage.

Limerick played their first championship match against Clare in 1944 with just six of the team that started the All-Ireland final only four years earlier. The team was in decline, and the All-Ireland-winning minors weren't coming through as planned. Michael Hynes put forward one plausible theory, echoing Tony Herbert's views about employment prospects in Limerick:

Work was scarce and you had two options that time, either join the army or go to England. I went to England and a lot more along with me, and that finished hurling for me. I would say the same thing happened the Limerick minor team of 1940. When you went to England you didn't do any hurling and that finished you. I was there from 1941 to '43 and once players had given up hurling, many never returned to it, even when they came home to Ireland.

Jimmy Butler Coffey felt that too much can be expected of minors:

Limerick were finished as a hurling force when they won the All-Ireland in 1940. You couldn't bring in the 1940 minors at that stage. Just because a minor might be a great minor doesn't mean he'll make a great senior player. At the very most, you should bring in a maximum of four players from a great minor team. You might not even get that many from a minor team that aren't that great. Too many of the old Limerick players went together within a couple of years and the replacements weren't there.

Seán Duggan played for Galway against that Limerick minor team:

Why didn't they make it? The standard of hurling was pretty high that time and that makes it harder to break through. I would have considered that to be a very good Limerick minor team. You must remember that Irish people have a reluctance to decide for themselves that they had their day. That's in every county and I think it's not an easy thing to try and break. History with men and women proves that we are all the same. I think that possibly some of the old Limerick team had their day but stayed on too long and weren't willing to move aside. When the time came to pass on the baton, they didn't do it. I think that's part of the reason the minors didn't come through. The same can be said of officials. Officials forget that they have had their day as officers of boards all over Ireland and they won't move away from it. Remember none of them are being paid but still they won't leap. It's bred into them that they will stay there till the end and keep the flag flying.

Tony Herbert believes the All-Ireland-winning minor team 'weren't good enough to step up'. The one shining light, Paddy McCarthy, was breaking through in 1944, but was succumbing to a weakness for liquor at an early age, as Tommy Cooke explains:

In 1941 after the match against Cork we were waiting for Mickey Fitzgibbon the treasurer because we were travelling home in the same car. Three or four of the Cork players came up to us and we were talking. I asked them if they knew Paddy McCarthy. 'Oh Paddy McCarthy,' they said in their Cork accents, 'sure he plays for a different team in Cork every Sunday.' He used to go to Cork and play for pints of porter, the poor divil. He was an only son and his mother was a widow, but he used to sneak up to Cork every Sunday and they played him illegally in club matches where he wouldn't be known. He was a great hurler, a big tall man. He once hurled a county final for Newcastlewest, and he had no togs, he only had a knickers on him, the day was fine. He was the captain of the 1940 minor team, but they didn't ever officially or publicly announce him as captain.

One ex-minor player who did come through in 1944 was Seán Herbert, but missed out on the All-Ireland minor success, as his brother Tony explains:

Canon Punch brought in his own rules when he was the chairman of the county board. I didn't have any time for him. My brother Seán was still underage for minor with Limerick in 1940. However, Canon Punch came along and suspended him for playing rugby. Seán was on a scholarship in the Crescent College at Dooradoyle and Canon Punch used to go down to the college and pick out the players who were playing rugby. He saw Seán's photograph on a rugby team picture. Seán was suspended and lost out on an All-Ireland minor medal.

His son Seán Óg Herbert concurs:

Having missed out on the All-Ireland minor medal through suspension he didn't want to miss out on hurling with Limerick any more. His suspension came after a schools rugby game at Thomond Park, when there were twelve players sent off. He had played the rugby game under a false name but Canon Punch found out and he hammered him with a six-month suspension. Paddy Reid the great Irish international used to call to our house and often said that my father was not only the best out half he ever played with, but one of the best all-round rugby players he ever played with. That is an amazing tribute because Paddy Reid would have played with the great Jack Kyle on the Irish grand slam-winning team of 1948. Because of the ban, my father never got to fulfil his potential on the rugby field.

Gerry Piggott agrees:

Seán Herbert was a great hurler. Getting suspended for playing rugby cost him an All-Ireland minor medal, and he never went on to win a Munster championship with the Limerick seniors after breaking into the team in 1944. I would say he was one of the unluckiest Limerick hurlers of all time, because he was one of the best, but was unfortunate to be around during a period when Limerick weren't successful. Seán was the best of the three Herbert brothers. The ban was a big thing at the time. There was a vigilantes committee for checking that GAA players weren't going to soccer and rugby matches. They had to make Mick Mackey a vigilante because he was going to rugby games and he would only end up getting suspended. He was delighted because he could go to all the matches, but I don't think he ever reported anyone. Jack Lynch in Cork and Jim Young were suspended for going to a rugby function.

Willie Keane believes Mackey's new role suited him:

Mick became a vigilante. Prior to his appointment, he spent more time in Thomond Park than anyone else attending rugby games. He wasn't going to report anyone, that's for sure, and I can't ever remember hearing of any GAA players suspended as a result of being reported by him.

A couple of ex Tipperary players threw in their lot with Limerick in the early 1940s. One transferee, Jimmy Cooney of 'the Cooney case' fame, played a number of games while Jimmy Butler Coffey also transferred but was restricted by injury:

I played a National League match with Limerick in the 1940s but that never really counted. I was finished with Tipperary and my hurling was nearly at an end. I got a very bad stroke in a League match for Tipperary on the side of my right ankle. I never went to a doctor or anything but that injury finished me as an inter-county hurler because it slowed me down. I was working in Limerick and I was cycling morning and evening in and out from there. The injury was very serious but I didn't realise just how serious until I had to take one or two days off work. When I played with Limerick I was really gone past playing senior inter-county hurling.

Limerick beat Clare convincingly in the 1944 Munster championship with Dave Conway in goals. Mickey Walsh was picked in goals for the Munster final, which ended in a draw, a game known as the 'bicycle final' because of the numbers cycling there due to petrol shortages during the Emergency. Mick Rainsford is quite blunt, but honest, in his assessment of the new goalie:

The trouble in Limerick is that we always take the wrong option when we pick teams. He left in six goals and wouldn't stop a cow, yet we put him into goals for a Munster final. In the replay they selected Dinny Malone from Fedamore in goals, the man who should have started the drawn game. I believe that if Malone started the drawn game, there would have been no need for a replay.

John Mulcahy agrees:

Mickey Walsh was attending UCD. Dick Stokes was friendly with him so he brought him down. I was at that match in Thurles and two

Pat Mackey prepares to walk on to the field with his father
Mick for the 1944 Munster hurling final.

balls crossed the line that didn't even hit the back of the net. They
only rolled behind the line. Whatever way he put down the hurley
when they were hopping into him, he wasn't quick enough, and they
were two very soft goals. I met Jackie Power coming off the field and I
said, 'Ye will win the next day with a different goalie.' 'I'm afraid,' he
replied, 'you cannot win a match twice.' They got Dinny Malone of
Fedamore for the replay and he stopped everything but they were still
beaten. Jackie Power was right: you cannot win a match twice.

Fr Liam Ryan believes Walsh was selected in good faith:

That was the first Munster final I was ever at and I was very young
at the time. Mickey Walsh was a student in UCD and became an

agricultural instructor afterwards. Dick Stokes brought him down. He was in goals for UCD and played well for them. I can't recall Walsh ever playing for Cappamore, and for that matter I can't recall Stokes ever playing for Pallasgreen either, though he may have for a short period of time. Any time Stokes played for Limerick, his club was listed as UCD as far as I can recall.

Timmy Ryan had fond memories of the comeback:

The one game I got the greatest thrill out of was the match against Cork in 1944. I think we were down six points going into the second half and we came back and drew level. We actually went ahead by a goal and I remember that John Quirke raced across the field and dropped a very soft ball into the goalie and it rolled in between his legs and if I had a gun I would have shot him. ('A Celebration of Munster Hurling', RTÉ Television, 1976)

Mick Mackey was beginning to wane, but the midweek Limerick Leader *column suggested that he'd proved his doubters wrong with a personal haul of 1-4. The selected team for that drawn game didn't meet with widespread approval, as a breakaway group of 'Gaels' picked an alternative team to take on the selected Limerick team. It is unclear if the game ever took place, but this* Limerick Leader *piece from June 1944 explains the scenario:*

Ahane's selection to represent Limerick in the Munster hurling final on July 16th has met with a share of criticism and now comes the announcement that a group of well-known Gaels have selected a team that they hold is good enough to beat the county side. They are offering a set of valuable trophies to the winners of the clash between them, which takes place at the Limerick Gaelic Grounds on Sunday week, 2nd July.

John Mulcahy explains that skulduggery was commonplace in team selection:

I was going in training for Limerick during the war years in a pony and trap that was sent to collect me. If the evening was wet, you were drenched before you got in. They were giving you double pneumonia instead of exercise. I was waiting one night to go in training and nobody turned up. I was going into Mass the following Sunday morning and I shouted over to the man who was due to collect me, 'You didn't call at all on Thursday night.' 'No,' he replied, 'I was sent elsewhere for two players. They are not worth taking in but the two of them are going to be on the Limerick team next Sunday.' He named the two players, and I said, 'Sure they aren't able to get on the Cappamore team.' 'Well they will be on the Limerick team next Sunday, mark my words,' was his reply. I went to the match and I saw that the two boys were togged out and were put on for about ten minutes. I said to him afterwards, 'You were right. How did they get their place when they can't get on the Cappamore team?' He replied, 'They were working for Mickey Fitzgibbon choosing eggs for the last week.' Mickey Fitzgibbon had an egg business and had the two of them working for nothing for the week and played them for Limerick as payment. The two of them are dead now, but they were always able to get soft All-Ireland tickets because they put on a Limerick jersey for ten minutes.

In the replay, Mick Mackey had a late goal disallowed when Din Joe Buckley threw the hurley at him and a free was given to Limerick instead. From the next play, the ball went up the field where Christy Ring buried it for the winning goal. To this day there are claims that Joe Kelly was inside the small square and interfered with Dinny Malone's hurley when Ring's shot was crossing the line. These have been defined as the moments when the mantle of power in hurling passed from Mick Mackey to Christy Ring. Inevitably this led to the great debate: who was the better hurler, Mackey or Ring? Willie John Daly is in no doubt:

There were only three men in my time, Mick Mackey, Jamesie Kelleher and Christy Ring. Mackey was a marvellous player and that Limerick team was a marvellous team. They were powerful men. There hasn't been a Limerick team anywhere near as good since. The one man of those three who stood head and shoulders above the rest, for me, was Christy Ring. They were all great men but I played with Ring and saw him playing before my time [as a Cork player] and after my time. Christy Ring was playing senior hurling for Cork for thirty years. Very few would play for that long. Ring was the greatest.

Mickey 'The Rattler' Byrne is not so sure:

Mackey and Ring were completely different types of hurlers because they had different styles. Mackey was more aggressive and more physical, whereas Ring was more stylish. You couldn't compare them. Both were great players in their own right. Ring was a big danger man for Cork but in a different way. Mackey would always have been the big danger when we played Limerick. We were more worried about Limerick than Cork back in the 1940s. Mick Mackey would have made the Tipperary team in the 1940s. He would have made any team and any team would have been glad to have him.

Donie Nealon agrees:

Mackey and Ring had different styles. Mackey had a bustling, strong, powerful running style with the famous solo runs. Ring was strong but was more of an opportunist. It was hard to compare them because they didn't play the same type of hurling. In their own right, Ring was regarded as the top Cork hurler of all time, while Mackey was the top Limerick hurler of all time.

Martin White is indecisive:

I have often asked the question who was the better hurler, Mick Mackey or Christy Ring. But I have always maintained that it is impossible to decide. You could throw Lory Meagher in with them as well. Lory Meagher was a real graceful hurler, whereas the others had power as well as great hurling. Mick Mackey was playing centre-forward. He was very strong, and was always going down the middle for scores. He could turn up anywhere. I remember playing against him one day; I was playing right-corner-forward and he was centre-forward. I turned at one stage in my corner and I got a rattle from a player. Who was it only Mackey. He was supposed to be playing centre-forward, and here he was at left-corner-back.

Christy Ring was different and could play anywhere. The first time I saw him he was playing right-half-back for the Cork minors against Waterford. He could pop up anywhere on the field. He would always pop up where there was danger and yet could still be down the other end to get a score. He had very powerful arms, was very strong, and when he got the ball it was very hard to take it from him and difficult to keep him from having a shot. The Mackey versus Ring debate is impossible to settle. One was as great in his way as the other was in his. Ring was playing at a time when there was a bit of a change in hurling. There was beginning to be more ballplay than in Mackey's time. Ring was playing with great ballplayers.

Fr Liam Kelly defends his close friend:

Mackey had great skill. The proponents of Ring versus Mackey as the greatest ever player will say that Mackey didn't have Ring's skill.

That wouldn't be accurate. Mackey had fantastic skill. Ring wouldn't compare with him in my book, but I am slightly biased, and am proud of being biased!

Michael Hynes said you couldn't compare the two greats:

It was a tougher game back then, more physical. You marked your own man that time and you could get away with slow players on a team because of that. Mackey was unbelievably strong, wasn't very tall but was well built. Mick had a great pair of hands and he had everything but it was his power and his courage that made him. Christy Ring's brother maintained that there was nobody stronger than Christy himself. And he was low sized as well. You couldn't compare them, but they were two great hurlers. There is no question about that.

Tommy Barrett explains the Tipperary psyche:

Limerick were always a threat in Mackey's time, you could never take Limerick for granted when he was around. Ring was better, though. Mackey had a style of his own, he carried the ball and he would knock over anything that was in his way. In Tipperary we would rate them in the following order: Ring, Mackey, Jimmy Doyle and Jimmy Finn.

Mick Rainsford says Mackey's strength made him many people's favourite:

Mackey was the best hurler I ever saw. He was gone well past his best when I saw him, but anyone I spoke to who saw him in his peak always claimed that in their opinion he was better than Ring. Ring would sidestep a player, but Mackey would go through him, that was the difference. If you weren't strong enough for Mackey, you had no business trying to stop him. Himself and John Keane had great battles. They reckon that John Keane was the only man able to manage him consistently.

John Mulcahy compares himself with the best:

Ring would have been more classy than Mackey, but Ring had great men around him and maybe had better men around him than Mackey. Once I saw on a paper after a match, 'Mulcahy was as good as Ring, but he lacked the support that the Cork man enjoyed.' There was a player called Paddy Barry who made a lot of scores for Ring. Ring used to come to the creamery in Cappamore delivering oil, and would always come down here for a chat. He would want you to go down to the creamery square with a hurley, pucking a ball against a wall. He was mad for hurling.

Gerry Piggott believes Mackey was the best:

Mackey was a far better hurler than Ring. Mackey was the king. It was Mackey who was bringing the crowds to the games that time. He was drawing crowds to matches ever before Ring was even heard of. I thought the best games I saw Mackey playing were in Thurles in 1940 against Cork and in the 1940 All-Ireland against Kilkenny. Kilkenny weren't able to handle Mackey; nobody was able to handle him. You could never predict what he was going to do. I would imagine that the big counties were afraid of Mackey because of that. He had strength, speed, everything.

Arthur Graham agrees:

I thought Mackey was way ahead of Christy Ring even when he was going off. I won't say Christy Ring was standing up doing nothing for long periods of games, but Ring certainly wasn't going full tilt for the full game. He would be out of the game for three quarters of it, and would then spring to life. Mick was always going full tilt, and roaming the field away from his position. In a way Christy Ring was a luxury-type player whereas Mick was a seventy-minute player and would often be helping out a good distance away from his position.

Jimmy Smyth gives his view:

I saw Mick Mackey hurling, but I believe that you can't make a judgement on a player as a fifteen-year-old. In my opinion you are better placed to make a judgement having marked a player and played against them. You could have grown up thinking a particular player was a great player, but having played on them you realise they might not be that good at all. When I first saw Mackey hurling in Ennis nobody could stop him. Once he had the ball in his hand you could not stop him and he always scored. Ring came on the scene when Mackey was finishing. Mackey was past his best and Ring was approaching greatness. Ring was more of a classical hurler.

Mackey might have been going off when I saw him, but Ring was also going off for eight to ten years before he finished. He got the three goals against Limerick when he was old, and would have been recognised as going off. There was always someone who could hold any great in the history of the game, and the way to hold Mackey was to keep your mouth shut and play your hurling. It was the same with Ring. Say nothing and hurl. There was a lot of mouthing during games that time, but not near as much as there is now. I played on John Doyle several times but I never opened my mouth.

Jim Hogan is another in the Mackey camp:

Mick Mackey was the best hurler I ever saw, even at club level when he was going off. It was his power. They talk about Ring, but I played club hurling against Ring in Cork for three or four years when he was playing with Glen Rovers; I was with Sarsfields. But I would always consider Mackey to be stronger because he would always run in a straight line into the backs and topple them over. He got great goals for Limerick, but missed vital scores too. People went to see Mackey. They went to see John Mackey too, but it was all the women who were following John!

Christy Murphy recalls an interview with Ring:

Ring was once interviewed about the famous comparison. He told a story about a time when he outsmarted Mackey at a throw-in. They were both captains but Ring didn't want to play in a particular direction. Mackey won the toss, but having lost the toss Ring created a scene, pretending he wanted to play in one direction. Mackey fell for the ruse and decided that the way Ring wanted to play was the way to play. Ring's attitude in the interview was that, having outfoxed Mackey at that throw-in, he was a better player than him by virtue of being cleverer than him.

The debate rages on to this day, and while some find it difficult to compare Mackey to Ring, others believe that it should be declared with certainty that Mick Mackey was a far superior hurler to Ring. Some wonder which of the two counties could have won all they did without their hero. The general consensus is that while Ring won eight All-Ireland titles with Cork, some of those titles could have been won without him but that Limerick wouldn't have won any of their three titles without Mick Mackey.

SIX

ᢉᢣ

1945–9: SELF-DESTRUCTION

In 1945 the Cork team that had achieved four in a row were beaten by Tipperary. Anticipation was rising in Limerick that there was one last kick in the elder statesmen, particularly in the Mackey brothers and Timmy Ryan. Now that their bogey team Cork were out of the way, a great opportunity presented itself. However, Martin White believes that the Cork four in a row was already tainted:

In the early 1940s some of the Limerick players started to get old and they hadn't the replacements for them. Other counties such as Cork and Tipperary started to come good. It was something similar to what happened Limerick in the 1930s because you had Cork and Tipperary coming and that spoiled Limerick's chances of winning more. Any time Tipperary became contenders, they were always good, and it was always very hard to beat them.

Cork won four in a row from 1941 to '44, but I wouldn't give them credit for the four in a row. They won an All-Ireland in 1943 beating Kerry in the Munster semi-final, Waterford in the Munster final and Antrim in the All-Ireland final. Waterford were on the way down at the time and were very reliant on Erin's Own to provide them with players. Antrim beat Kilkenny in the All-Ireland semi-final so that meant that Cork won an All-Ireland without beating any hurling superpower. In 1941 there was a foot and mouth outbreak in Ireland and Tipperary and Kilkenny weren't allowed to play in the All-Ireland championship because the disease had been in their counties. Cork could play, and won that All-Ireland. Tipperary and Kilkenny didn't come back for a while after that, and Cork won All-Irelands in that period because Tipperary and Kilkenny weren't as strong as they had been.

A high-profile member of the Cork four-in-a-row team didn't appeal to Tommy Cooke:

The Cork lads in general were of a great class because if they met you the day after a match they were as friendly as could be. However, I couldn't say the same for Jack Lynch. Jackie Keane, a neighbour of mine, and myself went to Cork to see the tall ships the time they were there. When we arrived below at the docks it was 4 p.m. and they wouldn't leave us into the boat. They said there was nobody allowed in after 4 p.m.. I went back out onto the quay and found myself standing beside Jack Lynch. I turned to him and said, 'How are you, Mr Lynch?' and he just turned around and walked away from me as if I wasn't there.

Mackey had continually dabbled with the 'big ball' code throughout his career and before he pucked a ball in the Munster hurling championship of 1945 he lined out for Limerick in the Munster senior football championship. Jackie Power was also on the team. Limerick were by now a senior team and beat Clare by 6-2 to 3-3 before going down to Kerry by 5-8 to 2-7 after a heroic contest. Mick Mackey scored an incredible 2-4 off the legendary Paddy Bawn Brosnan. Ger Cussen of Galbally, a nephew of Padjoe Cussen who was on the Limerick team that day, recalls his uncle's thoughts:

Padjoe often spoke of Mick Mackey and Jackie Power playing football for Limerick. Mackey would have got the football headlines when he played because of his status in the game of hurling, but he felt that Power was the better of the two as a footballer. He said several times that Jackie Power was the most gifted footballer he ever saw playing in his lifetime. When Ger Power broke through in the 1970s, Padjoe always maintained that he had the same style and mobility as his father and it was no surprise to him that he had such a distinguished career with Kerry given how talented his father was as a footballer. Ironically that wasn't the only connection with the Kerry four-in-a-row team because Eoin Liston's father also played football with Mick Mackey in 1945.

In the Munster hurling championship, Limerick beat Clare by 3-6 to 3-3 at Ennis before going down to Tipperary by 4 3 to 2-6 in the Munster final at Thurles. Cork may have been out of Limerick's way, but Tipperary took their place as Munster champions in what was the final appearance for Timmy Ryan 'Good Boy'. Seán Herbert gave an inspirational performance, as his brother Tony explains:

Seán partnered Timmy Ryan at midfield and he got the better of Harry Goldsboro in the 1945 Munster final. I met Harry Goldsboro after the All-Ireland final that year and he said, 'We shouldn't have been in the final at all. It's ye who should have been there. Your brother Seán gave a lesson in hurling to me.' Limerick should have won that 1945 Munster final. They had Tipperary beaten that day and a row took place between the goalkeeper and one of the backs. They were so preoccupied with their arguing that they took their eyes off the ball while play was going on and the goal was scored. The Tipperary forward shot a ball into the back of the empty net when there was no goalie. The same thing happened the following year with Ring.

Jimmy Butler Coffey believed Seán Herbert was needed elsewhere:

Seán Herbert should have been playing at left-half-back marking Mutt Ryan from Moycarkey that day. Mutt Ryan had a great game and scored the goal that made all the difference. He always maintained that if Seán Herbert was marking him the goal wouldn't have been scored. That was the goal that won the game for Tipperary.

Gerry Piggott took a memorable photo:

I took the photo of Timmy Ryan in 1945 on his last championship appearance with a box camera. I gave him that photo framed and all and he was delighted. He played with a broken finger that day, his hand wrapped up in plaster. He played very well, but Timmy never played a bad game. He could keep running for the day. He was well over thirty when he gave it up so he didn't leave inter-county hurling too soon. Paddy Scanlon was the only one of that team who left too soon. That Limerick team of that era were better than the current Kilkenny team but it was different hurling then. I don't think any modern Limerick player would have got their place on the team of the 1930s when Timmy Ryan and Mackey were at their peak, apart from Éamonn Cregan of the 1973 team and Seán Herbert from the 1940s.

Limerick were still struggling to recover the glory days. The controversy and internal strife that existed in the 1930s was simmering away in the 1940s and had an impact on that 1945 Munster final. Ahane were starting to lose popularity because they were winning so much, as Mick Rainsford explains:

To a certain extent Ahane dictated a lot. That wouldn't be any secret. Tom Conway was a natural defender, but was a poor forward. It was always reckoned that certain players dictated that if they weren't chosen on the Limerick team, they'd refuse to play with Ahane. Ahane played Young Irelands in the county championship prior to that 1945

The Limerick team, captained by Mick Mackey, that lined out in the 1945 Munster senior hurling final. *Back row (l–r):* Dinny Malone, Tommy Herbert, Mick Kennedy, Derry McCarthy, Pat Reilly, Mick Mackey (Capt), Thomas O'Brien, Budge O'Grady, Michael Minihan, John Mackey, Joe Hayes, Paddy Kelly, Paddy McCarthy, Unknown Supporter, Dr Jim McCarthy, Unknown Supporter, Robbie Lawlor. *Middle row (l–r):* Tom Conway, Timmy Ryan, Paddy Fitzgerald, Jackie Power, Seán Herbert, Paddy O'Shea, Dick Stokes. *Front row (l–r):* Tim Larkin, Johnny Clohessy.

Munster final and they reckon that only for switching Jackie Power into full-forward and taking Tom Conway out of it, Ahane wouldn't have beaten Young Irelands. Yet Limerick went to Thurles and Conway was playing at full-forward on the Limerick team. They reckon he had one ball inside in the square that all he had to do was tap it into the net on the ground and he rose it and threw it up and Cornally cleared it 70 yards. We have made several unforgivable mistakes like that when picking teams down the years. It was politics that cost us right throughout the 1940s.

John Mulcahy recalls a similar incident with Conway:

I played with Tom Conway for the county, and in one game against Cork I came in with a ball. Conway was still there in the square. I could have scored the goal myself but he was more loose and I gave him the ball. Whatever fooling he did with it, he threw it up and the Cork full-back pulled on it and drove it out the field.

Paddy Kelly was seen as a fine prospect but it wasn't happening for him at inter-county level. Gerry Piggott explains:

Paddy Kelly of Ahane was the greatest half-back in the country and he couldn't make the Limerick team. He hadn't the same interest in inter-county hurling as he had in club hurling. Mick Mackey paid him that tribute, saying he was 'the best club hurler in the country'. Thomas O'Brien was also a fine half-back and himself, Kelly and Jackie Power were the half-back line of Ahane, and Seán Herbert played there as well sometimes. They were like a stone wall and couldn't be passed. I would think Power was a better back than a forward. When Paddy Clohessy went off in the All-Ireland the switch of Power to defence made a better team of Limerick that day.

Michael Hynes also paid tribute to Kelly's ability:

Paddy Kelly was one of the greatest half-backs that ever caught a hurley when playing for Ahane, but put a Limerick jersey on him and he wasn't able to step up. But it has to go on record that he was one of the great club hurlers of all time.

Mick Rainsford expands further:

Paddy Kelly of Ahane was the best club hurler I ever saw and got a rake of chances with Limerick but he just wasn't able to hurl with Limerick. But give him a green and gold jersey of Ahane and nobody could touch him and if he could have hurled like that for Limerick he would have been a great one. It's not a surprise that Mick Mackey rated him so highly. Paddy Fitzgerald of Askeaton was a lovely forward who played for Limerick, and he also played with Munster in the 1940s when it was hard to get on the Munster team. He was from Askeaton, but was a painting contractor and he played with Rathkeale for a while because he was working there. They got to the county final against Ahane when he was playing for them. There was a timber fence around the Gaelic Grounds that time, and it was easy to break off the boards because they were there such a long time. At half time we got into the sideline. I remember being over alongside Paddy Fitzgerald and Paddy Kelly, and Fitzgerald spent the whole time appealing to the Rathkeale selectors to move him away from Paddy Kelly. 'Move me away from Paddy Kelly, there isn't a man in Ireland who would beat Paddy Kelly today. I am wasted here', but

Mick Mackey and Christy Ring, the two greatest legends in
the game of hurling, await the outcome of the toss before
the 1946 Munster final.

they left him there instead of moving him to where he could have
made some contribution. He didn't get a puck of the ball.

*In 1946, Limerick dethroned the All-Ireland champions Tipperary, winning
by 3-5 to 2-2 at Cork. However, the hard luck stories didn't end, as they fell
rather meekly to Cork in the Munster final, losing by 3-8 to 1-3 in what was
Mick Mackey's last championship start. Fr Liam Ryan explains:*

The biggest disappointment for Limerick was in 1946, when Cork
beat them well. Though I was very young at the time, my recollection
is that people generally felt Limerick were very unlucky not to have
won the Munster championship in the two previous years, 1944 and
1945, and that they were a better team than Tipperary.

*In 1947, Limerick humiliated Tipperary, beating them 6-8 to 2-3. The
final appearance of Mick Mackey in a Limerick jersey came late in the game
when he replaced Paddy Fitzgerald of St Patrick's. It was a far cry from the
days when Mick Mackey and Ahane dictated team selection. Canon Punch*

The Limerick team that lined out in the 1946 Munster final. *Back row (l–r)*: Jim McCarthy (UCD), Mick Mackey (Ahane), Paddy Fitzgerald (Askeaton), Jackie Power (Ahane), Mick Ryan (Young Irelands, Dublin), Jim Sadlier (Young Irelands), Dick Stokes (UCD), Thomas O'Brien (Ahane). *Front row (l–r)*: Derry McCarthy (Dromcollogher), John Mackey (Ahane), Paddy Collopy (St Patrick's), Jimmy Tobin (Kilfinane), Tom Cregan (Croom), Seán Herbert (Ahane), Peter Cregan (Ahane).

was approaching his peak as a dictator, and perhaps Mackey's departure was a combination of both that and an acceptance that his time was up. Fr Liam Ryan believes Mackey deserved better on his final appearance:

It was a most indignant way to end the career of Mick Mackey and was very similar to the way the Irish rugby selectors gave Ronan O'Gara his hundredth cap in November 2010. It was a disgrace, for all he had done for rugby, to give him his 100th cap like that [as substitute]. Likewise Mackey, having had the career he had, deserved better on his last appearance than to be brought in as a sub like that. I can't remember which GAA star once said, 'I never retired, they just stopped picking me.' The same thing happened to Mackey. I'd say for any senior player, especially Mackey, to find himself a sub was an indignity.

Gerry Piggott was in the team photo but Mackey was not:

I came into the old Athletic Grounds in Cork and there was only barbed wire to keep back the crowd. I had to walk around to try and get a place, and saw some of the Ahane supporters sitting on a seat inside the touchline. They lifted up the wire for me and I got in. Next thing, Thomas O'Brien called me over and gave me his coat. Before I knew it, I had three or four coats belonging to the players, and ended up in the photo. Mackey wasn't in that photo because he was a sub on the day.

Mickey 'The Rattler' Byrne acknowledged the loss of Mackey:

Limerick weren't as strong without Mackey because Mackey was the kingpin. No team could be as good without the class of a player that Mackey was. He was a great man togged off and was very physical. We went up to Cloyne to Ring's funeral in later years and I had my photo taken with Mackey and Tommy Doyle. John Maher and Mackey used to have great battles. There was very little between them; they were both as good as each other and they would break even most of the time.

There used to be murder between the Mackey brothers on the field against Tipperary. The game was that Mick would get the ball out the field, he would solo in and he would handpass the ball over to John. Then if John made a faux pas or missed the ball or lost it, they would be jawing at one another then, and giving out to one another. When Mick got the ball he would solo through on goal and John would wait loose for it. We knew that if Mick got the ball, it was always going to John above anyone else, so we knew if we marked John closely it would blot out some of the attack. There were different tactics in those days.

Gerry Piggott puts Mackey's status into words:

Mackey was the king. When Mackey got the ball in Thurles or anyplace else the crowd erupted. The crowd got behind him and it's not around opponents he would go at all but straight through them and the crowd loved that. Mick Mackey would take any man on, but John had more hurling craft but didn't have the same interest, not in later years anyway. Mackey was the best man to solo with a ball at that time. The Tipperary backs at the time were all 6 footers the likes of Ger Cornally, Dinny Gorman and John Maher. Mackey was only 5 foot 10 but he would power through them like a dose of salts. I saw Mackey on great Railway Cup teams, and he had the same effect on the crowd. He had that effect no matter where he went, even in the county championship. At club level, Ahane were a great team, but nobody was as good as Mackey. I'd say he wanted to stay on in 1947, because he loved hurling.

Jim Fitzgerald agrees:

When Mackey got on the ball the crowd would nearly lift the field when they saw him going on a solo run. It was he who brought the solo run into hurling properly, in that he did it all the time whereas others only did it sometimes. I haven't seen many capable of doing similar power-driven solo runs since. I would agree that he had the same effect on the crowd in club hurling, and even if there weren't many at a game, they created an atmosphere as if it was a full house.

As the width of the bas has increased down the years, it has become progressively easier to solo. In Mackey's time the solo run was more challenging. Dick Stokes was a keen observer of his style:

Mick's hurling style wouldn't be something to be imitated because there was nobody who hurled like him. He had a unique method of hurling. He was a very strong, well built man, very active and the big thing, a lot of strong men can't use their strength, but Mick was very well put together, so to speak, and could use it and could think as well as everything else. He might not have been as good as other fellows in the air, but my God, when it came down he could take it. He was able to throw fellows out of his way in a very regular way and in a very purposeful way. In other words it was always where the ball was and not in any way just loose, knocking fellows about for the sake of knocking them about. It was always constructive. He was always on the ball and when the fellas were knocked about, he was gone with the ball, but that was his method of doing it. He was unique in that respect. He could go up the middle. He never had to go up the sideline or anything like that. (Colm Keane, *Hurling's Top 20*)

Brendan Fullam believes Mackey was in decline before his retirement:

Mackey was born in 1912, so he would have been thirty-five in 1947, and in an era when it was man-to-man heavy hitting he had it all given. I think it's fair to say that his last great hour came in 1944, three years before his retirement. There was a song and the last line of a verse said, 'Christy won the match on the call of time.' I think that match was the call of time for Mick Mackey as well.

Life without Mick Mackey: The first game played by the Limerick senior hurlers after the final appearance of Mick Mackey was the 1947 Munster final. Mackey was involved as a mentor. *Back row (l–r)*: Bob McConkey (Young Irelands), Paddy Clohessy (Fedamore), Mick Herbert (Ahane), Toddy O'Brien (St Patrick's), Mick Ryan (Young Irelands, Dublin), Jackie Power (Ahane), Jim Sadlier (Young Irelands), Thomas O'Brien (Ahane), John Mackey (Ahane), Paddy Fitzgerald (St Patrick's), Timmy Ryan (Ahane). *Front row (l–r)*: Mick Mackey (Ahane), Dr Dick Stokes (Pallasgreen & UCD), Derry McCarthy (Dromcollogher), Owen O'Riordan (Young Irelands), John Mulcahy (Cappamore), Peter Cregan (Croom), Seán Herbert (Ahane), Tom Cregan (Croom). Mascot: Unknown.

Despite the departure of Mick Mackey, Limerick had a Munster final ahead of them and Mackey appeared in the team photo in his plain clothes, smoking a cigarette. Having grown in influence over the decade, Canon Punch was really beginning to call the shots by 1947, and his role in Mick Mackey's departure wasn't to be understated, as Seán Ryan (Malachy) explains:

I first saw Limerick in the 1947 Munster final from above on my father's shoulders in Thurles. From what I know, Canon Punch didn't want Mick Mackey and he had a big say because he was chairman of the county board at the time. However, Canon Punch wanted John Mackey but the local story here in Castleconnell is that John went away hiding on the morning of that Munster final. It was the local priest, Fr White, who found him walking the fields and took him to the match. He was down at Moran's farm, which was then owned by Niall Moran's granduncle Willie Moran. That's the local story here. I remember Mick Mackey running up and down the sideline in that final. John Mackey wasn't fit, didn't want to hurl, and all he seemed to be trying to do from my perspective was drive Con Murphy into the back of the net. In my opinion Mick Mackey would have won the match for Limerick that day because there were only three points in it at the end. John had lost interest in hurling at the time, wasn't fit and had it all done. Mick was twice as fit as John and still played club hurling until 1951. Even though Mick was gone heavy he still had class and ability.

In John Mackey's case it was easier to hide than to stand up and openly refuse to play. The lack of freedom to make decisions in that era cannot be understated and would be unknown to the modern generation. By now Canon Punch had serious influence and was a feared individual, in line with most of the clergy of the time. One assumes that the power struggle between Punch and Ahane to control the selection of the Limerick team was at fever pitch, and it is interesting that Mick Mackey was in the team photo wearing his clothes. It's unclear how many factions were operating on the political side of team selection, but it seems that Canon Punch and other county board members, the Mackeys along with other Ahane members, and Dick Stokes would all have tried to exert influence. In true Limerick fashion, the self-destruct button was pressed in that Munster final. Paddy McCarthy had been sent a taxi fare to get a lift from Galway to the game, but given his fondness for the liquor, he drank the money and thumbed to Thurles. A member of the clergy spotted him on the road and reported the matter to Canon Punch. Despite the best efforts of the players in the dressing room, Punch was determined to make him pay. Johnsie Donoghue from his own club was to be the beneficiary. Mick Rainsford tells the tale:

Canon Punch was dictator. One of the corner-backs got injured, and the obvious man to put in was Paddy McCarthy. And what did Canon Punch do? He sent in Johnsie Donoghue, and Johnsie wasn't in a couple of minutes and he scored the own goal for Cork, and then they took him off and they put in Paddy McCarthy. But it was too late because that goal had beaten us.

Jim O'Donoghue elaborates:

Limerick were playing well, and Johnsie had only come in as a sub at corner-back. A ball was coming in and going wide. Whatever way he blocked it, it skidded into the goals. There was consternation. Johnsie was an average hurler, wasn't bad but wasn't outstanding, a good trier. He would fill a gap in a League match when Limerick were short or when players might not always turn up.

A well-placed source offers the following:

Johnsie Donoghue was not worth his place but Canon Punch wasn't beyond putting in his own lads onto the team. Jack Keane was a selector with Punch in some years and they often had a run in. The canon used to say when proposing someone that he belonged to a decent family, etc. Jack Keane used to say, 'Look canon, I don't care if he came out of a wheel of a caravan at the side of the road if he is good enough, but I will not let someone be picked that isn't good enough regardless of his background.'

Craobh Ruadh was a pseudonym columnist in the Limerick Leader *around the time who would have not shied away from controversy. He was truthful, brutally honest and didn't pander to the GAA powers that be, who even in modern times like the media to be politically correct. In his column of Saturday 26 July 1947, Craobh Ruadh laid the blame for the Munster final defeat solely at the door of the selectors:*

Limerick lost Sunday's game because the selectors lacked the courage and determination to pursue the policy mapped out by them in all matches prior to the championship bouts. This is the chief reason for our failure, and to the five, seven or nine who sat down to select the Munster final team must go the blame for the defeat. Would the Limerick side who beat Cork in the Thomond Tournament have won the 1947 Munster final? They would have had, and comfortably at that. Cork had chances since then but no outstanding improvements. Limerick likewise.

Craobh Ruadh may well have departed voluntarily but one could be forgiven for assuming that he was dispensed with because Canon Punch went in to the editor and threatened him with his stick. The power that the establishment hold within the local media to this very day cannot be understated and took root back in the old days. Traditionally it has always been accepted that if members of the establishment are targeted in the media, the bullets are coming from within

The Limerick and Cork teams in the parade before the 1947 Munster final at Thurles. *Limerick team (back row, r–l):* Jackie Power (not shown), Toddy O'Brien (not shown), Peter Cregan, Mick Herbert, Tom Cregan, Seán Herbert (partially hidden), John Mulcahy, Owen O'Riordan, Mick Ryan, Dick Stokes, Derry McCarthy, Thomas O'Brien, Jim Sadlier (turned), John Mackey, Paddy Fitzgerald. *Cork team (front row, r–l):* Seán Condon, Fr Murphy, Willie Murphy, Dr Jim Young, Tom Mulcahy, Con Murphy, Jack Lynch, Jerry Riordan, Mossie Riordan, Joe Kelly, Con Cottrell, Din Joe Buckley, Paddy O'Donovan, Christy Ring, Alan Lotty.

their own inner circle. It's widely known that in modern times a county board officer demanded the removal of a free-spirited columnist from the Limerick Leader *and succeeded in his request.*

Surprisingly, there was little media comment on the impact Mick Mackey might have made on the 1947 Munster final, but Mick Rainsford believes he was missed:

In 1947 they considered that Mick Mackey was gone and that's why he didn't play against Cork. He had a lot of hurling done, and he had got heavy and was starting to go off. But he wasn't finished. If that man got a ball he would have known what to do with it.

John Mulcahy says you needed to be tough to play the game in those days:

Mackey was the best hurler I ever saw. It was terrible tough that time. He would get a ball and he would head towards the goals, and he would knock two or three of them out of his way and throw it on in front of him and go after it and rise it again, and he would take it in his hand again when he was facing a man. I wouldn't agree that John Mackey was a classier hurler. You had to be a strong man, you couldn't score a goal without being badly hurt. You took a lot of punishment, you had to take punishment and Mick Mackey took more punishment than anyone.

Jim O'Donoghue gives his thoughts:

Around that time, a neighbour used to give me money every day to buy him the *Irish Independent* on the way home from school. Naturally on the way home I used to read about the matches. I wasn't at a particular Munster championship match in Thurles and Cork beat Limerick well, but one paragraph sticks in my mind. 'Mick Mackey of Limerick was the best player of the day, he rallied the Shannonsiders time after time and often beat three or four opponents.' Mackey was the hero even in defeat.

Life went on without Mackey, and Limerick played two League finals against Kilkenny at Croke Park, drawing 4-5 to 2-11 in November 1947 and winning the replay in March 1948 by 3-8 to 1-7 with John Mulcahy scoring two goals. Gerry Piggott recalls John Mackey following Mick into retirement:

In 1947, Mick had too much weight put on, which meant he wasn't as fit as he had been in his prime. Limerick got to the League final against Kilkenny without him and won it after the replay in Dublin. I went to the 1947 League final replay by car. There were five of us in a Mini Morris. John came on as a sub and he won the match for them. That was the finish up of John.

John Mackey hadn't regained his enthusiasm for the game, as Tony Herbert explains:

He went on as a sub against Kilkenny in the 1947 League final replay. I was in Dublin at the time and playing for Dublin at that stage. My brother Seán told me to bring my togs, that John probably wouldn't have any gear with him and they were thinking of bringing him on. They brought him in and he destroyed them [Kilkenny]. He frightened the life out of them.

Jim O'Donoghue gives an insight into the management team:

Canon Punch was one of the old-style priests, you tipped your hat to him as you did to every priest of that era. It was a different era and they were men with titles. He had an awful lot of say in the county board. I never had any run in with him and he used to go to all the matches. He didn't seem to take a direct part on the sideline or sending in substitutes but perhaps he was dishing out the orders on the sideline. But I do know that he was strictly obeyed and always expected that you gave him respect and reverence. The drawn game was played in November 1947. I was only nineteen and I came in near the end of that League. Punch was always involved. He wouldn't be the main man in the dressing room, though he would generally say a few words. To me Jackie Connell was the main man.

Mickey Fitzgibbon also had a lot of say. Mickey was the treasurer, and organised things, but not so much on the field. Himself, Jackie Connell and Canon Punch and Paddy Shaughnessy were the main men. When I first married, I married Paddy Shaughnessy's niece. He had a bit of a say and was mainly on the city board but was on the county board too. To me it seemed to be Jackie Connell who made the switches. The first day we went up for the League final we had only eighteen players, but I didn't get a chance. After Limerick drew the first day there was hullabaloo, and twenty-five players turned up for the replay. In Barry's hotel they were giving out the jerseys, the starting fifteen got theirs and the stronger subs got the rest. I was togged out but got no jersey so I had to wear an overcoat. Even at half time we didn't go into the dressing room and I was sitting on the sideline with Paddy Creamer and a couple of the other subs having a chat.

Players hadn't the transport then that they have now. They were different times, and that's why they didn't always turn up for matches. I was in Tommy Casey's car, and we went to Barry's for a meal after the final and then we went to the dance. I had to be down to work at 9 a.m. the following morning. You had to be or else you would get a black mark. Of course we were late leaving Dublin because a couple of the lads were shifting women. We left Barry's hotel around 2 a.m. and strolled into Limerick about 5 a.m. on Monday morning.

The momentum from their League win carried Limerick to victory against Tipperary for the third year in a row in the Munster championship by 8-4 to 6-4. Ultimately it made no difference, as in the Munster semi-final they were yet again beaten by Cork, by 5-3 to 2-5. They were unfortunate that fate decreed they would play Cork in the semi-final. Would an easier draw have made a Munster title more likely? John Mackey was finally allowed to follow Mick into retirement. Jim Hogan recalls a game involving the Mackey brothers around that time:

Stalwart Ahane hurlers – brothers Mick (*left*) and Seán Herbert pictured after their Limerick League triumph in 1948.

I remember being at an Ahane versus Treaty Sarsfields game at Adare as a young lad and the match was abandoned. That time there weren't too many stewards around, and Treaty had a very big following. Their supporters used to come out from town on double-decker buses. The Adare pitch is about a half mile back the creamery road and at that time there were no dressing rooms. Some of the players togged in the field and for the big matches both teams togged out in the same pub, which was a disaster if there was a row. The pub is now Bill Chawke's but it was known then as Murray's, across the road from the village hall.

John Mackey was playing full-forward for Ahane and Mick was in the corner. The game was only on about ten minutes when Mick got a ball and crossed it to John. John buried the full-back, the goalkeeper and the ball – the whole lot – into the net. At that the supporters invaded the pitch. There was a wire paling around the field and the players jumped this to get away from the crowd and ran down the road about a half a mile to the village. As young lads we sat in front of the village hall and waited for the action to start. There was a swinging door on Murray's pub like you'd see on the cowboy films. Next thing a player comes out, with another player on top of him,

An Ahane senior hurling team from the late 1940s. Mick Mackey is seated at the front to the right of Timmy Ryan.

and this was going on for a while. They were fighting away. I think they called guards from everywhere to eventually sort it out. We sat on the wall of the village hall for an hour watching it. That's my earliest memory of Mackey.

One of the biggest hitters on the club tournament circuit, Ahane played Thurles Sarsfields in 1947 in the Newport Tournament. Ahane lost by two points and for the record, the Ahane team was as follows: Paddy Creamer, Mick Herbert, Tom Conway, Paddy Enright, Seán Herbert, Jackie Power, Paddy Kelly, Timmy Ryan, Thomas O'Brien, Neddy Stokes, John Mulcahy, Jimmy Butler Coffey, Mick Mackey, John Mackey, Dan Mescall. Quite a team! The game has been labelled the greatest club match ever played and Gerry Piggott was there:

I would agree that the 1947 game against Thurles Sarsfields was the greatest club match ever played. If there was an All-Ireland club championship in the 1930s and 1940s Ahane would have dominated back then. They were a great side.

Ahane had also played Glen Rovers of Cork the previous November, and Mick Rainsford was impressed by a clash between two of the game's superpowers:

One of the best club matches I ever saw was that clash between Glen Rovers and Ahane on a wet day at the Gaelic Grounds. There is a photo of Mick Mackey and Christy Ring together and Mackey looked heavy in it so it was near the end of his time. Glen Rovers had Din Joe Buckley, Paddy O'Donovan, Dr Jim Young, Jack Lynch, and Ringy. I'd imagine they had Josie Hartnett on the team but we didn't know him. Ahane had the Herberts, Jackie Power, Paddy Kelly, Thomas O'Brien, Timmy Ryan and the Mackeys. It was a mighty game. I think the Glen beat them by a couple of points.

As was commonplace for ex-players in those days, Mick Mackey became a referee in 1948 and took charge of a senior hurling championship match between South Liberties and Young Irelands among other games. In those times becoming a referee was regarded as an honour for a former inter-county player, even though these days inter-county players seem to believe that becoming a referee is beneath them. In 1949 Limerick beat reigning All-Ireland champions Waterford in the first round of the championship by 3-8 to 2-3 and seemed well placed to face Tipperary in the Munster final. However, they were beaten by 1-16 to 2-10 in a game where referee Con Murphy of Cork disallowed a Jackie Power goal and gave some very handy frees to Tipperary, which were scored by Jimmy Kennedy. Seán Ryan (Malachy) recalls the goal that wasn't:

Jackie Power went through for a goal, and Con Murphy the referee blew him back and gave a free out instead. It was a wet day with a heavy ball, and from a free Limerick went for a goal but it was saved. There were nine or ten players lined up in the goals facing a free in those days.

Jim O'Donoghue has his own memory of the game:

I missed out on getting my place for the Tipperary game in 1949. John Martin was at half-back. Nothing against John Martin, but I thought myself I would have got my place on that team, and I would have been on Jimmy Kennedy who was a lovely nice clean hurler. Martin was a good hurler but a loose marker. Gerry Fitzgerald was called in when Limerick were a goal down. Jackie O'Connell shouted, 'Gerry, get in there, we need a goal.' That was the closest I came to getting on, I would have been in the running that day. However, I could have played with Ahane instead of Young Irelands, who I was hurling with at the time. Pat O'Reilly approached me to play for

Ahane but I had already given a commitment to Jim Sadlier that I would play for Young Irelands. If I did play for Ahane, I might have got on the county team more often because Ahane had a major say in picking the county team.

Mick Rainsford was satisfied with Martin but unhappy with the politics:

I was at the match with Gus Driscoll and Fr Seán Donnelly. We were outside the gate at 10.15 a.m. that morning. We were inside on the sideline at 10.45 for a game that was starting at 3.30. We were mad! It was a big thing that time, a Munster final. Jimmy Kennedy got ten touches of the ball, scored two 70s and eight 21-yard frees. He didn't hit another ball, John Martin didn't give him a smell of it, but he had ten points when the final whistle blew and we were beaten. Bill Maher was brought in out of the cold and selected at corner-forward but the man couldn't hurl. He was a Kilkenny man and I remember years later Seán Murphy was presenting a programme on RLO [Limerick local radio station] and they had John Mulcahy from Cappamore on the show. As I turned it on I heard John Mulcahy say, 'In 1949 we had a man corner-forward, I won't name him, but he wouldn't have got his place on the Solohead junior hurling team.' I knew who he was on about straight away. We had Gerry Fitzgerald on the sideline that day who was a great hurler, and the Munster Railway cup star Derry McCarthy wasn't on the panel, which was a disgrace. When Jackie Power went through and scored the great goal, the referee Con Murphy saw Maher pushing someone out the field and the goal was disallowed.

Bill Maher was the stationmaster at Limerick Junction railway station. He was also involved with Castletroy Golf Club and was well in with Dick Stokes. Stokes had pushed the case to select Mickey Walsh in 1944, and again pushed the case of Bill Maher in 1949. But Maher also had other allies, he looked after a number of people associated with Ahane GAA for jobs on the railway, much to the discontent of other GAA people who might have liked similar employment opportunities. His selection on the 1949 Munster final team sounds like a two-pronged tit-for-tat deal, by pandering to Dick Stokes and mixing with the elite in Castletroy Golf Club and by providing 'jobs for the boys' in Ahane GAA. One Limerick stalwart said the following:

I blame a lot of the Ahane players for that because they all got jobs in the railway at a time when it was hard to get jobs. Maher got his place on the Limerick team for giving them jobs. That was right blackguarding, and it cost Limerick a Munster title, denying a lot of great Limerick players a Munster medal. Some were working at level crossings; others were working on the railway lines; others were stonemasons and a couple more of them that weren't even able to drive a nail were carpenters. Maher got on the team in return. I was disgusted with the situation myself, and the game wasn't long on when I spotted that he was no good. Dick Stokes backed up the selection of Bill Maher, just like he did with Mickey Walsh back in 1944. Maher did Stokes some turn at some stage. When Maher came to Limerick he got into Castletroy Golf Club and got involved at committee level where Stokes and himself became great friends. I had a row with Stokes over his selection. Derry McCarthy, one of the finest hurlers we ever had in Limerick, didn't make the team that year because his face didn't fit.

Another Limerick stalwart said the following:

I can't contradict that Stokes would have been trying to facilitate pals of his on the team. He did it with Mickey Walsh and he did it with Bill Maher, another cuckoo. Both were players without credentials who were selected on Limerick teams for Munster finals. I suppose it's fair to say that Ahane were running the show for CIÉ that time as well. Jackie Power, Tom Conway, Thomas O'Brien, Seán Herbert, Mick Herbert, Paddy 'Krujer' Byrnes, Tom Tierney, Tommy Benn, Tom Garry, Jim Conway and Paddy Enright were all associated with the Ahane club and were working with CIÉ either on the railway or on the buses.

John Mulcahy played in the 1949 Munster final:

Bill Maher wasn't able to get his place on the Solohead junior team. I was working at Ballykisteen stud at the time, because we were building all the stables there. They made a pure laugh of me. 'Ye had a man playing against Tipperary and he wasn't able to get his place here on the Solohead team.' He wasn't even a sub against Waterford in the semi-final. Mick Bresnihan of Fedamore was dropped for him after scoring two points. Gerry Fitzgerald of Rathkeale came on and scored two points against Waterford and he wasn't on five minutes. Gerry Fitzgerald didn't get the goal that day, I got the goal against Waterford but the papers got it wrong. That time, players used to follow the ball into the net and be pulling away at it. By following in the ball and walloping it into the net you are giving time to the camera to get your photograph taken. I saw John Mackey at it several times, he was photographed in every paper scoring a goal, but the ball would have been gone into the net a minute before he tore in after it!

Willie Keane explains team selections in the 1940s:

In those days, any newspaper reports were more of an inquest afterwards rather than any preview in advance of the big game. It meant that nobody knew for sure who was going to play until the day of the match. While the team would have been sent to the programme printers, it might not have been made known to the public until the morning of the game, meaning that it was difficult to question any selection of a player.

Fr Liam Ryan gives some background on Maher:

I wasn't totally familiar with Bill Maher's selection for that Munster final, but it was understandable why there was surprise that Gerry Fitzgerald hadn't been picked. Gerry Fitzgerald had come in as a sub against Waterford and got the scores against the All-Ireland champions that effectively won the match for Limerick. And they didn't pick him for the final, which was a surprise. There was great expectation ahead of the Munster final in 1949 after beating the reigning All-Ireland champions. And having beaten Tipperary for the three previous years, people felt that 1949 was Limerick's year, especially with Cork out of it, but unfortunately it didn't work out like that.

Bill Maher was living in Castletroy. All I remember from the game is that Con Murphy disallowed Jackie Power's goal, and it was Bill Maher who was said to have committed the foul, that's if it was ever a foul in the first place. Despite being nowhere near the ball, he was blamed for the goal being disallowed. You didn't need to give away frees with Con Murphy refereeing, he awarded frees for very little. Maher was subsequently very involved in the hurlers' association, an association of old hurlers mainly to play golf, which is still in existence. Dermot Kelly got together with a number of ex-Tipperary hurlers and founded it when he was working in the bank in Thurles. Liam Moloney was the secretary for a long time. In the early days they used to play matches among the old hurlers, but that didn't work out too well and then they started playing golf.

*The non-selection of Derry McCarthy in 1949 was a major sore point with
many Limerick supporters, and those in west Limerick in particular believe he
was blackguarded. He is known to have been openly downhearted at missing
out on selection for Limerick that year. McCarthy was an outstanding hurler in
his own right, but some believed that at times he provided scores on a plate to
John Mackey rather than take them himself and that ensured his place on the
team. While McCarthy was an outstanding Railway Cup player and a natural
forward, sometimes talent is not enough to break down the political barriers and
he may well have needed the support of the Mackeys to secure his place. When
the Mackey brothers departed so did their influence on team selection, and Derry
McCarthy suffered because Canon Punch would have had more control.*

*Punch had been a priest in the Dromcollogher-Broadford area for a period,
and there are numerous theories mooted. One is that McCarthy played minor
hurling illegally for Meelin in Cork and that Punch took a dislike to it many
years later. Another is that McCarthy wasn't selected on the Limerick team for
a suit length tournament in Offaly and his mother attacked Canon Punch. For
that tournament in question, it's believed that there were only fifteen sets of suit
lengths, meaning that the replacements on the sideline didn't receive any. Party
politics had a massive bearing on team selection also. If a player was aligned
to the wrong party or even associated with the wrong politician within what
would be deemed the right party, it could prove very costly. In one east Limerick
club, for instance, players travelling in cars to games were selected to travel with
others by management based on political alignment. This broke up natural
friendships between regular travelling companions to the detriment of that club.
Either way, Limerick were weaker in 1949 without Derry McCarthy and it
was detrimental in terms of the result.*

*When the Munster final was over, the county championship took precedence.
Canon Punch had decided that Ahane were too powerful and were winning too
much so he made a few changes and amalgamated Croom and Young Irelands
for the sole purpose of beating Ahane. At that time, a junior club hurler could
play junior with his own club and also senior for the nearest senior team within
the division. Being the only senior team in the east, Ahane had the pick of the
entire division. Canon Punch also put a stop to that, although Michael Hynes
believed they exploited the rule when it favoured them:*

What I would condemn the Ahane club for, from the war years
onwards, was that they depended too much on outside players, and
in my own opinion the approach was to win at any cost. And I think
it did a share of harm to the Ahane team at the time. From the 1930s
to the '40s there was no problem, it was from the 1940s on that there

was a problem with Ahane. And it led to Canon Punch bringing in the famous rule blocking junior players from playing with Ahane and amalgamating Croom and Young Irelands. That in turn led to the incident with Michael Herbert. I thought Ahane brought in too many outsiders from outside the parish in those years. Our own players that might have been good enough didn't get a chance. We won a minor championship in 1941 with Ahane but Seán Herbert was the only one from that team who made it onto the Ahane senior team.

Willie Keane says there was demand for change:

The county in general were getting fed up of Ahane, winning year after year with no opposition. It's only human nature that people would want change.

Jimmy Butler Coffey saw how some players benefited:

Because of the rule made in the early 1940s, you could play with Ahane and also play with your own club. Paddy Creamer, John Mulcahy and myself won county championships with Ahane. After a few years they found that it wasn't working. There's a photo of an Ahane team from the 1940s, and it's more like a Limerick county team than an Ahane team. Ahane were still good after we were stopped from playing with them. There was a young lad from Annaholty called D'Arcy, a great friend of my brother who got his place on the team. Ahane natives like him who were good hurlers hadn't been getting their chance previously, but were now getting their opportunity.

It's understandable that limiting the pick of Ahane on its own would be worth consideration in the best interests of hurling in the county. However, the double blow of weakening them and then amalgamating arguably the second and third best teams in the county could be seen as nothing other than a conceited attempt to undermine Ahane. The game between Ahane and Croom/Young Irelands took place two weeks after the Munster final, a game remembered for the blow to the head of Mick Herbert.

On the call of half time, Seán Herbert was tussling with Tom Cregan, and Mick was walking up the field to the row. Joe Cregan got to him first, however, and hit him a severe blow on the head with his hurley. That moment is widely acknowledged as a huge turning point in Limerick hurling, after which Limerick were no longer a consistent hurling force. People feared to speak of that day for many years, and indeed until the publication of Unlimited Heartbreak *younger members of the Herbert family hadn't realised the impact that it had on*

Limerick hurling. The game was eagerly anticipated because there was trouble expected. Croom and Ahane had a natural rivalry, which brought its own bitterness, and this would have only intensified with the weakening of Ahane and the amalgamation of Croom and Young Irelands. In the irony of all ironies, the incorrect refereeing decision by Con Murphy which robbed Limerick of the 1949 Munster title also dramatically altered the course of Limerick hurling and helped shape it into what it has become today. Michael Hynes explained:

If the goal scored by Jackie Power was allowed, Limerick would have been in the All-Ireland final. There was so much trouble expected in that Croom/Young Irelands match that they couldn't have risked playing it if Limerick were preparing for the All-Ireland. So if Jackie Power's goal had been allowed, the Mick Herbert incident may never have taken place.

Mick Rainsford agrees:

If we had won the Munster final, that game would have been deferred until after the All-Ireland final. Dessie O'Malley's father, also called Dessie, wouldn't normally have gone to such games but he went to that match because there was trouble expected. Several other people who didn't normally go did likewise. They all wanted to get rid of Ahane, but it was very costly to Limerick hurling to get rid of them. Limerick came back in future years, but it took a long time and I don't think we ever really recovered. Other teams should have worked harder to reach the standard set by Ahane. The one thing I noticed about Ahane was that ten minutes into the second half they used to always lift their game. If you weren't able to lift it in those ten minutes, you were gone. Unfortunately, we have no more of that where Limerick hurling is concerned.

Paddy Clohessy refereed the game, and perhaps wasn't the wisest choice given his history of conflict with both Croom and Ahane as a player. The game itself has been overshadowed by the controversy, but Rainsford has a clear recollection of the performance of Mick Mackey:

Ahane got two 21-yard frees in that match, and the very second the referee had the whistle blown Mick Mackey had the ball in the back of the net before the Croom backs were even waiting for it. He was as fast as lightning from those frees. No messing, and no waiting around. But Ahane were still beaten. Croom/Young Irelands didn't even win the county after dethroning Ahane, they went on and were beaten by

St Patrick's. They broke up as a combination soon afterwards, and the Young Irelands club possibly within a couple of years. They didn't last too long anyway. A lot of people say they had done the job they were set up to do, to beat Ahane.

The incident is believed to have started over a row between Seán Herbert and Tom Cregan as to which club owned the match ball. Jim O'Donoghue was at the game:

Mick Herbert was a tough man at full-back and he would cut you in two, a man of steel when he was togged out, a fine cut of a man. I saw him down in Cork one year when he was marking Séamus Bannon and he nearly killed him. However, I have never seen him play better open hurling, pure hurling, than he did that day. There was nothing passing him and he was sending the ball way down the field 50 or 60 yards which was a long puck at that time. There was always a needle between Croom and Ahane because Croom were the next best team to them in the championship for a number of years. In my opinion, Seán Herbert started the row. Seán had a terrible temper, and he would throw the head in a minute. A little melee started between himself and Tom Cregan. Paddy Clohessy blew the whistle for half time and did nothing about it, more or less saying, 'Ye can do what ye like.' Three or four got involved. Joe Cregan was playing corner-back for Croom, and he came in and hit Mick Herbert down on the head. I played matches when Joe Cregan was on the team and he was a nice fellow. I remember being on the embankment on the sideline, and when they took out Herbert we all thought he was dead. I think Joe just lost the head for a second, unfortunately. Then there was the court case that followed and the whole episode ruined Limerick hurling.

John Mulcahy says Mick Herbert was no angel:

I remember beating Cork in a tournament in Coachford for suit lengths. A line ball came in high, and a Cork player called 'Hitler' Healy went up for it and he leapt up higher than Mick Herbert and tapped it over the bar. And it seems coming down he accidentally hit Mick Herbert, but Herbert didn't lie down. The young lad apologised, and Mick Herbert said, 'It's alright Hitler, it's alright.' The puckout was taken and the ball came back in. Herbert hit him a bang down on top of the head and the young lad had to be taken off. Herbert got away with that down in Cork and I was a witness to that.

In the same game, John Mackey was supposed to have scored an illegal goal. The Cork crowd were shouting, 'Give him a brown one, give him a habit.' They used to dress dead people in a monk's habit when they were putting them into a coffin to bury them that time. There was no such thing as putting a suit on them, it was a habit like the monks used to wear.

Willie Keane concurs that Herbert had a reputation:

In the Munster championship that year against Waterford a row took place in the goalmouth and I remember the goalposts swaying for a couple of minutes after the row. Mick Herbert was involved and Curran the Waterford full-forward got a broken nose. Jim Weir the goalie was carried off and looked as sick as any man ever looked. Mick Herbert had a habit of drawing the trouble on himself and it was probably a case of give a dog a bad name. Joe Cregan saw him as a threat and got his retaliation in first.

Fr Liam Ryan recalls an incident from the Munster final:

Mick Herbert split the Tipperary full-forward wide open that day, quite deliberately. I was standing right behind it. He was marking a fellow called Gorman, I think he was from Holycross, and he got a goal. Paddy Creamer was in goals, and Creamer said afterwards that he asked Mick what happened. Mick replied, 'He won't do it again', and said something like, 'When the next high ball comes in we will see what happens.' The ball came in on top of them and Herbert hit him quite deliberately. The ball broke inside and Creamer caught it. He said afterwards that he dropped it over the line for a 70 because he got such a fright. He also said that the blood was pouring out of Gorman's head, that he was like a stuffed pig and that he just wanted to put the ball out of play to stop the match. He pulled on Gorman quite deliberately. I can still see it to this day.

Mick Rainsford recalls that Herbert was given sound advice:

After that Munster final, Timmy Ryan 'Good Boy' spoke to Mick Herbert and told him, 'Hurl the ball. You are good enough to beat all them fellows by playing the ball and forgetting about the off-the-ball stuff.' That match against Croom/Young Irelands was the only day I ever saw Mick Herbert hurling the ball and he was clearing balls 70 yards that day, until the row started and it finished all that.

Fr Liam Ryan agrees:

It was ironic that on the day he played his cleanest game of hurling he got the near fatal blow to his head. To this day they don't know why Cregan hit him. It wasn't over anything Herbert had done in the first half. Herbert was lucky to survive, but Limerick hurling didn't survive. It destroyed Limerick hurling.

But Joe Cregan was no angel either, as Tony Herbert explains:

Joe, Peter and Tom Cregan all hurled for Limerick. Tom and Peter Cregan gave long service, but Joe only played for one year at corner-back, in the 1949 championship, and hadn't the best of records. My brother Mick said to me that Joe Cregan had broken Ned Daly's hand in the championship game with Waterford that year. Waterford reported it to the county board. Daly was one of their best players, and Joe Cregan broke his hand with a late pull. There were five Cregans playing in that match that Mick got the injury, and Mick decided he was taking them all on. He dropped the hurley and put up his fists and got the belt of the hurley on the back of his head. Joe Cregan broke the hurley off his skull.

Jimmy Butler Coffey was close to the action:

Mick Herbert was an outstanding hurler, he was going to be one of the great ones, but he was hard. He was a better full-back than Pat Hartigan who came afterwards because he was sharper. Mick Hickey was there before him and was tough, but he wouldn't be in Herbert's class. Herbert was really powerful but he could hurl too. He could fly out to a ball, break it down and drive it up the field. I remember the day he was struck, I was at the match and we were walking down at half time with Denis Malachy and Tom Malachy and we got talking to Seán Herbert [possibly after Seán Herbert's row with Tom Cregan had ended]. Seán was looking around and he said, 'Jimmy, I think Micheál is in a row.' So we went down anyway and Micheál was stretched out. Some people still say it wasn't Joe Cregan who struck him, even though he got jail for it. There was a crowd around and it's very hard to be definite about a man, about who exactly struck him when there's a crowd around. They were saying, 'Let him up, let him up.' He was struggling for his life on the field. You wouldn't know what to say or do at a time like that, when something like that happens and someone is struggling for their life.

Tony Herbert was glad he missed the game:

I was supposed to be going down to the game with Dan Givens but he couldn't start the car. Maybe it's just as well. We heard that night on the news that Mick got the belt of the hurley in the head and was in critical condition in hospital. We probably would have got involved in the row. Dan Givens was a fiery man, he would go through anything because his wife was from Castleconnell as well. She was one of the Joyces. Her brother Paddy Joyce used to hurl with Ahane and was very much involved. We would have ended up in jail. Joe Cregan served the full nine months. He got twelve months but it was a holy year that year and because of that all prisoners in jail were released three months before their time was up.

Fr Liam Kelly recalls Mick Mackey's disgust:

I saw Mick Mackey playing on the terrible day of the assault on Mick Herbert in 1949 and he always said that the incident finished him and hurling. He played on for two years afterwards but was only going through the motions. He was so disgusted with that game. I was very young at the time but I have a vivid memory of Mackey walking off the field that day, and his face was completely covered in blood and he didn't have a hurley in his hand. He had been hit several times and was split open down across his head. He had no hurley, didn't even have a weapon to defend himself. It was savagery. The game in general was tough. The build-up to the game was the most stupid thing of all, amalgamating Croom and Young Irelands for the sole reason of beating Ahane. It was all engineered and galvanised by the Reverend Dean Punch.

Arthur Graham believes Mackey didn't ever seek conflict:

Mick usually went into rows to keep the peace more than anything else but if he got a belt from behind, as happens in these peacemaking situations, it could be different. He was such a strong man that if he got hold of you, you would know all about it. I remember the aftermath of the incident that evening, people cycled back into Limerick with their rosary beads. There was a rosary said for him out on the street. I wasn't there but a lot of neighbours were in there and there was apparently a very big crowd there. Herberts lived almost across the road from us. My father had a telephone at the house before anyone because my father was the OC of Sarsfield barracks during the war years. Paddy Herbert [Mick's father] used to come down every evening and phone the hospital in Dublin.

Jim Hogan was also at the game:

I can still hear the crack that Mick Herbert got down on the head that day. That was Canon Punch's fault without a doubt, putting Croom and Young Irelands together to beat Ahane. Canon Punch was a menace, he was the chairman, he was everything. He was the only steward at most of the matches, going up and down the sideline with his umbrella, hitting people to make them go back behind the line. He was a steward at the Ahane versus Treaty Sarsfields game in Adare where the big row took place, dressed in his hat and collar. When you think back on it, it was a joke. He would be keeping the crowd back and the people were genuinely afraid of him.

Michael Hynes had his own views:

I blame Paddy Clohessy for it. Clohessy walked up, picked up the ball and blew the whistle for half time. Instead of breaking up the melee between Seán Herbert and Tommy Cregan, he walked away and let them at it. I am not 100 per cent sure that the row was because of who owned the ball. Paddy Quilty and myself took Mick Herbert into the hospital. I can't recall any ambulance crew being there on the day. After he got the blow to the head, he collapsed, and he got up and he faced down the goals at the city end and he collapsed again. I would imagine that he didn't really know where he was. He wasn't out cold. The crowd didn't go silent because a lot of people in the crowd didn't realise how serious it was. I was holding his coat the same day, and I went out to the centre of the field. Dr Jim McCarthy of Croom was there and he said, 'Get him in to a hospital as quickly as you can.'

Shell had a contract in Shannon airport at the time refuelling aeroplanes, and they had their own transport in and out from Limerick to Shannon to collect their staff, a minibus that would carry eight or nine people. We flagged down a Shell bus coming in from Shannon airport. I knew the driver Joe Lynam because I worked with Shell, and I flagged him down as it was passing. We got Mick out onto the road and the Shell bus stopped and took him into Barrington's. I met Mickey Roberts inside in Barrington's and he told me he was going to operate. We got him into the bed, and Mick's head had swelled considerably at the side where he received the blow. Mickey Roberts operated on him. Mick regained consciousness the following day and was transferred to Dublin afterwards.

What Mickey Roberts did, in layman's terms, was to relieve the pressure on the brain, and Mick had to be transferred to Dublin for a final operation because they didn't have the expertise to do it in Limerick. In Dublin Dr Coll from Bruree assisted in the operation, while Dr McConnell from Belfast was the main surgeon. Dr Pat Cummins went to Dublin in the ambulance with Mick. He wasn't back down home until after the All-Ireland hurling final because I recall his brother Éamonn Herbert and myself went to Dublin for the All-Ireland. It was up to see Mick we wanted to go more than anything else. Tipperary beat Laois out the gate the same day and a lot of the Tipperary team went to see him after the match.

Gerry Piggott was at the hospital:

It was a sad day for Limerick when Mick got struck and it finished Limerick hurling for a long, long time. He must have been a powerful strong man to survive as long as he did. I was outside Barrington's hospital and I came home with Mick Mackey. He was living outside in Thomondgate at that time and we came over Thomond Bridge about one in the morning. People weren't sure if he was going to survive or not. The row started when Paddy Clohessy blew the whistle at half time, but he shouldn't have been refereeing the match at all. He was too excitable a man and he wasn't suitable for refereeing. But the whole thing was ridiculous, a county and a city team amalgamating. All they wanted was to beat Ahane. And they finished Limerick hurling between them. It was Canon Punch and Mickey Fitzgibbon who were behind it all.

Tony Herbert knew some of the medical team:

On the day Mickey Roberts operated on him, he was out golfing and they brought him in. There was also a Dr Crowe from Tipperary involved and he had been at the match. He played rugby with Blackrock and Ireland. They lived in Ballsbridge, they had a pub in Ballsbridge and it's still there. They brought Mick up [to Dublin] in a special ambulance but there was a complication and the haemorrhage started again.

I got Dr Joe Stewart, a great referee here in Dublin, to recommend someone to carry out the operation. So he recommended Adam J.

McConnell, who operated on Mick in the Richmond hospital. It affected Mick badly afterwards. He used to suffer from epileptic fits regularly after the incident and he had to take special tablets to prevent that. The brain would come in contact with the skull at certain times and it used to create adhesion and it would swell up.

It finished Limerick hurling. Most of them lost interest and it finished Ahane. I don't think Limerick hurling has ever recovered. Teams sprung up after that, but a lot of weak teams from west Limerick became senior. If Ahane had remained strong, those teams would never have been good enough for senior. Most of the players from the west Limerick clubs would be regarded as junior hurlers. There was a hurling tradition in areas like Kilmallock and Effin in south Limerick, but teams with no hurling tradition from west Limerick got up to senior without being good enough for it.

Seán Ryan (Malachy) expands on the repercussions for hurling in the county:

It had a big effect on Limerick hurling and had a massive effect on Ahane. It put an awful dampener on things. Players didn't have the same enthusiasm going out hurling. It cast a gloom over everything here. When someone almost loses their life, it has that effect no matter what the circumstances. A surgeon from Scotland was over on holidays. He missed the train back that Sunday evening, and as luck would have it he was still around when they brought Herbert in. He was part of the operating team with Mickey Roberts. Herbert had a plate in his head until 2004 when he died and to lead the life that he did as a councillor, TD and MEP was remarkable, a sign of a very determined man.

Éamonn Cregan offered the following in Unlimited Heartbreak*:*

I always remember Jackie Power saying that the Mick Herbert incident wasn't the reason Limerick hurling went down, but that it was because Limerick lost to Tipperary that year. The incident did have an effect though. We were born in the city and you never saw a young fella walking with a hurley in the city in the 1950s, because we had an inferiority complex. Why I had an inferiority complex I don't know. We played hurling in the People's Park and we played hurling in the Bombin Field. You were an oddity if you walked down O'Connell Street with a hurley in your hand. I assume that came from what happened in that match. In Cork they walked freely around with hurleys in their hand.

Brendan Fullam is unsure:

I was very interested in Jackie Power's assertion, quoted by Éamonn Cregan in *Unlimited Heartbreak*, that it was the Tipperary game in 1949 rather than the Ahane versus Croom/Young Irelands game which led to the demise of Limerick hurling. I wouldn't disagree that it was a combination of the two events, but to me the Croom/Young Irelands game was the worse of the two. Limerick would have won the All-Ireland that year had they beaten Tipperary, because Laois folded in the final. Dermot Kelly said to me that into the 1950s Limerick players weren't talking to each other and it was because of the Mick Herbert incident. I can still see and hear Mick Mackey saying to me one day in Killorglin, 'That incident in 1949 set Limerick back twenty years.' He was right. Even though a young team came out of nowhere in 1955, twenty years brought us up to 1969, and Limerick won the League in 1971. So realistically it took twenty years to recover.

Canon Punch got his way, and Ahane were finally dethroned as county champions. It must be borne in mind that what happened in the Ahane versus Croom/Young Irelands game was commonplace in those days, but in most cases the injured player would receive a gash to the head, get stitches and resume playing. Herbert was probably struck no harder than anyone in any game at the time – certainly no harder than he had struck opponents himself. However, the incident was to have massive repercussions for himself and his family for the rest of his life. But it's important to understand that Joe Cregan, no more than any player at the time who struck an opponent on the head, did not intend to leave Mick Herbert so severely injured.

☃

1950: DAMNING EVIDENCE

*J*oe Cregan was arrested and charged in the days after the game and remanded
on £100 bail with two additional sureties of £100. Croom/Young
Irelands had beaten Ahane but were in turn beaten themselves by St Patrick's.
The trial began in October 1949 and it was proposed that Mick Herbert be
called to give evidence. But because he had not sufficiently recovered by then,
Cregan remained on bail and the case was deferred. In early 1950, the trial
eventually went ahead at Limerick Circuit Court. Mick Mackey was a key
witness, along with a number of others who had played in the game. Cregan
was sentenced to twelve months' imprisonment for causing grievous bodily harm
to Mick Herbert. The following is a full account of the trial as it appeared in
the Limerick Leader *of Wednesday 11 January 1950:*

INCIDENT AT HURLING MATCH
Sequel before Circuit Judge
ALLEGED BLOW OF HURLEY
Found Guilty on one Count

The trial of Joseph Cregan, a member of the Croom-Young
Ireland senior Hurling Team, on a charge of causing grievous
bodily harm to Michael Herbert, a member of the Ahane
team, concluded at Limerick Circuit Court this evening.

The accused had been arraigned on three counts and the
Jury after an absence of four hours found him guilty on the
third count – That of assault, causing grievous bodily harm.

Supt. Colleran then gave evidence as to the character of
the accused, and Mr Fitzgerald B.L., in an address to the
Judge, made a strong plea for leniency.

The Judge put back the accused for sentence until tomorrow morning.

A Member of the Croom-Young Irelands hurling team, Joseph Cregan, Skagh, Croom was arraigned at the Limerick Circuit Court yesterday before Judge Barra Ó Briain and a jury and charged with causing grievous bodily harm to Michael Herbert, a member of the Ahane hurling team.

The charge was a sequel to an incident that took place during the interval of a match played at Limerick Gaelic Grounds on Sunday 14th August 1949.

The accused pleaded not guilty. Mr William Binchy B.L. (instructed by Mr M. Power, State Solr) prosecuted and Mr M.V. Fitzgerald B.L. (instructed by Mr T.E O'Donnell solr) defended.

Michael Herbert (24) said that on Sunday August 14th he was full-back on the Ahane team which played Croom-Young Irelands. Just as the referee had signalled the half-time interval he noticed that his brother Seán was in some difficulties. On his way to the centre of the field where the struggle was taking place, witness experienced a sensation and did not remember any more until he found himself in Barrington's hospital. Later he was transferred to the Richmond hospital, Dublin and was operated on twice by Dr McConnell.

Mr Binchy – 'As a result of the hurling incident, did you experience much pain?' 'Yes I did.'

Cross-examined by Mr Fitzgerald, witness agreed that during the interval he got the impression that his brother Seán was in danger and that he was going to his assistance but he did not recall having said to anyone, 'If you want to fight, come out here, and I'll give it to you.' However, he could have said it.

INJURIES DESCRIBED

Dr M.J. Roberts, ear, nose and throat specialist, recalled that on the evening of the match, Michael Herbert was admitted to Barrington's hospital. He was then in a serious condition and in a dangerous state and had to be operated on quickly. In the course of performing the operation witness found a large blood clot on the left side of the skull. There was a very large fracture extending right around the skull, and in the middle of this, a big bone driven into his brain, right under the tissue. Underneath the skull itself there was a large blood clot, which had to be removed.

Asked by Mr Binchy if he could explain the halt in Michael Herbert's speech that was so noticeable while Herbert was giving evidence, Dr Roberts said that the halt in Herbert's speech was due to the fact that he was a right-handed man, while it was the left side of the brain that suffered the injury.

Patrick Clohessy who refereed the match in question said that during the interval there was a minor scuffle between Seán Herbert and Thomas Cregan. Witness separated the pair and then spectators rushed onto the field and he did not see the incident which caused the removal of Michael Herbert from the field of play.

SPECTATORS USUALLY CAUSE TROUBLE

To Mr Fitzgerald, witness agreed that spectators were usually the cause of any trouble that took place at these games. Guard Thomas McHugh said that he was a spectator of the match in question. During the interval there was a scuffle between players and that spectators gathered around them. Then a player from the respective teams came up on the outside, and he (witness) got the impression that words were being spoken. The Ahane player dropped his hurley and then was struck on the side of the head with the hurley. He could not say who had used the hurley, but was positive that it was a member of the Croom team. The injured man, Michael Herbert, was stunned.

To Mr Fitzgerald, witness agreed that during the course of the scuffle, he saw some hurleys being waved in the air.

Mr Fitzgerald – At an identification parade held at Croom did you pick out a different man from the accused?

Witness – I did.

SCUFFLE DURING INTERVAL

John Mackey recalled that he was playing for Ahane on the day in question. During the interval there was a scuffle between Seán Herbert (brother of the injured man) and Tom Cregan (brother of the accused), and they were separated. The accused at this time was standing beside the witness and Michael Herbert was on the outside of the crowd. Witness heard Michael Herbert saying to Tom Cregan, 'If you want a fight, I'll give it to you.' Michael Herbert then dropped his hurley and when witness turned around again he saw Joe Cregan with half a hurley in his hand. 'I caught hold of him,' continued witness, 'and pulled away a few yards, but when I didn't see anybody cut or bleeding, I let him go. Immediately after letting him (Joe Cregan) go, I saw Michael Herbert who seemed to be in pain with his hands up to his head and he wasn't able to support himself.

To Mr Fitzgerald, witness said that the accused was quite close when Michael Herbert spoke to Tom Cregan.

Mr Fitzgerald – Why did you turn around?

Witness – I turned around because I saw another brother of Cregan's with a hurley and I thought he was going to hit Michael Herbert.

DID NOT SEE ANY BLOW STRUCK

Continuing, witness said that he did not see any hurleys raised in the air, nor did he see any blow struck.

Mr Fitzgerald – You don't know what broke Cregan's hurley?

Witness – No; I just had my suspicions.

EXCHANGE OF BLOWS

Michael Mackey recalled that he was also playing on the Ahane team on the 14th August. Just before the half-time whistle blew, the Ahane goalie pucked out the ball which fell at midfield. Seán Herbert caught it in his hand and was tackled by Tom Cregan. The whistle sounded and the pair exchanged blows before the witness separated them. In the meantime the spectators came rushing on to the field and when witness looked round he saw Joe Cregan with the handle of a hurley in his hand. He (Joe Cregan) was being accused by spectators of striking Michael Herbert who was lying on the ground. The Ahane secretary Michael Minihan was giving him assistance. Next he saw Michael Herbert jumping to his feet. He was staggering and waving his hands and witness then took hold of him and left him in the care of some St John's Ambulance men. When accused by spectators, witness could not say if Joe Cregan had replied, 'The accused made an attempt to pull my hurley out of my hands,' continued witness, 'saying that it was his but I held on saying it was mine.'

Mr Fitzgerald – Did you see hurleys raised in the air?
Witness – No.

HURLEY BROKE IN TWO

Daniel Mescall said that he played on the Ahane team in question. Just before half time, Seán Herbert and a man named Cregan fought for possession of the ball. When the whistle sounded they started boxing and witness pulled Seán Herbert away. Tom Cregan was also pulled away into the crowd. At this stage Michael Herbert was looking into the crowd, he had not a hurley in his hand. Then another man named Cregan, whom witness knows now as the accused, came up, and with his hurley clenched in both hands struck Michael Herbert on the left side of the head. The hurley broke in two and Michael Herbert put his two hands up to the side of his head, gave a groan and then seemed to get delirious. Later at an identification parade held in Croom, he [Mescall] picked out the accused as the man who struck Michael Herbert.

Cross-examined by Mr Fitzgerald, witness agreed that there was a general melee going on at the time.

HERBERT HAD NOTHING IN HIS HANDS

Michael Minihan, secretary of Ahane hurling club, said that when the crowd came onto the field at half time he saw Michael Herbert coming around from one side and Joe Cregan coming from the other. Herbert had nothing in his hands but Cregan had a hurley. Almost immediately Cregan raised his hurley and struck Michael Herbert a hard blow on the side of the head.

Mr Binchy – Have you the slightest doubt who struck Michael Herbert?

Witness – No.

Mr Binchy – Who was that man?

Witness – Joseph Cregan.

To Mr Fitzgerald, witness said that Michael Herbert was playing full-back for one team, and Joseph Cregan in the full-back line of the other team.

Mr Fitzgerald – Cregan will say that his hurley was broken by another player.

Witness – I would not agree.

Thomas Hayes, who was a substitute for Ahane, told of having seen one of the Cregans striking Michael Herbert with a hurley. At an identification parade he identified Joseph Cregan as the one who had struck Herbert with the hurley.

Thomas Bridgeman gave evidence of having seen Joseph Cregan striking Michael Herbert on the left side of the head with a hurley.

Cross-examined by Mr Fitzgerald, witness said that when the blow was struck Michael Herbert was on the outskirts of the crowd which had gathered. He did not see any hurleys in the air.

EVIDENCE OF SPECTATORS

Donal Brennan said he was a spectator at the match and was about midway in the field. At half time he noticed a scuffle between Seán Herbert and Tom Cregan, and later he saw Joseph Cregan striking Michael Herbert on the side of the head with his hurley. To Mr Fitzgerald, witness said that he would not be more than 20 yards away when Michael Herbert was struck.

Thomas Byrnes remembered that Michael Herbert was on the outskirts of the crowd in the centre of the field at half time. He saw Joseph Cregan striking Herbert on the side of the head with a hurley. The hurley snapped in two. To Mr Fitzgerald, witness agreed that he was a fervent supporter of the Ahane team and that he lived in Castleconnell, the headquarters of the club.

Denis Coffey who was a spectator at the match recalled having seen Michael Herbert moving towards the centre of the field at half time. He was not carrying his hurley. When

Herbert was on the outside of the crowd, Joe Cregan came from the other side of the field and struck Michael Herbert with his hurley. Witness had no doubt as to the identity of the person who struck Michael Herbert.

Mr Binchy – Who is that person?

Witness – The accused.

To Mr Fitzgerald, witness said that he was a supporter of Ahane. He knew the Cregans for a number of years and knew them one from the other.

John Doyle corroborated the evidence of the last witness, saying too that he had no doubt as to the identity of the person who struck Michael Herbert.

IDENTIFICATION PARADE

Sergeant J.T. Caulfield said that on August 26th, he conducted an identification parade at Croom. There were eleven people on the parade including the four Cregan brothers, one of whom was the accused. The first person called did not identify anyone, but Mescall and Hayes picked out the accused as the man who struck Michael Herbert. Guard McHugh then pointed out a man named Hartigan from Croom who he said looked like the man that had struck Herbert.

STATEMENT BY ACCUSED

Inspector Griffin, who was conducting the investigations, said that on the 15th August he visited Croom where he saw the accused. After being cautioned, Joseph Cregan made the following statement: 'I have been cautioned that I am not obliged to say anything unless I wish to do so but that whatever I do say will be taken down in writing and may be given as evidence. I am 28 years and married. I reside at Skagh. I am a farmer by occupation. On yesterday Sunday the 14th August 1949, I was playing in the full-back line with the Croom-Young Ireland hurling team against Ahane at Limerick Gaelic Grounds. We played until half time and there was no row during the first half. Sometime around half time I saw my brother Thomas and John Herbert having a bit of a tiff. I saw them giving each other a few digs with their flats. The ball was in play around them at the time. I saw the people in the sideline going into the pitch and I went down to where my brother Thomas was to make the peace. I did not get as far as my brother Thomas and John Herbert as there was a crowd around them, but as I tried to get to them, three or four people rushed me, one of whom was a player and the others were spectators. The first of these people had hurleys and had them raised up. I then put up my hurley to guard myself, and my hurley was broken with a wallop of a hurley.

COULD NOT SAY WHO BROKE IT

I could not say who broke it. I did not know any of the people who rushed me. The only person I knew at the time was Jim Sadlier, a player in the Croom team, and I saw him around about at the time my hurley was broken. I did not see my brother Thomas or John Herbert or Michael Herbert around the place where my hurley was broken. Michael Herbert played full-back for the Ahane team. I did not come in contact with him during the game. When my hurley got broken, I threw away the handle of it and went into the dressing room. When my hurley got broken I ran away from the people and as I was running I got a few tips of a hurley in the back. I could not say who hit me. I struck no one with a hurley. I did not see Michael Herbert being struck with a hurley. I am positive I did not hit him when I came out of the dressing room to resume the play after an interval of ten or fifteen minutes. I saw Michael Herbert being taken off the field. I was told by somebody whom I know that Michael Herbert was struck. I think that he was struck with a hurley. When I was in Sadliers having a meal one of the players – Timothy Glynn – remarked to me, "You are in the black books after today." I said, "For what?" He said, "For striking Mick Herbert." I said, "I had nothing at all to do with it, I struck no one with a hurley."'

EVIDENCE BY ACCUSED

Joseph Cregan, the accused, said in reply to Mr Fitzgerald that he was a member of the Croom-Young Ireland team and had also played for the county team. He had never been put off. On the day in question he was playing left-full-back.

The statement made by him to Inspector Griffin was correct and he had nothing to add to it.

Cross-examined by Mr Binchy, accused denied having heard Michael Herbert addressing his brother. He did not see the Mackeys – either John or Mick – around when the incident was supposed to have taken place.

Mr Binchy – Are you prepared to contradict John Mackey when he says he held you?

Accused – I don't remember anyone holding me.

Continuing, accused said that no one accused him of striking Michael Herbert. He did not remember meeting any of the Mackeys nor did he make any attempt to get Mick Mackey's hurley. When he (accused) was rushed, he just put up his hurley and he could not say whether it was a player or spectator who broke his hurley. When he came up to the crowd, an Ahane player and a number of supporters attacked him. The first bunch that came to attack him had hurleys.

Mr Binchy – I suggest that there was no attack on you; isn't it a fact that some of the spectators charged you with striking Herbert?

Accused – No.

Mr Binchy – Are you able to say who struck Michael Herbert?

Accused – No.

It was true that Timothy Glynn, a member of the Croom team, mentioned to accused that he (accused) would be in the 'black books' for striking Michael Herbert.

BREAKING OF HURLEY

Francis Costelloe recalled the half-time incident in which Seán Herbert and Tom Cregan were scuffling. Later he saw Joseph Cregan backing away from three Ahane players who had their hurleys over their heads. It was during this incident that Joseph Cregan's hurley was broken by an Ahane player.

To Mr Binchy, witness said that it was Paddy Kelly of Ahane who broke Joe Cregan's hurley.

Mr Binchy – Did you hear the accused saying that there was only one Ahane player attacking him and that the others were spectators?

Witness – There were three Ahane players.

Continuing in cross-examination, witness said that he did not see anything happening to Mick Herbert.

Mr Binchy – I take it you approached the accused and told him you were able to give this evidence?

Yes sir, I did, about three weeks after the match.

Patrick Morrissey recalled that at half time, Joseph Cregan was charged by three or four Ahane players and his (accused's) hurley was broken in his hand by an Ahane player. Witness was about 50 yards away at the time.

SETTING BACK DEFENDING HIMSELF

To Mr Binchy, witness said that he was at the match with the last witness. The accused was not being charged by spectators at the time witness saw him. There were three or four Ahane players and he was setting back from them, defending himself.

Mr Binchy – What were the remaining members of the Croom team doing that they did not come to the accused's rescue?

Witness – They were around.

John Hickey gave evidence of having seen a civilian striking Michael Herbert with a hurley. He could not say what happened the hurley as a crowd formed around Herbert almost immediately.

Cross-examined by Mr Binchy, witness said that he saw a civilian strike a man but did not know who was struck until he heard afterwards. It was around about December that witness met Cregan for the first time after the match. On the second occasion, he met the accused by accident in a public house in Croom. People were talking about the match and he told the accused that he would be prepared to tell the court what he saw on the day of the match.

RESUMED HEARING TODAY

When the hearing resumed this morning, the one other witness for the defence, Robert Nix, was called. He said that he was a commercial traveller living in Limerick and had always been associated with the Croom/Young Irelands hurling team. On the day of the match, said the witness, I was sitting at the side of the pitch, and just after the half time whistle went, the crowd invaded the pitch. Being interested in the Croom players, I went out to bring them to the dressing rooms. On my way out there was a crowd of a few hundred people or maybe more in the centre of the pitch. I saw two hurleys being beaten off each other, one being broken into splinters in the air. I didn't see the two people implicated but I understood from what I heard people say that it was Joseph Cregan and Patrick Kelly. I saw Cregan shortly afterwards coming from the spot where I saw the hurley broken.

Questioned by the judge, witness said he was not able to say that the accused did not hit Herbert. Addressing the jury, Mr Fitzgerald said that in all vigorous games there was always the risk of injury to players. He thought it was a tribute to the control exercised by the GAA and particularly to the skill and sportsmanship of the players that there were so few cases of serious injury in playing pitches throughout the country.

JUDGE'S CHARGE

In his charge to the jury his lordship said it was manifest from the great public interest displayed during the hearing that more than the jury had followed the evidence very carefully.

Dealing with the blow inflicted – by somebody – on the head of Herbert, his lordship remarked, 'It is not thanks to the man who struck him that he is alive today and it would not be the first time that a man has been killed by the blow of a hurley.'

Later when dealing with the evidence of the prosecution witnesses, the judge commented, 'Many more than those who gave evidence must have seen this deplorable incident. It reflects no great credit on them that they haven't come forward.'

Cregan was sentenced the next morning, and the following is the report of the sentence as it appeared in the Nenagh Guardian *of 14 January 1950:*

TWELVE MONTHS' SENTENCE
ON LIMERICK HURLER
SEQUEL TO PLAYING PITCH ASSAULT

At Limerick Circuit Court on Thursday, Judge Barra Ó Briain sentenced Joseph Cregan (28), farmer, of Croom, Co. Limerick to twelve months' imprisonment for having caused grievous bodily harm to Michael Herbert during a hurling match between Ahane and a Croom-Young Ireland selection on the 14th August last. Passing sentence, the judge said anybody could not but be shocked at the brutality and lack of sportsmanship displayed by the accused, whose conduct was a grave blot on the annals of the most historical and finest of Irish games. He expressed the hope that accused or anybody like him found guilty of such conduct on the playing field would be prohibited forever from playing. In his present unfortunate position, Cregan could take consolation in the fact that the medical skill had saved Herbert's life.

And so the most controversial and detrimental episode in the history of Limerick GAA came to its conclusion. Mick Mackey, in his role as peacemaker, tried to separate Seán Herbert and Tom Cregan when the row started, but by then it was too late. Sometimes in that situation blows are struck without any rational thought or any consideration given to the consequences. There were wrongs on both sides and on the part of the referee, but Limerick hurling was the biggest loser of all.

❧

EIGHT

1951–4: TERMINAL DECLINE

*T*he Mick Herbert incident finished Limerick as a hurling force and cast
a gloom over hurling in general throughout the county. Only five of the
team that started against Tipperary in the 1949 Munster final were there to
face the same opposition in 1950 – Jim Sadlier, John Martin, Dick Stokes,
Tom Boland and Neddy Stokes. Limerick were beaten 4-8 to 0-8, a respectable
enough scoreline without a whopping ten first-choice players from the previous
year's final – Paddy Creamer, Mick Herbert, Joe Cregan, Seán Herbert, Thomas
O'Brien, Paddy Fitzgerald, Tom Cregan, Bill Maher, Jackie Power and John
Mulcahy. Division was rife in the county at this point, particularly between
Ahane and Canon Punch. Brendan Fullam was at the Tipperary match:

At one stage in the game, the forwards had driven a few balls wide a
little hastily, and Dick Stokes waved his hand in the air a few times out
of pure frustration. Limerick were awarded a long-range free and he
went out from his position at corner-back, took the free and through
pure determination drove it over the bar from about 80 yards out.

Mick Rainsford lists the departure of players:

That row knocked Limerick hurling back years and knocked the
guts out of it. It was terrible. It also meant that Limerick were very
depleted in the early 1950s. The full-back line prior to the row used to
be Mick Herbert and the two Cregans but they were obviously gone.
Jackie Power was gone. Thomas O'Brien of Ahane was gone. Seán
Herbert was gone. That was half a team wiped out. It was terrible.

Seán Ryan (Malachy) believes the loss of Mick Herbert was incalculable:

He was an awful loss to both Ahane and Limerick. He was a massive
presence as a full-back and he was an awful hard man. It's hard to
know if Mick Herbert was better than the modern full-backs because

hurling has changed, but he would possibly hold his place with any of them. There wasn't a pick of weight on him. He was fast and he was as strong as a horse. It caused a massive rift in the county at the time. Limerick were losing a lot of players naturally at the end of the 1940s that were starting to go off. You have cycles in players, and it's very hard to replace good players. But that incident accelerated their departure.

Naturally enough, the Kilkenny man Bill Maher wasn't seen in a Limerick jersey again, while John Mulcahy and Paddy Creamer were suspended, as Mulcahy explains:

Myself, Paddy Creamer and Jimmy Butler Coffey played for Ahane as well as our own club Cappamore, and Canon Punch brought in the rule to stop us playing with them. He then allowed Croom and Young Irelands in the city to join up and yet deprived us of playing with Ahane. We refused to turn out with Limerick over that decision and were suspended for the year because of our protest.

Fr Liam Ryan remembers the departure of another player:

They suspended Paddy Fitzgerald [St Patrick's] for playing inter-firm soccer and I think he received a suspension of two years for 1950 and 1951. From 1950 on Limerick hurling was a disaster, a third of the team picked for several League games never showed up in the dressing room for those games. Some may argue that there could have been a natural turnover of players due to some of them coming to their natural end, but the Herbert incident totally compounded it. It created complete apathy in Limerick hurling for many years, marked by the number of players who were picked especially for the League who just couldn't be bothered showing up. I don't think the Cregans even played for Croom afterwards. It killed the spirit and any life that was in Limerick hurling. Any previous rows back through the years were one person against another, but the Mick Herbert incident was different and tore the heart and soul out of Limerick hurling.

Michael Hynes explained the impact:

Seán Herbert didn't hurl after 1949 for a while, Jackie Power was going off anyway but that incident finished him. They would definitely have won an All-Ireland in 1949 without question only for the disallowed goal in Cork, because Laois would have been their opponents in the All-Ireland final. They would have had the same team in 1950 and even though Jackie Power would have been a year older, they would still have been contenders. The Mick Herbert incident had a massive impact in that it even stopped people going to matches. Limerick had lost one of its best up-and-coming stars.

P. J. Keane says jealousy was a factor:

Ahane had won sixteen county championships in the 1930s and 1940s. My view is that there was a lot of animosity towards Ahane in the rest of the county because of their level of success. I think that has bedevilled Limerick hurling, concentrating on inter-club stuff rather than the good of the county. I don't see that in Kilkenny.

Not everyone was sympathetic towards Herbert though, as Rainsford explains:

I worked in Ballynanty at the time where they were building the houses. Mick Herbert was still in hospital and there was a great Treaty Sarsfields crowd working on the building site. For a long time they had no sympathy for him and anyone you would talk to reckoned Mick Herbert didn't get half enough. It was said that he played against Treaty one day and he gave one of their players a kick in the private parts and that's why they didn't like him.

Seán Leonard told me that the first time he came onto the Limerick team against Galway at the Gaelic Grounds he was marking Joe Salmon, a great hurler. They were outside pucking around before the game and Mick Herbert came over and said, 'Seán, you know who you are marking?' 'I do,' said Seán, 'Joe Salmon.' 'You know what you should do at the throw-in?' says Mick. 'Let out six inches of the hurley, and when the ball is thrown in give it to him into the private parts.' The throw-in was different that time, and they used to be eight-a-side lining up for the ball. Seán said to me, 'I never spoke to the man [Herbert] after.' Seán Leonard would play a hard game, man for man, but that was it. He would never go out to injure anyone and didn't do anything to Joe Salmon. He had no time for Mick Herbert after that. But it's ironic that the one day Mick Herbert hurled the ball was the day that finished him as a hurler. But on the other hand, if he hurled like that against Tipperary below in Cork, they would have won the Munster final.

John Mulcahy recalls the Treaty incident:

He kicked a Treaty Sarsfields player in the private parts, and would have been killed that day only Paddy McCarthy from Newcastlewest ran up along the sideline and threw in a hurley for him to defend himself. Murphy was the name of the man that he kicked. The Murphys and the Fitzgeralds and a few more Treaty Sarsfields players were all related. Once you went at one of them, you went at them all. He gave him a kick and there was no meaning to it at all. That wild streak just seemed to be in him.

Fr Liam Kelly recalls Mick Mackey's viewpoint:

The one game that Mick often spoke about losing was the 1949 Croom/Young Irelands game which he was always sore about, but not because they lost. It was a bad memory for him all his life. He never got that game out of his system and was pained that it dragged hurling through the mire that time. He was the first to acknowledge that Mick Herbert was no angel and he used to say, 'Mick Herbert was no saint, as tough as they come, he would take man, ball and the whole lot, but he was a bit rash and didn't take any prisoners.' In more modern times Mick Herbert's nephew Pat – who I believe could have been a great coach with Limerick – was something similar. He always pulled first and asked questions later.

On some occasions, Mick Herbert was reminded of this incident, as an old-timer explains:

A row took place in Herbert's pub one night. There were two groups of people drinking there on the night who didn't really get on well with one another and as the night wore on, and more drink was consumed, they started to get rowdy. Next thing a row started, and there were stools and tables flying everywhere. Mick and a few more locals took decisive action and cleared the lot of them out the door. One of them shouted as he was being removed, 'Joe Cregan didn't hit you half hard enough!'

But despite the hangover from the Mick Herbert incident, the politics and skulduggery didn't stop at boardroom level. The county board by their actions were leaving nobody in any doubt as to who was boss. The well-known hatred Canon Punch had for Ahane reached a new low when he unceremoniously suspended the legendary Jackie Power for six months because he didn't play against Tipperary. The following report appeared in the Limerick Leader *from the June county board meeting in 1950:*

PAINFUL DUTY

'And now,' said Father Punch, 'I have a most painful duty to perform in having to suspend Jackie Power and Dan Mescall of Ahane for six months for failing to notify the Board of their inability to play for Limerick against Tipperary in the Munster championship game.'

Mr Minihan (Ahane) – I understood that these players had sent word that they would be unable to play. I would like it to go out from this meeting that the Ahane club had nothing whatsoever to do with the calling off of these players from the county team. In the case of Jackie Power, the Board is showing very little gratitude in suspending him after fourteen years' loyal service to both the GAA and his county. It would look very bad to suspend a man like Power at the end of his playing career.

Father Punch – We are not suspending him, he suspended himself. I issued a warning at the last meeting of this Board, that players who did not turn out for the county team would automatically suspend themselves. I would not be doing my duty as Chairman of this Board if I allowed this kind of thing to continue.

RUMOUR CONTRADICTED

Mr O'Connell – I would like to contradict a rumour, which was current all over the county, to the effect that this Board failed to provide transport for Power from Claremorris to Limerick for the game. I wrote to him instructing him to hire a car in Claremorris to bring him to Limerick and left him the choice of coming on either the Saturday before or the Sunday of the game. This Board has never failed to provide transport for their players and I wish to contradict this deliberate falsehood.

Rev. Fr White C.C. (Ahane) – I would appeal to the Rev. Chairman not to suspend these players.

Fr Punch – Again I say I am not suspending them. They suspended themselves.

Mr Minihan – There is not a member of this Board who would wish the suspension of Power and I suggest that the Board vote on this matter.

Fr Punch – As far as I am concerned, these players are now suspended and there is nothing further I can do in the matter.

Jackie Power responded in the Limerick Leader *a couple of weeks later:*

LIMERICK–TIPPERARY MATCH
LETTER FROM JACKIE POWER

(To the editor, *Limerick Leader*)
A Chara – I read report of County Board Meeting of Saturday 24th June, at which Mr J. O'Connell, Sec., Limerick County Board, stated that he wrote to me re. travelling arrangements. I wish to state that I received no instructions whatsoever in writing from this man as regards travelling to Limerick on the day of the match and in view of not having definite instructions, I took it for granted that the Co. Board officials did not think it worth the expense. I am sorry for any disappointment caused to supporters of the Limerick team as I had trained and was anxious to play.
Mise Le Meas
JACKIE POWER

Jackie O'Connell, the county secretary, replied a week later:

LIMERICK–TIPP MATCH
REPLY TO JACKIE POWER

A Chara – With reference to Jackie Power's letter, which appeared in your issue of 8th instant, in which he alleges failure on the part of the County Board to provide transport for him from Claremorris for the senior hurling match Limerick versus Tipperary on the 18th ultimo, I shall be glad if you will give me space to state briefly the facts as given by me to the County Board at its meeting on the 24th ultimo.

Twelve days prior to the match, I notified Jackie Power at Claremorris, where he was then working, of his selection on the Limerick team. As he regularly came home to Annacotty each weekend (this was the condition that made it legal for him to play for Limerick), I made arrangements for a car to collect him at his home in Annacotty on the day of the match.

On Thursday prior to the game as final arrangements were being sent out, Mr Michael Kennedy, a member of the Selection Committee, informed me that he had received on that morning a letter from Jackie Power stating, inter alia, that I (County Secretary) was expecting him down as usual for the weekend, but he was afraid he would not be down this time, that he had exhausted his leave. Mr Kennedy spoke on the phone to Jackie Power and informed him that my instructions were to hire a car to bring him from Claremorris to Limerick for the match with Tipperary. He was given the option of travelling down on the Saturday evening prior to or the Sunday morning of the match according to his choice. He (J. Power) agreed to hire a car as instructed and promised to be at Fitzpatricks at 1 pm on the Sunday of the game.

About 8 pm on the Saturday evening prior to the game, Mr Kennedy brought me a letter which he had received from J. Power, in which the latter stated that as he had decided to give up hurling, he would not play for the county on the following day, and accordingly would not travel as arranged.
– Mise Le Meas
Seán Ó Conaill
Secretary Limerick County Board GAA
11th July 1950

John Mulcahy recalls some more skulduggery:

In 1951, Jim Sadlier was selected for the Munster Railway Cup team, but Sadlier wouldn't go. I was selected instead of him and we won the Railway Cup but I never received a medal. Many years later, shortly before Séamus Ó Ceallaigh died, I visited him. Out of the blue, he said to me, 'You didn't ever get your Railway Cup medal.' I was shocked when he said it and was about to deny it because I was ashamed to admit not getting a medal having played in the game. I said to Ó Ceallaigh, 'Why do you say that?' He replied, 'Because I know where that medal went, it went to Mickey Fitzgibbon.' Fitzgibbon gave the medal to his own nephew Jim Sadlier instead of giving it to me. I was disgusted. It reminded me of an incident that took place years earlier when I was rushing out the door to a minor hurling game. I hit off an old man outside the door with the hurley and gear as he was passing. He caught hold of me and said, 'Where do you think you are

The Limerick team that lined out in the 1951 Munster championship against Tipperary with some of the star names back on board after the Mick Herbert incident. *Back row (l–r)*: Seán O'Shea (Patrickwell), Mick Ryan (Young Irelands, Dublin), Thomas O'Brien (Ahane), Tom Long (Feenagh/Kilmeedy & Dromcollogher), Jim Sadlier (Young Irelands), Neddy Stokes (Pallasgreen & Ahane), Timmy Murphy (Treaty Sarsfields), Paddy Creamer (Cappamore & Ahane). *Front row (l–r)*: Dermot Kelly (Claughaun), Johnny Dooley (South Liberties), Donal Broderick (Dromcollogher), Seán Herbert (Ahane), Dick Stokes (UCD), Derry McCarthy (Dromcollogher), Gerry Fitzgerald (Rathkeale).

going?' I said, 'I am going to play a game of hurling at Doon.' 'Oh,' he replied, 'a game played by fools and run by crooks.' He wasn't too far wrong at all!

In 1951, Limerick were strengthened by the return of Seán Herbert, Thomas O'Brien, John Mulcahy and Paddy Creamer. It mattered little, though, as Tipperary beat them 3-8 to 1-6 in the Munster championship. Mick Mackey retired from club hurling in 1951 after a long and distinguished career (though some have a vague recollection of a brief comeback the following year). Ahane had been beaten by Treaty Sarsfields in the county semi-final at Kilmallock in his last championship match. Some believe the game was as rough as the 1949 Ahane versus Croom/Young Irelands game, with everything except a repeat of the Mick Herbert incident. Jim O'Donoghue explains:

That match in 1951 was the last club match he played. He was playing on Johnny Fitzgerald from Treaty Sarsfields. Before the game, the Treaty players were saying to Fitzgerald, 'Watch Mackey now or he will clip you.' Fitzgerald and Mackey had as tough a tussle as ever took place on a hurling field and there were plenty of other incidents in the game. There was a saying, 'Hit one Treaty Sarsfields man and you hit all fifteen of them.' There was always plenty of backup! Around that time I was playing in a tournament one day at Ballysimon for the Mental Hospital team in Limerick. Mick was playing for the opposition. I was young and light at the time and was going up the wing and Mick came across. He was very strong and he hit me a rattle of a shoulder and drove me about what seemed 100 yards over the sideline. He would hit you a rattle like that if he got a chance.

His final appearance wasn't all plain sailing, as Tony Herbert explains:

Mick Mackey got put off in the county semi-final against Treaty Sarsfields and he retired after that. The referee that day was Rody Nealon from Newtown near Nenagh. He was Donie Nealon's father.

Fr Liam Kelly recalls a tough match:

Mick Mackey's last appearance for his beloved Ahane came in 1951, a defeat to Treaty Sarsfields in the county senior hurling semi-final. *Back row (l–r)*: Mick Minihan, Tom Conway, James 'Todsie' Mackey, Frank Kelly, Tommy Casey, Tommy O'Brien, Jerry O'Riordan, Mick Mackey, Dick Leonard, Fr White. *Front row (l–r)*: Maurice O'Brien, Paddy Kelly, Paddy Byrnes, Seán Herbert, Paddy Enright, Arthur Graham, Joe McMahon.

He actually played at full-back in that game against Treaty Sarsfields. There was blood and murder in that game too like in the Croom/Young Irelands game. The state he was in afterwards was unbelievable. They were savage towards one another in that game. Treaty Sarsfields were a city team and they all had nicknames, such as Dasher Cronin, Pigeon Mitchell, Hatchet, etc.

Maurice Regan was at the game:

There were two or three of the O'Sheas playing for Treaty Sarsfields at the time. Mick O'Shea was the best hurler I ever saw, I never saw anything like him but he damaged his knee. He used to get the ball, solo through and put it over the bar, time after time. He won matches on his own, but he was a sprinter as well. He made a comeback but he only played a few matches, one of them was the opening of the pitch in Bruff. Cork had a good team that time, and he was on one of Cork's better players and he ran rings around the Cork player. The Cork players are talking about him to this day. They couldn't believe how good he was. The knee went again after that match. One of the O'Shea brothers was centre field against Ahane in the club game, and Mackey was switched out to centre field. O'Shea would take off on a solo run, show the ball to Mackey, and dummy him. After it happened a few times Mackey's temper was rising and he was trying to take out O'Shea. If Mackey met him, he would have killed him with his strength and power alone. Mackey was a gallery man, but my father always claimed that John Mackey was a better hurler, but he was a different type of person off the field. When the match was over John was gone home and didn't bother much about it any more until the next game or training. Whereas Mick was always a gallery man, he was more inclined to stay around to meet people. He was a popular character, but milked the attention a bit. At the same time if he got a belt in a game, he would put up with it and he got a lot of belts it seems.

Paddy Tuohy recalls the magic of Mackey:

Treaty Sarsfields mounted an attack on the Ahane goal late in the game. The ball hit the upright, rebounded high back into play, and Mick Mackey swooped on it overhead, one handed, and drove it 80 yards out the field. The crowd at the game thought it was absolutely unbelievable that at the end of his career he still had the savvy to do that.

John Mulcahy felt the time was right:

Mick Mackey finished of his own accord, and it was time for him. If he didn't go when he did, you would only have players coming along and saying, 'I held Mick Mackey scoreless.' He was gone heavy and he was gone slow so it would have been easier to get the better of him. There was a player called Clifford from Fedamore who played on him in a club game and he was boasting that he held Mick Mackey scoreless. I said to him, 'You wouldn't hold Mackey's hurley in his heyday.'

Fr Liam Kelly says Mackey regretted not departing earlier:

Mick always said to me that he stayed on too long as a player and he always felt that Christy Ring did too. He often said, 'Ringy stayed on too long, sure he was still hurling at forty-seven years of age.'

John Ryan played with Mackey a few times prior to his retirement:

When I played with him, he wasn't the Mackey of old, and I never played championship hurling with him. One night, a challenge match took place in Ennis between Ruan, the Clare champions, and Ahane. I wasn't playing because I had broken my collarbone in a game in the Gaelic Grounds. Mackey played full-back, the match was very close and Ahane were hanging onto a two-point lead. The Ennis referee wanted Ruan to win the match so he gave a soft 21-yard free. The Ahane corner-back blocked it and the ball as cleared. A couple of minutes later he awarded another 21-yard free and someone else blocked it. Soon afterwards he gave yet another 21-yard free. Jimmy Smyth was taking it, a man who was able to score 21-yard frees better than anyone, no matter who was facing him in goals. He was lethal from them. I was standing near the goals and as Smyth was about to hit it, Mick Mackey let a roar out of him, 'You'll never score it.' Mackey caught the ball in his hand and he drove it 80 yards up the field. That stands out in my memory. He was kind of in charge of us in those few years. Like all great players, he wouldn't have been a great man manager because he was thinking on a different level to everyone else. True greats find it very hard to train an ordinary hurler, because they expect everyone to do things as they did them. I remember playing corner-forward for Ahane in the Gaelic Grounds one day and I got the ball over in the corner. I made an attempt to rise it and Mackey let a roar at me to pull. I eventually pulled on it and it went into the far corner of the net. We were togging for the next game and he was giving a speech about ground hurling. 'I'll mention no names now,' he said (in reference to me), 'but I think after the last game, we realise that the ball has to be played along the ground.'

Over a period of a couple of years, Ahane had lost the Mackey brothers, Timmy Ryan, Jackie Power and Mick Herbert. When a strong club loses such quality players it can have long-term repercussions, as Donie Nealon explains:

Ahane were a very strong club at that time, and it often happens that the county team suffers after the decline of a very strong club. Ahane were probably providing 50 per cent of the Limerick team and when the power of Ahane dissipated Limerick entered decline. We came across that here in Tipperary as well, where our makers in the 1950s and '60s were Thurles Sarsfields who won ten finals in that era. When Thurles Sarsfields went into decline Tipperary went into decline. Ahane were the great power behind the Limerick team. When a bleak period follows a very successful one it can often be very difficult to bring through replacements. From the 1940s to the mid-'50s Limerick didn't win much at minor grade, and that's where new players come from.

Ahane were still fond of recruiting outside players, as Jim Fitzgerald explains:

My brother Paddy 'Danno' Fitzgerald played for Ahane in the early 1950s. He used to work for Pat O'Reilly and Ahane would take any good hurlers they could get their hands on. At that time we had no cars or clubhouses and we togged out on the sides of ditches. We enjoyed our lives. Out the country there was no such thing as rugby or soccer, it was all hurling, that's what we lived for. Anyone who was able to hurl would want to play for Ahane if they got the opportunity.

Limerick hurling settled down a little in 1952, though it would never be the same again. Seán Herbert was selected on the Railway Cup team, as Mick Rainsford explains:

He would have returned for the love of the game and wanted to play for Limerick again and he was selected on the 1952 Railway Cup team. An old passionate Tipperary man called Tom Moloughney worked with me on the houses in Ballynanty. One day he said, 'Seán Herbert was picked on the Munster team out of sympathy because of what happened to his brother Mick.' 'Tom,' I replied, 'in the Munster championship match at Thurles last year [1951], Seán Herbert hurled Phil Shanahan of Tipperary out of it.' 'Mick Rainsford,' he said to me 'don't let anyone tell you that a Herbert could beat a Shanahan in the Munster championship because he couldn't.' Moloughney was a real Tipperary man and the arrogance was there to prove it.

Limerick were beaten by Cork in the 1952 championship by 6-6 to 2-4. There was a change at boardroom level in 1952 when Canon Punch stepped down as chairman. He hadn't gone away, however, as he filled the position of president. His replacement as chairman was Pat O'Reilly of Ahane. Michael Hynes wasn't sorry to see Punch step aside:

I think Canon Punch was bad for Limerick hurling and in my opinion he did nothing good except put Limerick hurling back for years and years. Pat Reilly of Reilly's field took over as chairman.

Jim O'Donoghue says the new chairman was admired:

I don't know why Punch stood down, but as players we wouldn't have known much about the county board meetings. I knew Big Paddy Reilly from the time he came in to work to ask me to play for Ahane and he would have been a respected figure.

Fr Liam Kelly holds strong views on Punch:

He did more damage than good to the GAA in Limerick in his lifetime as chairman. He was completely arrogant and you couldn't deal with him. I knew him reasonably well and he said several things to me that were very questionable. He exaggerated everything he did. He once described Dermot Kelly to me as 'the worst hurler in the world'. He just had a set on him. That sort of stuff used to annoy me intensely.

Dermot Kelly jokingly agrees that Punch may have had a point:

Canon Punch barely talked to me when I played and didn't seem to have a lot of time for me. I don't know why. He might have got it right when he called me the worst hurler in the world, though!

Fr Liam Kelly explains the views of the hurling greats:

Canon Punch also had a set against Mick Mackey. Mick had no time for him either. Mick felt that he was a hopeless chairman and felt he was dictating to everybody. He felt that the way he ran meetings was a disgrace, that it was a one-man show and that was it. Canon Punch was very intolerant of anyone else's views and if anyone opposed him, which Mick did, they weren't to be listened to. John Mackey was completely turned off by this carry-on. Jackie Power who was an absolute gentleman once said that Limerick would have won at least ten more All-Irelands but for the county board. He didn't mention Punch's name, but everyone knew what he meant. Power and these guys had no time for what used to go on, and they had no time for the county board. As a result, the county board had no time for them either. In fairness, Ahane won sixteen county championships out of eighteen, and you are bound to be unpopular when you win that much. But despite their success, Mackey and Power and these guys would never be arrogant. Mick was a character on the field. I am one of the few that would have known him very well in his private life and he was a terribly shy fellow.

The lowest point for Limerick hurling came in 1953, a disastrous 10-8 to 1-1 defeat by Clare in the Munster championship at Ennis. Jimmy Smyth scored 6-4 but has always been reluctant to speak about his performance:

That day in 1953 is something I rarely speak about for the simple reason that it must have been very hard on some Limerick people to accept a defeat like that. Clare have taken some heavy beatings over the years and it hasn't been easy for us to take.

It is said that four Limerick players never turned up on the day but Mick Rainsford was one of those who suffered the pain of defeat:

Weren't the four players who didn't turn up lucky they stayed away! We went down by train to the match. I will never forget it. It was terrible. I remember talking to Seán Herbert about it afterwards and he said, 'Even when we were five goals down, I still thought we could beat them.' Seán had gone back playing for Limerick for the love of hurling and because he wanted to play for the county again but losing to Clare below in Ennis finished him. Dermot Kelly scored the goal and I always believed that Timmy Murphy scored the point, but the paper doesn't credit him with it. Timmy Murphy captained the team that day and was the only Treaty Sarsfields man on it. Jimmy Smyth scored 6-4. Séamus Ryan (Jim) was in goal that day. He was just after picking a ball out of his own net and he pucked it out, but it only went out as far as the 21-yard line and Smyth doubled it back into the net for him. I'd imagine they were totally demoralised at that point. We went to see Clare against Cork in the next round, and for the first ball that Jimmy Smyth got, four backs tackled him and hit him hard. They might as well have taken Smyth off after that. Clare kept playing the ball to Smyth, who wasn't able to waggle, instead of playing it to the two Greenes who were winning any ball that came down their side. And yet Cork were lucky to beat them without Smyth playing well. That was a good Clare team around that time though.

In 1954 Limerick were beaten by Waterford in the Munster championship. Limerick could only muster a single point on this occasion. Mick Rainsford again disputes the scorer:

Michael 'Mousey' McInerney of Treaty Sarsfields always said to me that he had a record of his own. He claimed he held the record for being the top scorer for Limerick in the 1954 Munster championship. Seán Leonard was credited with the solitary score in the newspapers, but 'Mousey' always claimed it. I remember being at that game, it was terrible. They were two bad years, 1953 and 1954.

Just fourteen years after that September day in 1940 when Limerick were sitting on top of the world, they had plummeted to the depths of despair. Once a feared hurling force, they now resembled a feeble club side playing a couple of grades above their level and unable to compete. An aggregate score of 1-2 in the 1953 and '54 Munster championship campaigns speaks for itself. They were truly at rock bottom. The 5-3 that Mick Mackey scored in one single Munster final years earlier amounted to more than the entire aggregate score Limerick could muster in the championships of 1952, '53 and '54. The inspiration of Mackey was needed to resurrect his county.

NINE

CR

1955–6: MACKEY'S GREYHOUNDS

Following his retirement, Mackey had been sporadically involved with the Limerick senior hurlers as a trainer, in both official and non-official capacities. In 1955 he was one of eleven selectors appointed. Jim O'Donoghue had played under Mackey prior to 1955:

Bob McConkey had trained us for the League that we won against Kilkenny a few years earlier. Mick took over at some stage after that, or at least would have had an involvement in some capacity. We generally trained for three nights in the Gaelic Grounds before a championship match but there was no training before League games. Mick was easy going as a trainer as far as I could see. It usually consisted of a puck around and then playing a game of backs and forwards. Sometimes we might run a couple of laps. Mick wasn't a man for training at all.

I remember one Saturday night a crowd of us went to a dance. We were playing Clare the following day in some tournament and after the dance we decided to go out to Shannon for something to eat which was most unusual because young people didn't go out to eat. Anyhow four or five of us went to Shannon and didn't get back into Limerick until about 5 a.m. That time you had to be a member of the confraternity, and we said we wouldn't go to bed at all, that we would go to Mass at 6 a.m. Of all people to meet coming out from Mass, who did I bump into only Mick, who was a great man for the confraternity himself. He said to me, 'Were you in bed at all last night?' 'I was,' I said. He replied, 'You don't look like it, you know you are playing today in Ennis. Go home now and get some sleep!'

By 1955 there was a serious drive to get the Limerick senior hurlers back on track. It was decided to clear out the old players and introduce some new blood, fresh from the scars of past controversies. Fr Liam Ryan explains:

143

They put out a very young team. There was also a myth then relating to a new rule that had come in called the 'non-stop' rule. Previously when a man went down injured the whole game stopped. In 1954 a rule came in that the play shouldn't stop if a player was injured; he simply went to the sideline. The myth was that somehow you needed young men to last the hour, which was total nonsense. For one reason or another Limerick put out a very young team in 1955 and not many of those who had been there in the previous five years had survived. Four or five did but that was all, it was practically a clean sweep. Of the experienced men Dermot Kelly was at most twenty-five, Gerry Fitzgerald from Rathkeale would have been the oldest at nearly thirty, Paddy Enright was next in line. Seven or eight of the team were certainly no more than twenty.

Limerick had won the 1954 All-Ireland junior championship. Paddy Cunneen, Jim Keogh, Jim Quaid, Jack Quaid, Vivian Cobbe and Aidan Raleigh graduated from that team to start on the senior team in the 1955 championship. Clare were making waves in Munster, while, almost unnoticed, Limerick slipped into the Munster final after a 4-5 to 3-5 win over Waterford. The Ryan brothers who were studying for the priesthood at Maynooth joined the panel in preparation for the Munster final. Fr Séamus Ryan explains:

We missed the first round against Waterford in 1955 because we were studying at Maynooth. Éamon and Paddy O'Malley of Cappamore played that day. The first match I ever played for the Limerick seniors was a challenge match against Kilkenny prior to the Munster final when I was put on for the second half. I had played minor for Limerick in 1953 and '54 and was still underage for minor in '55. However, Limerick were knocked out of the championship before I was home from Maynooth for the summer. I always seemed to be marking Liam Devaney at minor level and I found it a big step up from minor to senior.

Waterford were confident of victory, as Séamus Power explains:

We would have been expecting to beat Limerick in 1955. Let's face it, in Waterford we would normally give ourselves a chance, even on our worst days, against Limerick or Clare. If we didn't think that, we were at nothing. On the other hand, we would have always seen games against Tipperary or Cork as an uphill battle.

Fr Liam Ryan was the nineteen-year-old captain:

I was captain simply because the system at the time, and the system that still prevails, is that the county champions, if they have someone on the team, automatically provide the captain. I was only nineteen and the Munster final was my first time playing a championship match with Limerick, so I was in awe of others who had been around a while. Someone like Dermot Kelly probably should have been captain. I was certainly not a captain who led the team or anyone who inspired them or anything like that; it was the very opposite. I don't think the captain should automatically come from the county champions. Anthony Daly was a very successful captain, and the board, the players, all accepted him even though his club weren't county champions. All the captain does on a GAA field is call the toss of the coin and lead the team around the pitch. After that he has no duties and it's up to the sideline to make changes and all that. Being the captain in rugby means much more. There were eleven selectors. The county champions had two, and the county board had four or five, certainly the treasurer, secretary and chairman, while each of the divisional boards had representatives. They were all equal. Mackey was not the manager, as the media would have portrayed, and he had no more authority than anybody else.

Mackey may not have been the manager but he was the trainer of the team. Jimmy Butler Coffey was one of the selectors:

A letter came from Jackie Connell, the secretary of Limerick county board, stating that as county champions, Cappamore were entitled to two selectors. We had a club meeting and there wasn't a single name proposed at the meeting. Nobody was interested. I said I would go for the first match, because it would be a terror to let the Limerick team out without any Cappamore selector when we were county champions. Fr Noonan, the parish priest, then said he would join me. We were at the first couple of matches and we got on alright but eleven selectors was too many. If some of us were involved with a lesser number of selectors we might have made a better job of the team. I wanted to play John Mulcahy in 1955 but there were too many on the selection committee. If I had my way, John Mulcahy would have been on that team. It's a six marker whether we would have won the All-Ireland or not with John Mulcahy but he would have given us experience. John was a great hurler and an outstanding ballplayer, but you could never claim that he would have won us the All-Ireland.

Jimmy Smyth offers an interesting perspective on Mackey as a selector:

I never thought Mackey would be interested in management. I didn't think he was suited for it and it was a surprise to me when he took over because he wasn't that type of fellow. The players themselves must have played a major role that time because Mackey never spoke that much. I wouldn't think Mackey was a great man to give instructions or to sit down and study what he would do on the day of a match. He was a product of the old school from the 1930s and in the old school there was no coaching and management, you went out and hurled; the players made the decisions on the field. Mackey got the name for being the manager alright, but I don't think his role reflected that. However, he was there as a figurehead, which was very important with such a young group of players. Mackey was basically a player, and some players don't adapt to management. When he was on the field as a hurler he was able to see and read everything that happened from his position of centre-forward, but would not have had that same vision on the sideline. I would have been the same myself, I could see everything that happened on the field and knew exactly where the strengths and weaknesses of both teams were as I was playing in a game. However, I would not have had that same vision from the sideline.

Jimmy Butler Coffey agreed:

Mackey was a selector for a good number of years, but he wanted it one particular year and he was turned down and he didn't like it at all. I wouldn't count Mick Mackey as a great selector because he was too interested in the match. Mackey wasn't a great judge of a hurler really, or a judge of a match either. He might have made switches on the field as a player, he was very domineering that way, but that didn't mean he was a good selector on the sideline. Switches were fine if they won the match, but Mackey didn't care whether they won or lost, as long as he had got his way.

Maurice Regan says it takes a particular type to make a good selector:

It was always said that he wasn't great as a selector, but he was not alone. The same thing happened with a lot of great players and there were people that never hurled who made great selectors. I'd say Mackey would have been too much of a gallery man to be

The presentation of the Munster trophy to Fr Liam Ryan, captain of Mackey's Greyhounds in 1955. He remains the youngest ever Munster championship winning captain. His Cappamore clubmate and Limerick selector Jimmy Butler Coffey is on his left, wearing a suit.

concentrating enough as a selector. You would need to have the head for it to be a good selector.

Limerick won the 1955 Munster final 2-16 to 2-5 on a roasting hot July day when the young, free-spirited Limerick flyers whizzed around like March hares and left the Clare players trailing in their wake. Mick Rainsford explains a change to the 1955 Munster championship:

From 1949 onwards there was a fixed draw in the Munster championship and Cork and Tipperary were kept apart. That's why you had a sequence of Cork and Tipperary Munster finals at that time. In 1954 Clare got to the final of the Oireachtas tournament, beating Wexford after a replay. They felt they had a good chance of winning a Munster championship so in 1955 they insisted on the open draw. They drew Cork in the first round and Tipperary in the semi-final, whereas Limerick got Waterford. I reckon if Clare had said nothing and let the draw proceed, they might only have had Cork to play and might have got Tipperary in the final. I'd imagine they saw Limerick in the final and felt it would be a pushover. I don't know what Mackey was like as a selector in 1955, but it was always said that he roused them up going out on the field and roared, 'Clare never beat us in a Munster final, and they are not starting now.' We didn't see 1955 coming, it came totally out of the blue. I think we won because we were playing Clare in the Munster final. If we were playing Cork or Tipperary we wouldn't have had a hope, but you always believe you have a chance against Clare, especially when they hadn't beaten us in Limerick. Tradition and history are hard to change.

Tommy Barrett gives a Tipperary perspective:

It was a bigger surprise to us in Tipperary to be beaten by Clare than it was to watch Clare go on and be beaten by Limerick. We were the League champions having beaten Wexford in the League final in 1955, although the Rackards were missing off the Wexford team because their father died. We would have been expecting to beat Clare. We hadn't any injuries against Clare. They just came good on the day. They had Mick Leahy the corner-back, Haulie Donnellan, Jimmy Smyth. Limerick came as a surprise that year all the same.

Jimmy Smyth concedes that Clare took Limerick for granted on the day:

We did take Limerick for granted because all these Limerick players were young fellows with the exception of Dermot Kelly. Kelly was a great hurler and every ball he hit that day went over the bar. Donal O'Grady, who was on him, was a great hurler, but he was never switched on the day and I would blame the selectors a lot for that. In 1955 we saw Limerick as a team of nineteen-year-olds who got the handy draw whereas we had beaten the big guns, and we felt that we were favourites and would have recognised ourselves as being favourites. We were looking towards the All-Ireland really. We were looking one step ahead. On top of that, nobody on the Clare team played well whereas every Limerick player played well. In centre field we were being beaten all hands up. Tommy Casey was starting to dominate and was the main man early in that game before Dermot Kelly started hurling. Casey wouldn't have been rated a great hurler when he was in St Flannan's but he came out that day and played one of the best matches I ever saw him playing. Every Limerick player dominated. We didn't get our two goals until the last five minutes. They had annihilated us by that stage. Realistically it was 2-16 to 0-5. We weren't able for them. Dan McInerney, the full-back, wasn't in it, Nugent, wing-back wasn't in it, there was nobody in it. I was average myself, no more than average. I changed away from centre-forward where I had started off on Séamus Ryan. I didn't believe in any of the Biddy Early stuff and you would be surprised at the people who believed Biddy Early was the cause of us losing Munster finals. Limerick came out and took their chance when they got it. We weren't expecting them to be as good, but if we had played against them the following Sunday we might not have won, but it would have been a much closer game.

We would have had massive regrets over that final, but we were so used to losing it was just another loss. But having done so much, and beaten Cork and Tipperary to get there, it was devastating. We had beaten Wexford the previous November in the Oireachtas after a replay so we knew how to play against them. An All-Ireland semi-final against them could have gone any way, but we would have been there with a chance.

Mick Mackey rated Tommy Casey highly, as Fr Liam Kelly explains:

Tommy Casey didn't ever look like a great hurler, but was a very intelligent guy. I remember Mackey used to always say, 'A lot of people don't think much of him, but I do because he has a great head. A thinker on the field and always does the right thing.' He showed he was a thinker on the field with the positions he used to take up, and used to always do the right thing when he had the ball but wasn't a very stylish hurler.

Fr Séamus Ryan had huge admiration for Jimmy Smyth:

We were in St Flannan's in 1953 when Limerick were annihilated in the Munster championship by Clare and Jimmy Smyth was the main architect of that. Jimmy was a hero in St Flannan's, and I played with his brother Mike Smyth when we won the Harty Cup there. When Jimmy was a minor in a Munster final he scored an amazing goal where he soloed the whole length of the field. I always had great admiration for him because I think if he had been with Cork, Tipperary or Wexford, he would have been one of the great names remembered in the mould of Ring or Rackard. To think that I was marking Jimmy Smyth in a Munster final only two years after the 1953 annihilation was remarkable.

Mick Rainsford raises an interesting point:

Dermot Kelly couldn't go astray; no matter where he hit the ball from, it went over. The papers gave him 1-12 but in my opinion, he didn't get the goal. I remember Seán Leonard always said, 'Dermot Kelly got no goal, Gerry Fitzgerald got one and Vivian Cobbe got the other.' Leonard would get cross if you suggested that Kelly scored the goal. I went in to see the papers in the City Library years afterwards and got out the 1955 Munster final report and it went, 'Ralph Prendergast had the ball and he showed great unselfishness when he passed it to Dermot Kelly to score it.' Kelly knew that he didn't get the goal and he always lived off it. He wasn't man enough to say, 'I didn't get the goal.' He still got twelve points and no matter where he hit them from, they would have gone over. I'd say if he turned around and hit them the other way, they would have turned backwards and gone over the bar behind him. After that Limerick expected him to score that every day. He did it no more. He had one good day.

Seán Ryan (Malachy) agrees:

Dermot Kelly was credited with 1-12. However, I knew Gerry Fitzgerald very well and he always claimed that he scored that goal. I think Gerry Fitzgerald got a flick to it before it crossed the line, but he was never credited with the goal. The name on the record books is Dermot Kelly.

Limerick hurling history has raised many controversies about who scored goals in games. Damien Quigley and Frankie Carroll both claimed the second goal of the 1996 Munster final. Ned Rea and Mossie Dowling both claimed the historic goal in the 1973 All-Ireland final. And there was even controversy over a goal that wasn't: Rea's Effin team-mate Tom Bluett claims the disallowed goal against Cork in 1966, while Bernie Hartigan also lays claim to it.

It would appear that in 1955 Dermot Kelly took a shot, which was saved, and in the resulting scramble for the rebound the ball was sent across the line. In the absence of video evidence we will never know. In any event Dermot Kelly gave one of the greatest individual performances ever in the Munster senior hurling final and it compares to the 5-3 scored by Mick Mackey in the 1936 Munster final. Whatever about the goal, Kelly raised twelve white flags. That alone constitutes a serious performance and renders the dispute surrounding the goal irrelevant. Kelly himself was more worried about the result than who scored the goal:

I am not really interested in whether it was my goal or not, it was the fifteen players we had that day who won the match for us. It wasn't Dermot Kelly who won that match for Limerick, it was the fifteen great men of Limerick. Ralph Prendergast and Liam Ryan were like greyhounds in the half-forward line and I was just in the middle. At that time I got hold of press photographs with the goal in it, and the press said I got the goal. Don't you know the Irish would hammer you any way they could [laughing]. It was a great team effort, we caught them on the hop and we were lucky enough to beat them the following year. My father came into the room the following morning, he shouldn't have said it but he said I should give it up, that it would never happen again! In 1955 I started to run on the roads, which was rare at the time. I was living on the Ballysimon Road and used to run a circuit out by where B&Q is now and back in towards the city. While I wasn't that fast, it definitely improved my fitness that year.

Fr Liam Ryan gives his account of the goal:

Dermot Kelly didn't score the goal. To be fair to him he took a great shot, but Hayes saved it and Gerry Fitzgerald was running in and blasted it to the net. Gerry Fitzgerald scored the goal. I used to know Micheál Ó Muircheartaigh well because he used to come to the Fitzgibbon Cup in later years to pick the Universities All-Star team. I remember when Dermot Kelly retired from the bank I said to Micheál, 'Dermot Kelly retired during the week.' Micheál replied, 'I thought he retired in 1955!'

Fr Liam Kelly credits Mackey with the 1955 success:

Mick Mackey made a team out of nothing in 1955. Mick was his own man and cleaned the boards and brought in new players. He got rid of every fella that was in it. On that 1955 panel I would say there were about ten players under twenty, and Séamus Ryan was only eighteen, and he was the outstanding centre-back in the country at that time, a colossal man at centre-back. His brother Liam was captain, because Cappamore had beaten Ahane the year before. The Limerick team came from nothing. I would credit Mick Mackey solely with that. He was a very shrewd selector, very knowledgeable. Mick would always insist that he wasn't an educated man, and he wasn't either, but he had an incredible sense of what to do on a hurling field and he was a genius himself, of course. He was a bit of a rogue, even though he didn't deliberately try to be a rogue.

Gerry Piggott agrees:

Mackey must have been a good selector to get a Munster champion-ship out of that 1955 team. None of that team would have made the 1940 team, although some of them would have made the 1973 team. They weren't anywhere near as good as the 1940 team, though.

Dermot Kelly was inspired by Mackey:

At half time, Mick Mackey got up on the table in the dressing room. He was like Martin Luther King or John F. Kennedy. The words were flowing out of him, and he said, 'We have it.' That's where you saw the hurling passion coming out in him. Having Mick Mackey as a trainer was worth his weight in gold, because everybody was in awe of him at the time.

Ralph Prendergast was also motivated:

Mackey banged on the galvanised roof with the hurley at half time and said Clare have never beaten us in the Munster championship here and they aren't going to start now. I believed him and I vowed to myself that I was not going to be on a team that was the first team to be beaten. Of course, I was only nineteen so I was easily fired up and I am sure there were other young players who were equally motivated. I never played any opponent, it was up to them to stop me. I drifted into open space to use my speed advantage, as I was a 440-yards runner, which gave me stamina and speed. That allowed me to drift back from the half-forward line to the half-back line and I spent a lot of time foraging in a defensive capacity as well as being on the ball.

I considered Mackey to be a good motivator but he was a man of his time as a trainer. That was a different era before all the new coaching ideas came in. That time you ran around the field ten or eleven times, did a few short sprints and a small bit of hurling.

Willie Keane appreciated Mackey's knowledge:

Mick Mackey knew his stuff. You would be put through your paces in 1955 and again the following year. A few years earlier I remember he would test you in Reilly's field as a young lad, a small field with no escape! He never pulled you to one side to explain something but if you got up off the ground within a minute of being hit, you were OK.

Donie Nealon was at the game:

I cycled to the 1955 Munster final. Very few attended on the day, because they felt Clare were favourites. I believe there weren't many more than 10,000 at that match. Clare were raging hot favourites because they had beaten Tipperary and Cork. Limerick were highly impressive, giving a brilliant exhibition of fast ground hurling and movement. Mackey had them absolutely flying that day. They were very young and had no fear. They didn't seem to give a care. They put on an unbelievable and unexpected display.

Jim Hogan has nostalgic memories:

It was a scorching day and all the Limerick people went to Kilkee. We used to cycle to the matches and park our bicycles at the side of the Stella Ballroom on Shannon Street in the city. There was a bicycle park there for 2d and 3d. We used to park the bikes and get the jarvey cars out to the Gaelic Grounds. There was no traffic allowed out from town for big games so they had a fleet of jarvey cars. Nobody gave Limerick a chance that day because Clare had a great team. The famous Donal O'Grady/Dan McInerney story is one of those that was prominent in the aftermath. There were other stories and one of them was that some of the Clare players were on the tear the night before. Apparently they had bonfires prepared outside in Bunratty ready to light when the team were on the way home.

Jim Fitzgerald tells the famous Donal O'Grady/Dan McInerney story:

I was at the games Clare played against Cork and Tipperary. I didn't go to the Munster final because I thought Clare would win handy. It was a roasting hot day, and a few of us spent it above in the Clare Glens. We were listening to Micheál O'Hehir and we couldn't believe it. I was working in London a few years afterwards and I met Donal O'Grady. He told me that he had been working [back in Ireland] for McInerney Construction, either driving a lorry or helping on it. They crashed the lorry and his team-mate, big Dan McInerney the Clare full-back, was over him and sacked him.

He didn't want to run down Dermot Kelly, who to be fair played an excellent game that day regardless of who was on him but he told me that being sacked was the cause of him not playing well against Limerick. He might as well not have been there at all and he told me that he said to McInerney in the dressing room, 'You will never win a Munster medal as long as I am playing with you.' He was playing centre-back and apparently he didn't put in his best. He knew he was wrong and was a bit sorry over it, but he was sour at the time because being sacked meant he would have to emigrate.

An associate of a 1955 Clare hurler offers the following dimension:

As far as I am concerned, there was no such row between McInerney and O'Grady, and there was no foundation whatsoever to any of those rumours. I got that first hand from a prominent player who played in the game. There is no concrete evidence or proof anywhere that there was a crash involving a cement lorry. All those stories are buttered up as the years go by. The hard facts were that Clare took Limerick for granted, as they had beaten them by ten goals two years earlier. They had beaten them easily in a League game in March 1955 too. They were run off their feet in the Munster final. Limerick shocked the hurling world that day. Clare hurling didn't recover for years afterwards.

There is no point in blaming rows, they were blaming Donal O'Grady in the wrong for that defeat when every player around him failed. They were all caught out of position. Those rumours might have been started within Clare to deflect attention from other players who didn't perform. The reason Donal O'Grady wasn't changed off Dermot Kelly was because they were expecting him to come good. O'Grady was mainly responsible for bringing them that far and had won the 1954 Oireachtas for Clare. He was selected at centre-half-back on the Munster team with Pat Stakelum and Ben Twomey on the two wings, and they were the Cork and Tipperary centre-backs. At that particular time he was one of the best, if not the best, centre-half-backs in the country. There is no concrete proof either that Clare were drinking the night before the Munster final in 1955 but I can guarantee you they weren't drinking the following year and Limerick beat them by just as much again. I never heard about the bonfires being prepared and as the years go by everyone tells their own story. I don't believe in fairytales.

As Munster champions Limerick marched on to the All-Ireland semi-final where they were on top against Wexford in the first half but were beaten in the end. Many believe that if both Seán and Mick Herbert were still around, Limerick would have ended the year as All-Ireland champions. Séamus Ryan was overawed by the occasion:

Mick Mackey addresses his Munster champion Greyhounds in training prior to the All-Ireland semi-final against Wexford in 1955. *(L–r):* Jim Quaid (Feoghanagh), Seán Leonard (Monaleen and Ahane), Jack Quaid (Feoghanagh), Mick Mackey (Ahane), Fr Liam Ryan (Cappamore), Donal Broderick (Dromcollogher), Eugene Noonan (Dromcollogher), Ralph Prendergast (Claughaun), Séamus Ryan (Cappamore), Aidan Raleigh (Bruff), Dermot Kelly (Claughaun), Gerry Fitzgerald (Rathkeale) and Paddy O'Malley (Cappamore).

In 1955 when we came up to Dublin they told us that we could go off down the town from the hotel on the Saturday evening. We went to see Jimmy O'Dea the comedian of Maureen Potter and Jimmy O'Dea fame. On the morning of the game Micheál O'Hehir came into the hotel and introduced himself to us all with a handshake and wanted to get to know us. It just shows the kind of man he was. I suppose it might have been his way of getting to recognise us ahead of the game for his commentary.

It would have been nice if someone from the management had spoken to us the evening before the game and highlighted the importance of the occasion. I was awestruck in Croke Park against Wexford. I don't remember being nervous in the Gaelic Grounds before the Munster final because I was very familiar with the ground and would have played there as a minor. On the other hand, I do remember being totally awed by Croke Park, and of course nobody was going to get me over that, but I felt at the same time that there should have been more concern with the team and at least some words spoken. I can't remember anything being said, or even getting together for a team meeting in Dublin prior to the match. Ironically, it wasn't my first time playing in Croke Park, because I had played there with the Munster colleges a couple of years earlier, so both times I played in Croke Park we lost. Munster used to win most of those colleges games but Leinster were strong that particular year because St Kieran's had a lot on and they beat us that day.

Seán Ryan (Malachy) remembers Limerick's misfortune:

They were in hard luck in that game because Wexford got a goal that shouldn't have been allowed. One of the Keoghs ran through with a ball in his hand for about 40 yards and over-carried. Some of the Limerick players were very light but that was a great Wexford team they met in the semi-final.

The switch of Ned Wheeler into centre-forward on top of Séamus Ryan was instrumental, as Jimmy Butler Coffey explained:

At half time Wexford changed their team and the switches won them the match. Séamus Ryan blew the Wexford centre-forward Paudge Keogh out of it in the first half, so they put in Ned Wheeler, a big, powerful man, on him and that's where the damage was done. Eleven selectors was too many to work with. I said to Mackey, 'Look at this,' when Wheeler was moved onto Séamus, and he said, 'What can we do? There are too many other selectors to go to.' We couldn't make the change on our own. It was even very hard for me to force Séamus onto the team at the start of the championship because he was too young. When they saw him playing they decided he was worth his place. It wasn't his hurling at all, it was just that he was too young.

Fr Liam Ryan believes Mackey needed to take control of things:

When Jimmy Butler Coffey and Mackey wanted to make the change in 1955 in Croke Park maybe the mistake was to go to all the other selectors! Mackey could identify a change that needed to be made in a game like the one against Wexford, but strangely he didn't feel that he had the authority to take control. I'd say he would have been checking with others what to do. He knew what to do, but he wouldn't do it without getting consent. There wasn't a manager like there is today. There was nothing like that. He seemed reluctant to take complete control. He was in charge of training alright but that didn't give him authority over the team. All the eleven selectors were equal and he wasn't a manager in the modern sense at all. Having eleven equal selectors led to nothing happening and led to stalemate. You couldn't have a vote on the sideline. You would nearly have had to have a committee meeting. Someone should have taken complete control of the team on the day of the match, and Mackey didn't do that.

It's ironic that in Mackey's playing days he didn't think twice about taking control, perhaps even to the detriment of some results, yet as a selector/trainer, when he needed to take control he was reluctant to do so. Séamus Ryan agrees that a change would have been of benefit to the team:

I was on Paudge Keogh in the first half, and I always preferred to be marking a good hurler than a big, strong fellow because I was very young and light at the time. Ned Wheeler came in on top of me in the second half and he was a big man. I suppose he was pushing his weight around and pushed me out of it a bit. It definitely affected me. I certainly played far better in the first half.

Ned Wheeler says Wexford changed their tactics at half time:

If they were called Mackey's greyhounds, then they were definitely greyhounds in the first half, they were flying it. Vivian Cobbe and the boys were all over us, we couldn't cope with their speed. Mick Hanlon, a veteran at the time and a corner-back, stood up at half time and said, 'Lads, it's time we slowed them down to our own speed.' I remember in the second half Vivian Cobbe was soloing down the field and Jim Morrissey gave him a shoulder, driving him out onto someone sitting on the sideline and put him sitting on his lap. It wasn't a malicious shoulder, it was a clean shoulder and part and parcel of a great game then, but it defined our new approach in the second half.

Jimmy Butler Coffey recalled the immediate post-match events:

I remember Fr Noonan came to me and said, 'We must go up now and congratulate Wexford.' 'Go up you,' I replied, 'but I won't go, let a Limerick man and a great one, Mick Mackey, go up with you.' So the two of them went up. Fr Noonan wished them the best of luck and then Mackey spoke and they all cheered. They said, 'We are delighted to have the best hurler in the world here with us in the Wexford dressing room this evening.' They came back down to us and the trainer said a few words, 'I don't know how ye felt at half time, but we were definitely worried.'

Wheeler was in the dressing room:

I remember Mick Mackey came in and said, 'Lads, ye played my type of hurling.' I thought it was a great expression of admiration from such a distinguished man. We were very surprised that Limerick seemed to fade into the wilderness almost immediately after that All-Ireland semi-final. Every hurling county in Ireland was surprised that Limerick didn't come again, and that they seemed to fade away overnight.

Donie Nealon believes Wexford had studied their opponents carefully:

Limerick were unlucky to lose that All-Ireland semi-final that year. Wexford were cautious in advance of the game because Limerick had won the Munster final so convincingly. I would say Wexford did their homework on Limerick. If you draw too much attention on yourself in one match, your opponents for the next game have an opportunity to assess your strengths and weaknesses.

Brendan Fullam believes Clare would have gone one better:

I always felt Clare might well have beaten Wexford. Physically they would have matched Wexford, which Limerick didn't. That Limerick team were very raw, beautiful hurlers but very raw. Wexford were physical and seasoned and had been there since 1950. They were used to Croke Park and weren't going to suffer from nerves. Clare would have been a different proposition. Tim Flood [former Wexford hurler] said to me that if they hadn't won in 1955 they mightn't have won anything, and might have been gone.

On the domestic scene, Ahane regained their county championship in 1955 when they beat the Geraldine's by 4-4 to 2-2 at the Gaelic Grounds. Jackie Power returned to the Ahane colours after a sabbatical playing club and inter-county hurling in Kerry. Despite having lost the players from the East division, Ahane still had strong representation from outside in the form of the Monaleen players who would soon afterwards form their own club. Fr Liam Kelly explains:

Jackie Power was from Monaleen parish and being from the same parish I was very friendly with him. There was no club in Monaleen at that time so we had no choice but to play for Ahane. Power had played for Ahane as had my brother before me and it was an honour to win a county championship with such a distinguished great. In the county final we won in 1955 there were eight Monaleen men and seven Ahane men on the team. It was shortly after that that Monaleen decided to start their own team.

P. J. Keane explains that Mackey was respected within Ahane:

When we won the county in 1955, Mackey was no longer playing, but he was on the periphery of the club and used to come to the annual meetings. He was recognised as one of the elder members of the club, a distinguished individual. He was on the Munster scene as well, as the Limerick representative on the Munster council. After Mackey retired from playing with Ahane, it left a major void, so a parish league was run in a field behind Mick Herbert's bar. It ran for a year or two prior to Ahane winning the county title in 1955. It was a four-team fifteen-a-side adult league with subs and was highly competitive. Bridgetown and Montpellier had one team; Gardenhill and Castleconnell had another; Lisnagry had a team; and Ahane/ Annacotty were the fourth team. I was young at the time, but the crowds were massive, and the hurling was savage because there was such fierce local rivalry. Four teams would provide a total of sixty starting players and there were also subs, which enabled Ahane to get the players to win the 1955 county title.

Limerick beat Clare in the 1956 Munster championship by 1-15 to 2-6. They faced the mighty Cork in the Munster final but were beaten by 5-5 to 3-5 after a late three-goal surge from Christy Ring, who returned to haunt his old rival Mackey, including one hand-passed goal while on his knees. P. J. Keane recalls the circumstances:

That 1956 team beaten by Cork were a better team than the 1955 team that were Munster champions. I was sitting on the sideline at the 1956 match with my father and distinctly remember midway through the second half Ring left the field completely. He hadn't struck a ball in the game up to that and he spent about five minutes off the field selecting a hurley on the sideline. He went back on and scored the three goals. The problem wasn't with Donal Broderick the corner-back though, the problem stemmed from centre-back where Willie John Daly cleaned out Dermot Kelly. There was ball after ball raining

The Limerick and Cork teams in the parade before the 1956 Munster final at Thurles. *Cork team (back row, l–r):* Christy Ring, Willie John Daly, Gerald Murphy, Joe Twomey, Vincent Twomey, Josie Hartnett, Paddy Philpott. Limerick team *(front row, l–r):* Tommy Casey (Ahane), Willie Keane (Ahane), Jack Quaid (Feoghanagh/ Castlemahon), Fr Liam Ryan (Cappamore), Dermot Kelly (Claughaun), Fr Séamus Ryan (Claughaun), Ralph Prendergast (Claughaun), Vivian Cobbe (St Patrick's), Tom McGarry (Treaty Sarsfields & Claughaun), Jim Quaid (Feoghanagh), Donal Broderick (Dromcollogher), Paddy Cunneen (St Patrick's), Paddy Enright (Ahane), Benny Fitzgibbon (Treaty Sarsfields), Mick Tynan (Claughaun).

down on top of the Cork full-forward line and Ring, being a very good forward, would pounce. He was very strong, had a low centre of gravity and was so enthusiastic about everything he did that if he got a chance he would bury it. And he did, three times in the space of a few minutes. That stemmed from insufficient pressure being put on Willie John Daly. I remember talking to Mick Herbert about that at some stage afterwards; Mick was on that selection committee and apparently there was a lot of division over whether they would play Dermot Kelly in 1956 at all. To me that's what happened; people blamed Broderick but the problem was further up the field. Willie John Daly dominated.

Ring was fussy about his hurleys, as Andy Fleming explained:

When we went to Dublin on Railway Cup trips Ringy would let all the Cork boys off. The Cork boys are clannish, and would all go off together, but he would pal around with me all night. I would usually have been the only one from Waterford so I would have a single bedroom to myself with a single bed. Ring would come into the room about four in the morning. He would catch the bed and turn me upside down and pull me out of the bed out onto the floor. I'd have the hurleys under the mattress, and he would pick out one and say, 'You give me this tomorrow and I'll give you the best of the Cork hurleys.' The Cork hurleys were only pieces of rubbish, only bits of boards. Ring loved the hurleys I had and was very fussy about having good hurleys for himself. After that night I always hid my good hurley in the sleeve of my overcoat, and put it in the wardrobe so he wouldn't find it. I'd put the other one under the bed to trick him, and he would come in and take it. The next day I'd go out on the field with the good one and he would be sorry he didn't spot it.

John Mulcahy believes Cork got two soft goals:

Christy Ring palmed one in from the 21-yard line, which wasn't a hard shot. The other one was a simple shot again and it went in. Paddy Cunneen should have done better for those goals.

Fr Liam Ryan expands:

I have no recollection of Ring choosing a hurley in 1956 but I would agree that two of his goals were lucky enough. Willie Keane knocked one into the net. Paddy Cunneen would have had it covered easily, Keane came across him and struck it with the bas of his hurley into the corner of the net. Cunneen caught his hurley in the crossbar for the goal that Ring handpassed. He should have caught the ball instead of trying to bat it. Perhaps the forwards were coming in on top of him. Dermot Kelly was blamed for losing the match as there was nobody marking Willie John Daly. The whole Cork half-back line cleaned up. I wasn't great and Prendergast was even worse. Every ball that came down my wing went back as quick. The Cork half-back line got on top for the last twelve to fifteen minutes and that's what turned the match.

Willie John Daly wasn't concerned:

I was conscious of the game Dermot Kelly played in the Munster final the year before, but in my time as a hurler I worried about nobody. I went out and I played the game, and I marked the player I had to mark and did the best I could irrespective of who I was on. Some days I played well and some days I was well beaten. I never shook the hand of an opponent before a match but after the final whistle I'd be the first to put out my hand.

We were playing well in that final, even though we were down in the game. While the Limerick supporters were shouting that Ringy was finished and that the game was won, I don't think the players were thinking like that on the field. But Ring wasn't finished, and he proved that when he came back onto the field after changing his hurley. There was only one Ring, and Ring could do things nobody else could do. He proved that for almost thirty years. They were a good Limerick team, and were very nearly champions only for Ring, and they were on the verge of proving themselves. But for Ring we wouldn't have won it.

Mick Rainsford suggests some changes that could have helped Limerick:

In 1956, I reckon that Dermot Kelly should either have been put into the corner or taken off and 'Mousey' McInerney brought in to centre-forward. The other alternative was to bring Mick Tynan out to the half-forward line, because Willie John Daly cleared ball after ball. I think if Willie John was tied down, Cork would not have beaten us. 'Mousey' McInerney was a tough bit of stuff and would have stopped Willie John from clearing the ball. Kelly was poor the same day and left him clear as much ball as he liked. Some people reckoned that Willie John kicked him in the backside a few times. Whether he kicked him or not, I don't know, he had no bother beating him. And the following year [1957] the same thing happened against Waterford, he was centre-forward and he was still poor.

Dermot Kelly refuses to use a hamstring injury as an excuse:

The 1956 game was a bad day at the office, but it had nothing to do with the injury. I didn't play well on the day. It was just one of those things. However, I wasn't in the back line when Christy Ring wasn't picked up. It was a terrible tragedy, because that was a good team. The defence conceded three goals that day but they also left in a couple of goals late in the 1955 Munster final against Clare. There was a terrible mistake made in 1956 when Jim Quaid, who had a bad back, was left on for ages with his injury when he should have been replaced.

Jimmy Butler Coffey remembered some switches Ring made:

Séamus Ryan's display in Thurles in 1956 was the greatest display I have ever seen from a Limerick centre-back. Donal Broderick told me that Ring changed himself out to centre-forward when Cork were being beaten. He had been inside on Donal Broderick and didn't get a ball. Next thing he went on Séamus, and wasn't out there a couple of minutes when Séamus had cleared a couple of terrific balls. Jim 'Tough' Barry ran up around the goals and called Josie Hartnett and said, 'Josie, tell him [Ring] to go off him [Séamus Ryan], he will never win a ball off him.' After that he got the three goals. There was nobody marking Ring when he got his goals.

Jim Fitzgerald views things differently:

If they had left Donal Broderick man-mark Ring when he went back into the full-forward line, Limerick would have won because Broderick was playing a great game. However, Mickey Fitzgibbon put his own son marking Christy Ring when he went back in. It was always said that Ring got the three goals off Broderick but that wasn't the case. Mickey Fitzgibbon had a big say and wanted his son to be known as the man who held Christy Ring because Limerick were winning well.

Willie Keane believes Seán Herbert should have played:

I felt that if Seán Herbert had been there in 1956, we would have beaten Cork. He would have cancelled out Willie John Daly. Daly lorded it that day with the result that there was a constant barrage of balls coming in around the Limerick square. Seán Herbert was a good hurler to mark a man. Having him on the bench ready to introduce at the right time would have been the winning of the match. He was playing good enough club hurling to warrant being on the panel. Sometimes you have to play horses for courses and that was one of the times.

Fr Liam Kelly outlines the politics, which, unsurprisingly, were rife:

I remember for the 1956 Munster final there were only twenty players selected for the panel, and from what I remember only five selectors picked the starting team. I didn't think there were as many as eleven selectors, but the system was chronic at the time, every division was represented, perhaps only five selectors were able to turn up on the night to pick the team. Mick Mackey was a driver for the ESB at the time and he was broken down above in Loughrea. He contacted Jackie Connell the secretary and told him he wouldn't make it down, but to nominate Mick Herbert, who was also a selector, to represent him and cast his vote. Mick Mackey had told me that I was an automatic choice for a place on the team. I cannot recall who the other selectors were but I think there was an O'Connell from the west and Seán Cunningham from Doon was the east selector. I was guaranteed to get enough votes to be selected but somebody got at Cunningham and Benny Fitzgibbon got my place instead.

Benny Fitzgibbon was a Treaty Sarsfields player, Mickey's son, and I was very friendly with him because he was in my class in Munchin's College. His father and Canon Punch decided that he was going to be picked as wing-back instead of me. And I only got two votes eventually because Cunningham reneged, and I didn't get my place. That sort of shenanigans was going on at the time. Mackey was mad over it.

Even worse, there was a story attached to the substitutions on the day. After about fifteen minutes Jim Quaid went down injured. In those days all you were told was 'Get up out of that.' But Jim had a bad back, it was a chronic thing with him, and you don't mess around with a bad back. After they told him to get up, he did get up, but was obviously still struggling. After another ten minutes Mackey says to me, 'Quaid is coming off, and you are going on.' I was kind of excited and went straight on into the middle of the field. I had actually caught a ball and hit it. I think it may have been from a puckout or something. Next thing the referee gave a roar, 'Hey you, where is your piece of paper?' and I had to run back out to the sideline. Mick was over talking about me and getting my name written out. Next thing I noticed 'Mousey' McInerney out of the corner of my eye. 'Mousey' was also from Treaty Sarsfields, and Mickey Fitzgibbon and Canon Punch sent him in. I said to myself, 'There's someone else injured,' but while I was getting my piece of paper they sent in 'Mousey' instead of me. I went back in again and hit another ball, and next thing there was shouting and roaring from the Cork crowd about sixteen men on the field. The ref hadn't even spotted it, so he stopped and he looked around and he shouted to me, 'Hey you, get off.'

It's an indication of the messing that went on behind the scenes at that time, which was totally detrimental to success. Jackie Power had a collection of memoirs that he used to show me. As part of them he wrote, 'Limerick would have won ten more All-Irelands but for the county board.' I said, 'Jackie, you can't put that in.' 'Why can't I?' he answered, 'sure isn't it the truth!' He was right.

Christy Murphy tells a tale about the three goals from Ring:

I read an interview with Christy Ring in later years and Ring suggested that it was very arrogant of a young inexperienced Limerick team to think that they actually had a chance of beating a great Cork team. He felt that Limerick never had the match won, and never had a chance of beating Cork, because Cork were always capable of

The Limerick senior hurling panel, trained by Mick Mackey, which was beaten by a late Christy Ring goal in the 1956 Munster final. *Back row (l–r):* Ralph Prendergast (Claughaun), Benny Fitzgibbon (Treaty Sarsfields), Tom McGarry (Treaty Sarsfields & Claughaun), Fr Séamus Ryan (Cappamore), Tommy Casey (Capt) (Ahane), Willie Keane (Ahane), Paddy Enright (Ahane), Dermot Kelly (Claughaun), Mick 'Mousey' McInerney (Treaty Sarsfields), Fr Liam Kelly (Monaleen & Ahane). *Front row (l–r):* Jack Quaid (Feoghanagh/Castlemahon), Fr Liam Ryan (Cappamore), Jim Quaid (Feoghanagh/Castlemahon), Mick Tynan (Claughaun), Donal Broderick (Dromcollogher/Broadford), Vivian Cobbe (St Patrick's), Paddy Cunneen (St Patrick's), Gerry Fitzgerald (Rathkeale). Sitting: Paddy O'Malley (Cappamore), Stephen Long (Feenagh/Kilmeedy).

stepping up a few gears to secure the result when it really mattered. One of the three goals Christy Ring got that day should have been disallowed because he was in the square. However, his first action after scoring was to rush to the umpire and grab the green flag and he waved the flag himself. By doing so, he hoodwinked the referee who was distracted by the frenzy of excitement at a player waving the flag himself after scoring. The referee never stopped and thought about what had really happened and it was considered to be a clever move from Christy Ring.

Gerry Piggott says Ring didn't spare the timber:

Christy Ring was a dirty player. He was cute and would do a player in the quiet without getting caught. He was the king with everyone that time, so he never had a reputation for being dirty. Mackey in comparison was clean. He would use his body, but he didn't use timber, whereas Ring would always use timber.

Andy Fleming had first-hand experience of being timbered by Ring:

Ring was dirty alright. I played on him one day in Dungarvan and things weren't going well for him. About ten minutes from the end he came over and split me across the forehead and I got a few stitches after the game. I was on one knee on the ground and the first aid people were dressing it and he came over in his Cork accent, looked down over me, and said, 'I'm sorry I didn't do that to you an hour ago.' We ended up the best of friends afterwards.

Séamus Ryan had huge admiration for Christy Ring:

In 1956 Christy Ring came out and congratulated me after the final whistle. It was the best game I ever played for Limerick. Looking back, Ring wasn't as dangerous at centre-forward as he was around the goals. Perhaps he was trying to put me off my game, going around with wild eyes on him, fists clenched looking into my eyes, and totally different to when he came up to me after the game. It was a game we threw away. We had the winning of that. He came out all the way from corner-forward to centre field to me and he said, 'You had a great game, a pity you had to lose' or words to that effect.

I met him years afterwards coming out after a match in Cork and we walked back together to my car, which was parked near where he lived in Cork. He chatted away and it was very nice. I had often heard that he was a remote man but he wasn't that at all. He was a lovely fellow. I suppose if you were to draw a contrast between Christy and Mick, Christy was a hurling fanatic, an out-and-out hurling man, whereas Mackey didn't just confine himself to hurling. He was a sportsman and a popular star before the stars of our time. I suppose you could say that Ring was a famous hurler, whereas Mackey was a celebrity.

Fr Liam Kelly agrees:

I played against Ring on a few occasions and he was a dirty player. In my time he was going off a bit, and the older he got, the dirtier he got. He was always late on the pull and pulling from behind and stuff. However, I must say I knew Ring as a man off the field and he was a gentleman and I got on very well with him. Cork were a class side. They had the most skilful players and were in a league of their own from a very early age, even as minors. They would take the ball out

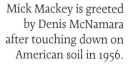

Mick Mackey is greeted by Denis McNamara after touching down on American soil in 1956.

of your eye if they could. They had great coaching even at that stage, before people had the title of coaches. All the older players always got involved in Cork. They put it back in, which is always so important. We had no fear of Tipperary when I was playing and I would say we beat them as often as we played them. We had no fear of Cork either but we just couldn't beat them.

Fr Liam Ryan compares Mackey's approach to that of the other selectors:

In 1956, amazingly, the crowd came on to the pitch around us at half time for a chat. We would have been talking to people from Cappamore for the first five or six minutes at half time and it was only about two minutes before the match restarted that Mick Mackey called us all together in a huddle. Jimmy Butler Coffey was there in 1955 as a representative of Cappamore as county champions. Mick Herbert was there in 1956 representing Ahane as county champions. Pat Reilly was there as well, as county chairman. Mackey was there by right as being an expert.

Mackey and Butler Coffey had different approaches. Jimmy Coffey would hit the table with a hurley and send you out fired up with fire in your belly and you would be afraid to let him down if you met him after the match having played badly. You never felt that with Mackey. He hadn't the same fire in addressing a team. Looking back on it I would say he was a reluctant speaker. I would put it down to the fact that he saw himself as one selector and therefore didn't feel that he had the authority to take over entirely on his own, which was a big loss because had he taken on that mantle, things could have been different. I remember in the 1956 Munster final the difference between the sideline approaches from both teams. Jack Barrett was up and down the sideline constantly shouting and using bad language to rile the Cork team. There was nobody corresponding for Limerick. Barrett was abusing the Cork players from a height for most of the game and had one or two others with him up and down the sideline. Nobody from Limerick had his voice heard from one end of the game to the other. Obviously Cork hated to lose more than Limerick.

From a vocal perspective, Jackie Connell and Mickey Fitzgibbon seemed very subdued in terms of their roles on the sideline and in the dressing room. I don't think they ever addressed the team formally. Maybe at meetings in the boardroom Fitzgibbon would have been very influential, but I never saw them getting involved on the day of the match. It was a case of the players being left out onto the pitch and very much a case of nobody passing a comment one way or another from the sideline for the duration of the match. So at half time, as I said, it was only with two minutes to go we were all brought together into a huddle. We had a chat with everyone else that day at half time except the management. We weren't even talking to each other until the last two minutes. There was very little emphasis on tactics. Training by modern standards was poor.

You went to the Gaelic Grounds two or three times a week and pucked the ball up and down the field. Four or five balls all on the ground, you'd imagine that nobody was ever going to take the ball into their hand on the day of a match. Then you did a few rounds of the field and a few sprints and a bit of backs and forwards. There was never any talk of tactics, I don't know what tactics could have meant on a hurling field anyway because it was all man to man marking at the time. It was amazing looking back on it that there was so much emphasis on ground hurling. First-time pulling, letting the ball go, especially from Mackey who rarely pulled on the ground himself. All the training was hitting five or six balls up and down the field for twenty minutes on the ground.

Mackey never stood in and participated in a game in training, even though he wasn't that old and not long retired from club hurling. He

Three of the stars of Mackey's Greyhounds – Dermot Kelly, Fr Séamus Ryan and Vivian Cobbe – along with 1956 newcomer Tom McGarry were honoured to be chosen on the Limerick All-Star team from 1954 to 1984. *Back row (l–r):* Tom McGarry (Claughaun & Treaty Sarsfields), Bernie Hartigan (South Liberties & Old Christians), Jim O'Brien (Bruree), Fr Séamus Ryan (Cappamore), Joe McKenna (South Liberties), Pat Hartigan (South Liberties), Richard Bennis (Patrickswell), Éamonn Cregan (Claughaun), Seán Foley (Patrickswell). *Front row (l–r):* Vivian Cobbe (St Patrick's), Jimmy Carroll (Hospital/Herbertstown), Éamon Grimes (South Liberties), Dermot Kelly (Claughaun), Jim Hogan (Adare & Claughaun), John McDonagh (St Patrick's & Bruree).

never togged out and never seemed to have the urge to step into a game. He never pulled me to one side to advise me. There didn't seem to be much personal counselling or advice at all that I can remember. I can't recall him taking anyone else to one side. I don't ever remember him giving one-to-one advice. He was a reluctant man in that regard, and wasn't like managers now at all. You would never hear him haranguing at all. He hardly ever raised his voice and while he would be talking, it was in a low-key manner the whole time.

Fr Liam Kelly recalls an amusing incident:

Mackey used be inside in the Gaelic Grounds training us and would be shouting, 'Pull on it, pull on it, pull on it, don't mind poking with it!' There was a famous incident one evening involving Ralph Prendergast, as stylish a player as I have ever seen, who was very young at the time. We were having a match in training, and Ralph took off down the wing flying on a solo run. He came back anyway and the next thing he heard, 'Don't ever do that again, I told you pull on it!' To which Prendergast replied, 'You did it yourself when you were playing, Mackey.' Mackey told him to be quiet. Prendergast was only a young lad of nineteen and he answering Mackey back like that! Mackey would appreciate that though, and he was often laughing about it afterwards.

Séamus Ryan recalls how players could be inspired by Mackey:

While I had played well in the 1955 Munster final, the best match I ever played for Limerick was against Cork in the '56 final. Mackey came to me and gave a few congratulatory words afterwards. He was good that way.

If we had won the 1956 Munster final, it would have steadied us. We had no big-name player with great experience. Dermot Kelly was the most talked about member of the team and was a colourful character but there was no established hurler who had made his name for Limerick who would have been a rallying force.

I always felt that if we were under pressure in matches and hanging on, we might collapse like we did against Cork, whereas had we won that game we might have had more confidence in other tight games. Looking back, we felt that had we won that one, we would have established ourselves as a hurling force and it would have given us confidence.

Team building is also important and there was none of that in our day. We rarely met each other. There was very little build-up to games, and that applied especially to us who were away in the priesthood. I can't remember any closeness between the members of the team because we just didn't know each other. Looking back, it was wonderful to have played in an occasion like a Munster final and a massive honour to wear the Limerick jersey.

Limerick had claimed their first silverware since 1947, but it proved to be a false dawn. As with most successful Limerick teams, there was the feeling that more trophies could have been won, even though winning the Munster championship is something to be cherished. As an aside, it's worth noting that in a gold medal tournament final at Bruff during this time, Willie Keane, playing at full-back, held Christy Ring scoreless, a remarkable feat.

TEN

ೞ

1957 ONWARDS:
WILDERNESS YEARS

While Limerick were winning titles on the field, inspired by the great Ahane team, all was not well with that club in terms of having proper structures in place. Given that it had produced so many great players, even allowing for the times that were in it, it seems amazing that Ahane didn't have their own field for many years, as a local explains:

Before he became county chairman, Pat Reilly was running the show and was instrumental in bringing in outsiders from other clubs. Ahane never concentrated on underage because we didn't have a field. There could have been fifty or sixty players playing hurling on one evening at Reilly's field. When Ahane were going well in the 1940s there was no minor team. When Neddy Stokes, John Mulcahy and Paddy Creamer played for Ahane, there were a good few locals who didn't get their place. Fr White, the local curate, then decided to organise the minors and put a bit of structure to it. Monaleen broke away and formed Ballysimon Faughs, and took away the Leonards, Mick McGrath, Eddie Browne (the singer), and the Doyles, though John Doyle stayed with Ahane. But the locals had already missed the opportunity, when outsiders came in and took the medals.

The committee spent years trying to decide on a pitch, and a number of people wanted to buy Mescall's pitch behind the school in Castleconnell but the Ahane people didn't have great regard for the Castleconnell lads. Eventually, the club bought boggy land that would need work near the railway gates in Lisnagry on the main Dublin Road for a small fee. That land was left untouched for a number of years. Pino Harris had the franchise for one of the major truck dealerships at the time and bought the land to open a warehouse in the early 1970s. That sale gave us the money to invest in Newgarden,

171

so for the first time Ahane had a pitch. There is a plaque below in the clubhouse with the names of the people who donated money to help with the development. Mick Herbert's name is not there because he knew that there was a clubhouse and it would be in competition to his own pub. He was called to about it at the time, and he wasn't pleased, and felt that it was taking the bit out of his mouth.

Pino Harris was a well-known associate of Charles J. Haughey. Given the Fianna Fáil association with Ahane through Tony and Mick Herbert, it's worth pondering if they knocked on Charlie's door to help out their beloved club. Perhaps the idle purchase of this unused land by Harris was a political favour to Haughey. If so, it's ironic that the money was spent on a pitch at a disadvantageous location to Mick Herbert. P. J. Keane outlines how politics has always been part of Limerick hurling, at both club and county level:

I was always giving out about the fact that Ahane hadn't their own field, even though when they were in their prime they opened every field in Limerick and Munster during the 1930s and '40s. Then they bought a field at the railway gates in Lisnagry. It was a bog, a disaster, and they never made a field out of it but at least they went ahead and bought something. They weren't progressive, I thought. Then as time moved on they bought the present field, which is away from the local villages. There was always a problem in Ahane with regard to locating the field, in that Lisnagry, Castleconnell and Ahane were three separate areas. If the field was in Castleconnell, the crowd in Annacotty or Ahane didn't want to play there and vice versa.

Pat Reilly was the chairman, and his plot used to be full of people trying to get a puck. Reilly's shop and Herbert's pub were near each other and sometimes Herbert's field was also used. In hindsight I used to think they didn't want to have a field in Ahane because Pat Reilly and Mick Herbert would lose business. That was the perception among some of us at the time. Whether that perception was right or wrong, to a person like myself with a deep interest in the club progressing there didn't seem to be any impetus in trying to get the thing going. But that was a reflection on the entire county. I saw people at club level in Limerick who went on to become treasurers of the county board and didn't know how to keep a cashbook. They didn't know how to keep accounts. Beyond keeping clubs afloat there wasn't any great vision and I think that percolated right up to the top of Limerick GAA. You didn't have the people with the acumen and the drive to move things on. The attempt to stop Ahane rather than raising to that level and matching them in 1949 stemmed from that.

The point raised by Keane is most interesting. In Limerick GAA, becoming a county board officer, to this very day, has nothing to do with ability and has everything to do with politics. The capacity to circle the wagons and gather votes has led many incompetent and agenda-driven people to reach the top, at the expense of those with great potential and vision. P. J. Keane went on to become a top-class hurler, and was recognised as one of the greatest Ahane players since Mick Mackey. However, he found things difficult at minor level given the animosity towards Ahane:

I felt it was difficult as an Ahane player to get on the county minors. Seán Cunningham was the East selector and he wasn't very pro-Ahane; you would want to be very good to be selected. I was born in November, which also made it difficult. The likes of Paddy Cobbe who was only a couple of months younger than me was at the right side of January and was underage in 1958 when Limerick won the All-Ireland but was fully up to the age in terms of physical development. In my final year, 1957, I got a trial but was very light at the time and I was on Liam Hogan of Bruree. He was a huge, strong man and he was up to the age. I wasn't able to manage him that well. We went down to Waterford for the championship and I was put on as a sub. I played very well and I got a couple of scores and thought it was enough to get my place in the Munster final. However, there was another trial prior to the Munster final and I was on Hogan again and couldn't handle him. From being on the team I ended up being dropped altogether. The night before the final I was hurling in the field with my brother Willie and Pat Reilly came over and said that one of the players had been injured. He asked me to travel instead and I got the boots straight away and went off the following morning. Liam Hogan was a very good hurler and was on Jimmy Doyle that day and was beating him. Limerick were playing with the wind in the second half and they put me on. So from being dropped from the panel, all of a sudden I was playing in a Munster final. Next thing a guy called Woodcock ran into me and broke my collarbone.

Having made his return from injury, Keane played in a Newport Tournament:

Ahane played Holycross before a huge crowd. We would tog out in my uncle's place, Lee's yard. I marked Pat Stakelum who was centre-back, and it's something I always regarded as a fierce honour even though he was coming to the end of his days. John Doyle was playing at centre-forward and I was amazed at his level of hurling considering he was a corner-back at inter-county. He was a far better hurler in terms of ability than he was ever recognised for. We were up by two points and Holycross got a controversial goal. All hell broke loose and we had to get around the referee to protect him. There was a lot of aggro from supporters because the goal shouldn't have been allowed. In one way, though, it was great to see them so enthusiastic because it showed they had a greater passion for the game than sometimes exists nowadays.

After running Cork so close in the 1956 Munster final, the wheels came off the wagon prematurely for the Limerick senior team. Although a young side with great potential, varying circumstances saw the players slip away gradually over the next few years. Apart from goals, Limerick scored five points against Wexford in 1955, five against Cork in '56 and five against Waterford in '57. Jimmy Smyth raises a valid point about the forwards' lack of scoring power:

I didn't expect Limerick to dominate hurling even though they had beaten us comprehensively in 1955. That result wasn't a flash in the pan because they were subsequently beaten by Cork in the 1956 Munster final, a game they should have won. They were a decent team and a good hurling team but they relied on Dermot Kelly getting the 1-12 in 1955 and it's very hard to get 1-12 a second time. There wasn't a great spread of scores from the other forwards, who were very fast players but contributed only 1-3 between them in 1955.

One of the first to go was Mick Mackey, as Fr Liam Ryan explains:

Canon Punch had a lot of deep prejudices and needed no reason. Looking for logic in Canon Punch was a mistake. It was the very same after 1956 as it was in earlier years, he had to get rid of Mackey. In the late 1940s the theme was that Ahane had to be got rid of, and then in the late '50s it was that the Limerick hurlers would go nowhere under Mick Mackey. Canon Punch was a man like that, who had deep feelings with no sense to them. He was no longer the chairman but was president. He was a respected figure because he had been there so long, but he certainly wasn't a man you would put in charge of a team. I can remember whenever you'd meet him at a match it was always the same recurring theme, 'Unless we get rid of Mackey we are going nowhere.' It wasn't that Mackey had done anything detrimental.

In the front row at a Limerick GAA convention in the 1950s are *(l–r)* Canon Punch, Pat O'Reilly, Jackie O'Connell, Liam Fitzmaurice and Mick Mackey.

Fr Liam Kelly believes Mackey should have been retained:

Mick wasn't involved consistently as a selector every year because of the system in the county board, depending on who were the county champions and other things. Reputations didn't matter if the politics went against you. There was nepotism at the time and if you were picked as a selector from the East, your priority was to get as many from the East division onto the panel as you could. There was no such thing as for the betterment of the county and Mick would have been all for the betterment of the county.

Willie Keane explains why Canon Punch didn't like Mackey:

The canon didn't like Mick Mackey because he was in the limelight. Mackey was used to calling the shots as a player since the early 1930s. The canon had to be the boss, but when he came on board it was too late for him to gain control over Mackey because Mackey had been there so long. Fame and success brings jealousy. You have to give credit to Mackey for being successful, but not everyone gave him credit.

Jim Hogan reveals more about Canon Punch:

A publican nicknamed Smiling Bill was building a new pub in Dooradoyle, what is now known as the Unicorn Bar. Canon Punch was by then a dean, and was the local parish priest at the time, living across from where Raheen church is now. Smiling Bill went to him as a matter of courtesy and told him he was going to build a pub, there was no pub at that side of town at the time and he was the minimum distance away from the nearest pub, etc. The dean told him that no way would he allow him to build a pub in the parish, but that he would curse it if it went ahead. Smiling Bill went to the bishop and told him the story. 'Listen,' said the bishop, 'that man is cursing Christy Ring for the last ten years and it's better he is getting.' He went away and built the pub, and apparently on the night it opened, Smiling Bill's wife fell and broke her hand. That was the dean for you, he was hated by everyone.

The flying wing-forward, Ralph Prendergast, departed for the US:

I was working in Clover Meats, and I was invited over to New York to play for the Limerick hurling team. I had a sponsor for a visa. A brother of the famous Derry McCarthy [former Limerick and Munster Railway Cup player], called Jim McCarthy in Long Island, was secretary of the Limerick Hurling Club in New York. He wrote to me and invited me out. Tim O'Connor who compiles the 'Bits in Brief' articles for Munster championship programmes has a brother Matt. Matt told them that I was interested in going and he set the ball rolling. I was there for seven years. I played for the Limerick intermediates when I came back but I can't recall playing for the Limerick seniors again.

Limerick were beaten at the first hurdle in 1957, losing by 4-12 to 5-5 to Waterford. Waterford had been making strides following their defeat to Limerick two years previously and were aiming towards greatness, as Frankie Walsh explains:

Pat Fanning came in as county chairman around then and changed the whole structure. Training was haphazard prior to that but Fanning and John Keane and the selectors got us together and said we had an All-Ireland title in us. We believed them and started to put in an effort. We trained under Keane, and concentrated on ballwork for most of the year. We got fit early in the year, and hurled from then on.

We didn't have training games among ourselves because they would have been too contentious. It was mostly practising our striking and practising running into positions in space to receive passes and that type of thing. We would have been very worried about Dermot Kelly in 1957, but we had Martin Óg Morrissey at centre-back and would have had our backs organised. Kelly was a great hurler, and on the day of the 1955 Munster final if he ran to the toilet the ball was going to follow him.

Mackey may have departed as a selector, but he was making the headlines in other ways. Cork played Tipperary in Limerick in the Munster semi-final, the game in which Justin Nelson took the famous 'What Mackey said to Ring' photograph. John Mulcahy explains:

There was an incident in the first half of that match. Mick Mackey, who was an umpire to Michael Hayes of Clare, was in the wrong, though it was a genuine mistake. A high ball came in from Martin 'Musha' Maher, and the Cork goalkeeper Mick Cashman caught it in his hand, and as he did, the Tipperary man jumped and landed in on top of his chest. As quick as the goalie was falling back into the net, he threw the ball around the post wide. We were standing behind the goals and it came back to our feet, but we never saw it coming back. We were fully convinced that when the goalie was driven back into the net that the ball was gone in with him. Mackey thought the same and put up the green flag. Next thing a spectator roared, 'The ball is here, the ball is here.' The Cork players were showing the referee the ball. They came in and looked at the goals to check if there was any hole in the net. Mackey knew he was wrong by then, and the referee didn't award the goal. Soon afterwards Michael Maher hit Ring a belt of a shoulder and gave him a tap of a hurley going past, breaking Ring's wrist. Ring is coming off in the photo with his hand in a sling.

The Tipperary forwards weren't pleased because they felt that when the goalie threw away the ball both he and ball were already behind the line. Without delay, Mick Mackey had waved the green flag, but the other umpire disagreed and said it wasn't a goal. Mick Hayes consulted with both umpires and was less than politely told by Mick Mackey (using choice language) that it was a legitimate goal and to disappear back out to the middle of the field. At that time Hayes was part of the National Council of Referees and was heavily involved in redrafting the rules of hurling. One of the rules involved giving the referee power to make a decision if two umpires were in disagreement. Hayes

The famous Mackey vs Ring photograph taken at the 1957 Munster final by Justin Nelson. Mick Mackey, an umpire for the game, allowed a Tipperary goal which the referee over-ruled. Christy Ring, leaving the pitch injured, has words with Mackey.

overruled Mackey and awarded a free to Tipperary and was within his rights to do so. Given Mackey's resistance to being overruled, Cork were annoyed and perhaps felt Mackey was exacting retribution for past sins by Cork referees. The backlash from Christy Ring was inevitable, especially as he left the field in pain. Jim Fitzgerald was at the game:

Ring had been playing at wing-forward and after a while switched into the square. There had been a few incidents and one involved Michael Maher where Ring broke his wrist. Kieran Carey was playing that day and between himself, John Doyle and Michael Maher, they also drove Ring out onto the concrete seats. Mackey was doing umpire, and Ring was walking off sore and hurt with his hand in a sling after getting busted on the seats. It took place at the city end, at the far corner of the ground [the Thomond Park corner]. Ring was mouthing, and you could see Mackey turning around saying something to him. Ring passed the first comment as he was walking behind the goals going off. Mackey was doing umpire. You could see Mackey turning around and as he did he was caught on the camera.

Johnny Wall asked Mackey about the incident many years later:

He laughed and said, 'I'll tell you so, but a lot of people have asked me that question and I never told them.' He told me that Ring said to him, using bad language, 'You never lost it, Mick', and Mick said back to him, in equally bad language, 'You never lost it either, Christy.' There are lots of other stories going around but that's the real true story as Mackey told me himself.

Séamus Walsh spoke to James 'Todsie' Mackey, a brother of Mick, on the matter and concurs with Johnny Wall:

Almost twenty years ago 'Todsie' told me that story, having heard the truth from his brother Mick. Contrary to opinion from other sources, the comment had nothing to do with Ring's injury and was actually in relation to Mackey being in a hurry to put up the green flag for the disallowed Tipperary goal earlier in the match.

Cork won the game by three points, 5-2 to 1-11. Waterford beat Cork then in the Munster final and Ring could not play due to the fractured wrist. The man in the suit, kneeling and looking up at Ring and Mackey in the famous photo by Justin Nelson, is Jack Molyneaux, who owned a pub in Mungret Street, Limerick and was a great stalwart of the local Claughaun GAA club in the city. He was a steward at the Gaelic Grounds that day.

Limerick reached the 1958 League final, described by former Irish Independent *GAA reporter John D. Hickey as the greatest game ever played. It was a match Limerick should have won, but they were beaten by Wexford. Even without Fr Liam Ryan, Fr Séamus Ryan and Fr Liam Kelly, they still almost won the game. They had only one day out in the championships of 1958, '59 and '60 and were beaten by Tipperary on all three occasions. Séamus Ryan explains why he wasn't always available for selection:*

I played in 1957 against Waterford in the first round, but my brother Liam didn't play because he was still in Maynooth doing exams. Waterford lost to Kilkenny in the All-Ireland that year. The seminaries were very enclosed places, it was a different world, there was no newspaper and no radio allowed. During our time in there they began to allow newspapers to be read. I remember Limerick were playing in the League final of 1958, a game we could have been playing in. We wouldn't have been able to listen to it but a kind professor left a radio outside on the window. In 1958 and '59 Limerick were gone from the championship in late May or early June, before we came home for the summer. In 1960 the championship game with Tipperary wasn't played until July so it meant we were available. Liam was ordained by then and played under an assumed name of 'Tom Ryan'. I was marking Jimmy Doyle in 1960 and we were beaten well in the second half. It's hard to know how we would have done in 1958 and '59 if we hadn't been in Maynooth but it would have been nice to have played for Limerick in those two years.

Ned Wheeler recalls the 1958 League final:

That was a great game of hurling. Josie Gallagher of Galway refereed that match, and I called to him years after and he said in his own sitting room that it was the best game of hurling he ever saw.

Brendan Fullam was at the game:

I was at the 1958 League final and it was a great game, contrasting styles, and again it contradicts the theory that the modern game is better than it was back then. Having won the Munster championship in 1955 with a very young team, Limerick supplemented the side in 1956 with players such as Tom McGarry. Again in 1956 they showed signs of what they could do but they just seemed to go downhill after that, whether it was through poor management or losing players. Jack Enright, from my own home place Ardagh, was at full-back in the 1958 League final. He would have been a very tight full-back and didn't give much away.

Jim Hogan was coming onto the scene at the time:

I was working in Cork from October 1954 until June 1958 when I secured a new job in Shannon airport. My first game for Limerick was in the 1958 championship against Tipperary. I had won a county with Sarsfields of Cork in 1957 so Weeshie Murphy asked me if I would play for Cork as they had no goalie at the time. I refused because it would have been treason! It was only when I spoke to James Lundon, the Athenry-based programme collector, recently that I realised I ended up being the fifth longest-serving player for Limerick and made twenty-four appearances. That is a remarkable statistic considering there were no qualifiers in those days and we played only one championship match per season for most of my fifteen-year career.

Jimmy Butler Coffey believed the Ryan brothers were a loss:

When the Ryans were available Limerick were great, and when they weren't Limerick weren't great. They could only hurl when they were home from Maynooth. When they were ordained they couldn't hurl any more, so when Liam played in 1960 against Tipperary it was made to look like a misprint in the paper so that people wouldn't recognise who it really was. In later times, there was no harm in what Fr Liam Ryan did, but within that era there was a problem playing as a priest. It wasn't allowed and he was wrong to play. Within the church it would have been seen as very serious.

Fr Liam Kelly gives his views:

Ordained priests weren't allowed to play and that meant that myself, Fr Liam Ryan and Fr Séamus Ryan were all retired at twenty-three. When Fr Liam Ryan played under an assumed name he was reported to the bishop. That was one of the rules I regretted most of all, though it had changed by the time the Fitzmaurices of Limerick and the Clarkes of Galway came along. Our bishop at the time in the Limerick diocese was Bishop Murphy and he was against the rule. He wanted us to play. Fr Liam Ryan was from the Cashel and Emly diocese, a completely different regime! The bishop there, Dr Thomas Morris, rapped him on the knuckles. The problem was that he had been captain of a successful Munster championship-winning team and you couldn't be playing under the assumed name of Tom Jones or Paddy Ryan if you were that well known!

To give you an indication of Bishop Murphy, I was always keen on golf because we were born beside Castletroy Golf Club. My father was a teacher, and a founder member of Castletroy. He used to go up after school and we would go up there with him. It was great for me because I could take up the golf when I finished the hurling. There were rules pertaining to golf and I couldn't play in the South of Ireland competition. You had to play under an assumed name and it was always put in inverted commas such as 'J Potter' or 'P Driver'. Some priests used to deliberately do it, but everyone knew it was a priest, so it was a giveaway straight away. I was doing it for a while and I think they were calling me McNamara. Eventually I got tired of it and decided to enter in my own name. I went down and I was playing against Dan Ryan in the first round who had won it the year before. Who did I see standing behind the first tee only the bishop. He walked over and shook my hand and said, 'Good Luck now Liam, you did the right thing today.' I was walking tall for the day. The rule was lifted in 1970 because enough of the bishops wanted to get rid of it by then and they secured a majority, but it was too late for me.

Fr Séamus Ryan disagreed with the ruling:

Looking back on it, it was all so petty and small. The Maynooth Statutes of the early 1950s said that we couldn't take part in violent games. It wasn't a blanket ban on playing games, it was a ban on violent games and hurling would have been interpreted as a violent game along with rugby. It wasn't universally applied but the bishops took a very strong line on it in Ireland when they were running the seminaries like ours. If you were a missionary priest like a Columban in Dalgan Park or a member of the Holy Ghosts in Kimmage, you were allowed play. I remember a Fr Barry from Cork was a Kiltegan Father and was able to play. So the rule wasn't universally applied, which made it difficult to accept.

Limerick lost the 1960 championship game to Tipperary by 10-9 to 2-1. Jim Hogan pinpoints a lack of preparation:

That 1960 game was a disaster. Tipperary were advancing and it was a lack of training on our part. If you go through the 1960s, Tipperary won three or four All-Irelands after beating us in the first round by maybe only three or four points. That proves they were organised and we weren't. I always considered the organisation and preparation to be a joke.

One suspects Fr Liam Ryan wished he hadn't played:

Tipperary were trying to make up for the previous year because Waterford had beaten them by 8-6 to 2-6. At half time that day against Waterford, the score was 8-3 to nothing. In our 1960 game there was a very strong wind blowing straight down the pitch in the first half and it had a major bearing on the result.

In the early 1960s, P. J. Keane would become a highly regarded hurler for Limerick and someone for whom Mick Mackey had huge admiration. Just like Seán Herbert, he was in the wrong place at the wrong time where success was concerned, but was generally regarded as a better player than some who were on All-Ireland-winning teams. However, his lack of success as a player stemmed from a lack of preparation, politics, and the premature departure of quality players:

In my career as a Limerick player, I would love to have played in Munster finals and All-Ireland finals but I never had that opportunity. It's amazing the transition between the 1955/1956 teams and when I came along in the early 1960s. An awful lot of what was a very young Munster championship-winning team were gone. It is one of the major problems with Limerick. Counties who are managed properly and are successful introduce fresh talent and always have a conveyor belt of talent and hold onto their players whereas Limerick always seem to be in a rush to get rid of players too soon. The book *Unlimited Heartbreak* is a testament to that. The number of players who were left out or dropped before their time was unbelievable. Mike Houlihan and Dave Clarke were examples of players who still had something to offer. Mossy Carroll was deemed good enough to play Munster championship hurling in the vitally important centre-back position for Tipperary, yet Limerick left him go.

I started with Limerick in the early 1960s and would only have played with a few of the 1956 team. I played with Tom McGarry for a number of matches and perhaps with Tommy Casey for a few games. Granted I was away sometimes with the cadets and might have missed

The Limerick panel that beat Dublin 5-6 to 2-10 at Croke Park in the National League of 1963–4. *Back row (l–r):* Tom Bluett (Effin), Liam Hogan (Bruree), Tony O'Brien (Patrickswell), Ned Rea (Effin), Mike Heelan (Kilmallock), Mick O'Brien (Claughaun), Éamonn Carey (Patrickswell), J. J. Bresnihan (Hospital/Herbertstown), Bernie Hartigan (Old Christians). *Front row (l–r):* Jim Hogan (Adare & Claughaun), Martin Rainsford (Ahane), John McDonagh (St Patrick's & Bruree), P. J. Keane (Ahane), Kevin Long (Feenagh/Kilmeedy), Paddy Cobbe (St Patrick's), Séamus Quaid (Feoghanagh/Castlemahon), Larry Cross (St Patrick's), Frankie Costello (Banogue).

out on playing with some but it's still a huge turnover of players. If you compare a very young 1956 team to the 1963 team, there are none of the 1956 players on it.

I think a large part of the problem was the structure of the county board, with a lot of delegates having their own interest in promoting players from their own clubs to wear the county jersey instead of having a unified approach to achieve success. There was a lot of internal club politics and inter-club rivalry where team selection was concerned. We would be selected to play. We would go to the match and you wouldn't know until the very last minute who the team was. There was no organisation, no analysis of the opposition, no analysis of your own team, or a plan of action or any thought put into how you would play the match.

Tipperary were very professional even in the early 1960s but we always gave them good matches, especially in 1962. Tony Wall who was in the army with us would go down to Thurles three nights a week for training, because the chat would be that he was getting mileage. They were paying mileage! We thought this was amazing that they were so far ahead. They would train properly three nights a week and they had their own masseur, Ossie Bennett. They had a structure. We had nothing like that. To think that we could go down and try and compete with them when we just arrived down in the dressing room on the morning of the match.

Despite his undoubted quality as a hurler, Keane had one major weakness, as Fr Liam Kelly explains:

P. J. was only a young fella starting off in my time, and Mackey used to say to me, 'Don't let him start a row.' Limerick were playing Tipperary one day and P. J. was centre-forward and playing brilliantly. He got a ball, tore through the middle, raced in along past John Doyle and the full-back was there facing him. The full-back knew he wouldn't beat P. J. so he came across him to do him, but P. J. got past him and all he had to do was tap the ball into the empty net. What did P. J. do only drop the ball and go back out and hit the full-back a belt!

Keane doesn't disagree:

All we were told before games was to go out and pull and lash into the opposition. I think Tipperary players targeted the likes of me. They knew I had a short fuse and they played on that and exploited it. I had nobody there to calm me and advise me that they were out to rise me. Instead I was being told the opposite. They didn't have to tell me to be fired up because I was naturally fired up anyway. I didn't realise I was being set up a lot of the time by the opposition, and therefore the opposition played on the referee. If I was playing in the yellow/red card system it might have suited better. We were playing against the likes of Devanney and Doyle who would hit you off the ball, and they wouldn't get away with it now. But it all comes back to the overall lack of vision and awareness.

Mick Mackey wouldn't have had the vision needed to transform Limerick in the 1960s, and the people involved with him were all old school, the likes of Jackie O'Connell and Mickey Fitzgibbon. They wouldn't be into technology and the emphasis on weight training and nutrition you see in modern times. In the army we would have done weights, but we wouldn't have been into the benefits of weight training from an individualised scientific approach like the Munster rugby team or the Tyrone team under Mickey Harte. And there has to be balance in a weights programme. I was aware I was too light for inter-provincial level with Munster and I was meeting guys who were bigger and faster and stronger. I didn't know how to get heavier, I should have been doing weights but instead I decided to eat more.

In the 1930s people had physical lifestyles that compensated; they cycled and they did manual work on the farm. There were no hamstring problems because their legs were so strong; they were well conditioned and hardened. Times progressed into the 1960s and '70s and people went into different occupations. Everything changed, and some fellows got degrees. Some counties would have been more clued in than others. Mackey would have been light years away from what was needed and while it would have been of benefit to have him around, there was a need for someone who would be open to using modern methods with him.

At that time Limerick needed to put more emphasis on getting players who were away from home to come back. I would only come down on a Saturday and would go on to the match. I used to meet them in the dressing room and then leave immediately afterwards. There was no talk, no bonding or rapport. I didn't drink. I would go back to Galway and there was nobody up there to talk to about the match. I found that difficult. In Limerick I would have met neighbours at the creamery and talk hurling and talk about the match. I was separated from all that in Galway. I think there were Munster finals that could have been won with proper organisation. The raw material was there but none of us ever reached our potential. In hindsight I was very professional. I didn't drink or smoke. I had three or four hurleys going to a match when it was frowned on. I have seen other fellows turn up with no hurley and they would be thrown one out of a bag. How could you hurl with a strange hurley?

I would touch up my own hurleys, I took good care of my boots. There were some days I went out and I was flat, and there were other days I went out and I was flying. I never knew why, but it was probably down to diet. We didn't know enough about diet at the time. Prior to one Railway Cup game, I remember going around all the hospitals in Limerick looking for a painkilling injection for a broken finger. I couldn't get one. They thought I was on drugs. I remember there was a masseur for Limerick at one stage before a Railway Cup final and I wanted a rub and I couldn't get one. When Paddy Cobbe, John McDonagh and myself were playing we would get a cut, go to casualty ourselves and get stitched in there. In those days if you travelled to a game, you would get a fiver for taking a car. Paddy Cobbe brought two or three players to one match, and the county board were cribbing about the fiver.

In 1962 they were moving players and plugging holes the whole time. When I played Harty Cup with Limerick CBS we all knew our positions and were played in our best positions. We knew where any other player was going to hit the ball and were on the move accordingly, knowing where the ball would arrive. The transition from Harty Cup to inter-county was enormous. We had different players playing every day. We had endless switches in the course of a game. How could we win when we didn't have a static team?

Things were very amateur in those days. I remember once the car transporting us broke down in Charleville and we had to thumb to Cork to play a championship match against Tipperary. Another time Tommy Casey's car broke down just after we collected Mick Mackey in Ardnacrusha. We were waiting an hour for a replacement car. I was in Cork watching another game with Paddy Cobbe one day and Liam Moloney was playing a great game. There was another Moloney on the team who was playing badly and the selectors took off the wrong Moloney by mistake.

In 1961, Limerick were eliminated from the championship after a 4-14 to 4-5 defeat to Waterford. The game was played under the shadow of a six-month suspension given to Tom McGarry only a couple of weeks beforehand. McGarry was a talented GAA, handball and soccer player who had a high profile as a successful Railway Cup player. The media reports at the time suggested that several GAA players had taken part in an inter-firm soccer match, but McGarry was the only one suspended. McGarry's defence was that by virtue of being employed by a company, a player was obliged to represent that company in inter-firm competitions. The position of county board secretary Jackie Connell, however, was that no man could be forced to play foreign games against his will, and Limerick had to face Waterford without McGarry. Mick Mackey was back in the fold for 1962 and 1963 following huge public demand for his presence. Limerick beat Galway in 1962, drew with Tipperary and lost the replay heavily. Jim Hogan explains:

Galway always looked good on paper that time but just weren't at the races really until later years. They found it almost impossible to win a first round while they were in Munster. I thought we had Tipperary on the rack in the drawn game, which was played at the old Athletic Grounds in Cork. The old stand in Cork was like a cowshed, and you will see that in the photos. We used to come in through the gates and if there was a heavy shower there would be water up three or four inches around the turnstiles so they used to put planks down for us to walk on. We were defending the Blackrock goals when Jimmy Smyth blew the whistle early for full time. There was no love lost between Limerick and Jimmy Smyth. He was a great hurler, but was pompous and wouldn't shake hands with you. At the time John Moloney refereed a lot of our games and was one of the best referees I ever saw. I remember looking at the time when Smyth blew and realising that there was a few minutes left. Every one of the Tipperary players ran off out of the ground to the showgrounds at the back of the city end where we used to tog out sometimes. They smelt a rat and knew what had happened but they were out on their feet. They were brought back, but it was about ten to fifteen minutes before the match was restarted and they had got their breather. I can still see them running off the field through the entrance at the far side of the field. They were All-Ireland champions and we had them. We played well that day.

Tipperary were leading by a point at the time but were out on their feet. Limerick had all the momentum and were approaching the finishing line like a juggernaut. When they were off the field Tipperary refuelled, caught their second wind and held on for a draw. Jimmy Smyth explains the scenario:

I blew the match five minutes before I should have through a genuine mistake, and restarted the match. They drew the first match, and Tipperary won the replay. Limerick felt they were going to drive on and win the game, and their supporters booed me heavily at the end of full time. The game had ended level and they were looking for blood. They thought they should have knocked out the All-Ireland champions. I was on a loser whatever I did but I think I did the right thing. If I hadn't restarted it, the final score stood and there were no appeals in those days. When you make a mistake like that you never forget it.

It was different to the Jimmy Cooney incident in 1998 in that I restarted play and finished out the game. You couldn't let the game go with five minutes to go, it would have been very unfair. When you are playing a match and have to go out again and play the last five minutes, it's going to affect your play. That is another side to it. There are two sides to it, and to be honest there are some refereeing incidents that I don't think can be remedied at all. Look at Meath versus Louth in 2010, for instance.

I can't recall Mackey saying anything to me on the day. Mackey never interfered in things like that and he kept in the background. I suppose he had seen and done it all. The teams he had played on himself were in a lot of scrapes and that incident was only chickenfeed to Mackey in comparison to the scrapes he would have been in as a player.

Donie Nealon believes Tipperary had a lucky escape:

I would say we weren't ready for Limerick in 1962. Limerick hadn't really bothered us for a few years before that and we were extremely lucky to draw that match, but it was the winning of the All-Ireland for us because I can tell you it brought us down to earth fairly fast. We won the replay convincingly but were extremely lucky to get out of Cork that day with a draw.

Jim Hogan believes Limerick were better in 1962 by accident rather than design:

There was a lot of craic that time and we never took it seriously because we never had any reason to. On paper I will agree that the 1962 team was an exceptionally good Limerick team, with a lot of names recognised as being great Limerick names. John Bresnihan at full-back and Kevin Long at centre-back would have been recognised as two of the best Limerick players ever in their positions, along with Éamonn Carey and Tom McGarry. I would say the reason it wasn't taken seriously reflected on the management of that time. Club hurling wasn't great at the time either, and there were soft counties won by teams that didn't have to fight for them because they were way better than the rest. There was a lack of discipline as well. While it wasn't that long after the Mick Herbert incident, I wouldn't say there was a hangover from that.

It's hard to figure out what was the difference between 1962 and other years. I think we beat Tipperary in the League that year. We were close enough to them anyway and we knew it coming into the game. Mick Mackey would not have had too much of a role in our preparations. He never impressed me as a selector, but that doesn't mean he didn't impress others. I don't remember Mackey pulling anyone aside and giving advice but maybe others would have seen that differently. Everyone has their own experience and their own views on someone. I never had serious hurling conversations with Mackey but would have had with other selectors. I'd be asking them things, they'd be telling me things about what I should and shouldn't have done regarding puck outs and all this kind of stuff. Mackey never interfered, he took it that as inter-county hurlers we knew hurling, that we wouldn't be on the team if we didn't know hurling and he left us at it.

Seán Ryan (Malachy) believes Limerick were competitive:

Limerick had a grand team in 1962 and drew with what was probably the greatest Tipperary team of all time, by virtue of winning five All-Ireland titles in seven years. OK, Limerick were well beaten in the replay but when you have All-Ireland champions you get one chance, and you don't take things for granted in the replay. Owen O'Neill is a first cousin of my wife and he was a tough man in the early 1960s. I happened to look back at one stage and he was getting it tough from Mick Maher. I looked back down when the play was at the other end of the field and I saw Owen laying Mick Maher out flat with a belt of a fist on the field during the match.

In Unlimited Heartbreak, *O'Neill believed they needed hurling:*

My recollection is that all we did was physical training between the draw and the replay. We had a game of backs and forwards one night, and the backs leaked five goals in about ten minutes and Mick Mackey decided to call it to a halt. There was no more ball work before the replay. Tipperary had their eye in and had their game plan and we never got off the ground. Tipperary beat Waterford by a cricket score in the Munster final, so I feel we would have won Munster.

Mick Rainsford says there was only one team in the replay:

Tipperary destroyed us that day and Mackey was on the sideline in front of us, looking in at it. He gave up completely in the second half because it was all over. Realistically it was practically all over after twenty minutes of the first half. Tipperary blew them out of it.

Mick Mackey was also a Railway Cup selector for many years by virtue of his position as Limerick representative to the Munster Council. Séamus Power of Waterford was a selector with him and outlines the difficulties the weaker counties had with the big two, Tipperary and Cork:

I would remember more of Mackey from a Railway Cup perspective than anything else. The Railway Cup was a prestigious and a popular competition. It was an honour to get on the inter-provincial team, and it was a well-sought-after honour at the time. The competition on the selection committee was intense. The Munster Council representatives for each county usually acted as Railway Cup selectors. Mackey was the Limerick representative, I was the Waterford representative, Con Murphy was the secretary of Cork and the Cork representative and that's how we were selectors. In Tipperary we had Pat Stakelum who was both the secretary of Tipperary County Board and Munster Council representative. I was a selector with Mackey for the best part of ten years. We would all be looking after our own players; 90 per cent of the fifteen players were automatic. The big scramble would be for the places for players from the counties outside the big two (Clare, Waterford and Limerick), depending on what kind of a vein of hurling they were in at the time. They would be fighting for representation, and they might do a little bit of dealing behind the scenes to get the significant (or insignificant) one on the team. Myself and Mackey used to do a bit of juggling to get our own boys on. It would be a sort of a quid pro quo.

There were a couple of times where Tipperary and Cork were dominating and they wouldn't spare you, they wouldn't give you any sympathy. If they had their way they would want the entire fifteen between them, but they never got that. Myself and Mackey got on quite well in that regard. And Clare would back us too obviously, the three lesser counties would stick together. I wouldn't say we did anything underhand, but we certainly tried to make sure that no team went out without a Clare man, a Limerick man or a Waterford man. We always managed to squeeze them in, and in the better days we might get two or three on. There were days when Waterford were winning All-Irelands that they got four or five, as Limerick did. Mackey was good to fight his corner to get a guy on, he would be shrewd and he would see what other guys were thinking and saying, what way they were going. If there was a chance of slipping in a Limerick man he would pounce. Of course there were times when a Limerick man was standing out that the Cork and Tipperary selectors would have to agree. It wasn't all skulduggery, but there would have been a bit where the weaker counties were concerned. The weaker counties would have had their standout players, Jimmy Smyth for example.

Smyth knew how to work the system:

It was very hard to cope being in relative isolation to these guys. It would have been very hard to get on the team as a Clare man. These guys didn't pass to you much, so you had to be clever and pass to them when you got the ball, to make sure you were picked the following year. Nobody passed the ball in the Railway Cup. I played for eleven years and got two passes in that time. I got one pass from Jimmy Doyle and another from Terry Kelly of Cork. I got two goals out of those passes, but if I got more passes, I could have got more goals. I used to always pass to Ring. I remember a Cork man got injured in a Railway Cup game one day and Jim Barry warned him not to go off. He wanted to keep the full complement of Cork men because the next man in would have been a Tipperary man. There were some good Limerick players but it was hard to get them on the team when Tipperary and Cork were so strong in the 1960s.

Séamus Power offers his views on Jim 'Tough' Barry:

In the first round you would be playing Connacht or Ulster, which would usually have been only a cakewalk. One year we went up to the old Casement Park. There was thunder, lightning, snow and all sorts of weather. Ulster were winning by five or six points at half time against a much vaunted Munster team. Jim 'Tough' Barry was the manager of the Munster team. He was only the manager in name, a figurehead. He started giving the spiff to the lads at half time. Mackey banged the hurley off the table and said, 'Give over Tough (Tough was talking rubbish). All I can tell ye is that when this half time result gets out that the so-called stars of Munster are being beaten by five or six points by Antrim (that's what he called them, he didn't even call them Ulster), every single one of ye will be made a holy show of.'

We let the ball fly on the ground and the game was over fifteen minutes into the second half. 'Tough' Barry was rambling a bit when making his speech, and I know he meant well. He was a lovely gentleman. He minded the jerseys but nobody took him too seriously. I don't know where he got the nickname 'Tough', but it must have been a nickname given to him as a slag. He might have been known as the tough, but he was soft enough!

He got the name 'Tough' when a boxer in the 1920s, but based on the comments from Power, he obviously mellowed somewhat in later life. Unlike others, Jimmy Smyth had a high opinion of Barry:

Jim 'Tough' Barry would have been a first-class manager in my estimation and he made the decisions. He wouldn't have had that reputation in Cork though where he wasn't rated as highly. I never spoke to him as a player even though I was there a few years with him. At the same time, the management function was relatively non-existent in comparison with modern times. Once the players were picked on the team the players did the business.

Andy Fleming also respected Barry, but that was a couple of decades earlier:

Jim 'Tough' Barry was a tough man. One day when I was up there [in Dublin] for a Railway Cup match we went to early Mass and went to the Phoenix Park pucking around and were enjoying it. Next thing Barry pulled up and he was white in the face: 'Get up here now and get down to the hotel.' Everyone responded instantly. There was no messing out of him. I remember Christy Ring and Jack Lynch were there, but it didn't matter. He had great power over the team. Everyone did what he said. One day we were walking down O'Connell Street and a lesser-known player turned around and said, 'Hey lads, I'm not playing tomorrow unless I get paid for it.' He tried to round us up to back him up – Christy Ring, Jack Lynch, Jackie Power – but we didn't believe in it at the time. We played matches for the love of the game. Now the modern players won't turn on their heel without getting paid.

Frankie Walsh, the legendary Waterford hurler, also played on Munster Railway Cup teams. A story is told that on one occasion, in a tight call, Mackey voted for Frankie Walsh. Another selector queried Mackey on his vote, saying that there was another player of similar stature who should have been chosen ahead of Walsh if they were opting for a small man at corner-forward. 'Frankie Walsh might be a small man,' Mackey responded, 'but he hurls big.' Walsh himself had huge admiration for Mackey:

I always found Mick Mackey to be a very approachable man, a nice man to talk to and he would come over afterwards and say well done or something which was very encouraging. He was always very kind to me, I have to say. That time you didn't need motivation from the management, you were picked and you motivated yourself. Christy Ring was around and would motivate you enough on the field. He was loud on the field. One day Pat Fanning asked Christy Ring, 'How do you think Frankie and yourself will get on in the full-forward line?' Ring replied, 'Frankie and myself will get on well together if Frankie passes the ball to me.' The star names expected you to feed them the ball when you got it, and I must have got on alright with him because he scored 3-5 off Nick O'Donnell the same day.

Tommy Barrett worked as a selector with Mackey:

We wouldn't meet much that time, except on the day of a match. He was a character and would fight his corner to get a Limerick man on the team. Nobody would really disagree with him but he wouldn't select anyone who wasn't worth his place. We had players on Railway Cup teams who would go through a brick wall for you, and then we had players who wouldn't put it in and would only be going through the motions. Mackey was very shrewd in terms of being able to identify those who weren't prepared to fight tooth and nail for the win.

Jim Hogan was chosen for Munster:

I was the Railway Cup goalie for Munster in 1964 when Mick Mackey was a selector. Tony O'Brien of Patrickswell was a sub the same day. I wasn't successful though and lost out on a Railway Cup

The Munster team that won the 1963 Railway Cup final. *Back row* (*l–r*): Joe Condon (Waterford), P. J. Keane (Limerick), Jimmy Byrne (Waterford), Tom McGarry (Limerick), Jimmy Brohan (Cork), Michael Maher (Tipperary), Jimmy Smyth (Clare), Christy Ring (Cork), Jim 'Tough' Barry (Cork) (Trainer). *Front row* (*l–r*): John Doyle (Tipperary), Liam Devaney (Tipperary), Tom Cheasty (Waterford), Mick Cashman (Cork), Donie Nealon (Tipperary), Jimmy Doyle (Tipperary), Tony Wall (Tipperary).

medal because of John Doyle. We were playing against Leinster in the final and were winning by two points with a minute to go. The ball came across from the wing, and I went down to get it but John Doyle let a roar at me to let it off. I let it off, but it hit the post and came out and a Leinster forward came in and flicked it in. That goal beat us.

P. J. Keane was chosen for Munster on several occasions:

I would have made Railway Cup teams from 1961 to '65; whether Mackey would have influenced that or not I don't know. Maybe he had something to do with it. The one year we won it was in 1963. We drew on St Patrick's Day and won the replay on Easter Sunday. Mackey was very excited over the fact that a fellow Ahane clubman had won a Railway Cup medal and there were very few Limerick players on it in those years. He was excited that day that we won it. It was a tight game. I think I played OK and he was very pleased with me.

It was a very prestigious competition at the time, and I'm sad that it has been sidelined over the years and that the public perception of it has changed, primarily driven because the media perception of it has changed. The attendances started to go down because of a number of things. I believe the initiation of the All-Stars was a major factor because commercialism began to take over a bit. The All-Stars were picked by the media, who were running the show by picking them.

You are not picked to play on the All-Stars. You are only picked in a particular position because the media take a liking to you or because your county were lucky enough to get into the All-Ireland semi-finals or final. If they had them picked from Railway Cup teams they would play, and it would give them an incentive to play Railway Cup. How many players are selected nowadays and don't turn up?

Mick Mackey drifted as an official Limerick senior hurling selector in the mid-1960s. However, Jim Hogan can recall him being on the sideline on the famous day in 1966 when Limerick were robbed of victory against Cork after a disallowed goal:

Mackey was there in 1966 in some capacity. When the goal was disallowed Mackey was definitely involved with the team and would have killed the referee. The ball was in the back of the net when the referee blew the whistle. We were getting consistent for a couple of years before that and I thought it was a good Cork team but they got a lucky goal. Gerry Sullivan took a 70 and I can still see it hitting the highest part of the post, dropping down into the square and Charlie McCarthy flicking it in. That was the goal that beat us. In later years, Mackey could call into the dressing room sometimes depending on where the match was. I have a feeling or a memory that he got lackadaisical about attending games in later years and wasn't even going to all the championship matches.

There was very little change in some positions on the Limerick senior team over a few years when Mackey was involved. I always felt it was harder to get off the Limerick team than on it. I often played very bad matches but there was never a question of me being dropped. It was the same for players who were going off, or players who were going through a bad spell in the League; they were still picked. Andy Dunworth didn't want to play in goals. Mike Tuohy of Patrickswell played a few games and he was a gas man.

There's a good story told about him playing for Patrickswell in a tournament match. In those days there was more interest in tournament games than championship games because there used to be gold watches etc., things we couldn't normally buy. Patrickswell and Mungret were playing in the final, a local derby. There was a full-forward from Mungret called Foley, and Mike was reputed to be afraid of his life of this guy. Foley's mother was sick and was moved to the hospital before the match. Mike heard it, and was rubbing his hands delighted that Foley wasn't going to be there. However, the first man out onto the field was Foley. Mike went to commiscrate with him about his mother being sick, and Foley said, 'If you don't go back into the goals fast, you will be in the bed beside her!' Tuohy was a good keeper, though. Seán Sparling from Adare was a great goalie as well. I played with Claughaun to beat my native Adare in 1969. I was fairly popular that day, I can tell you! I can still hear them out in the embankment roaring at me.

But basically regardless of the competition for my position, I was Jim Hogan, I had been there since 1958 and I couldn't see myself being dropped. There was chopping and changing of certain players in the 1960s, but there was a core of seven or eight safe players who remained. Certain players were safe. Complacency could set in while others were chopped and changed and got no proper chance. Mackey would have been a selector through all that.

Training methods were unquestionably haphazard, but were the mentors who came from an earlier era, such as Mackey, to blame? In 1967 he was no longer a selector and in a radio interview questioned the dedication of the Limerick senior players prior to that year's championship defeat to Clare:

I don't think the youngsters of today have the same interest as we had anyhow. I believe that a number of players from the Limerick team weren't available for training for the Clare match and on three or four nights I believe that only four or five players turned up. (Mick Mackey interviewed by Liam Campbell, RTÉ Radio, 1967)

Limerick had made strides in the minor championship, winning Munster titles in 1963 and '65 on the back of the great Limerick CBS Harty Cup teams. Glenroe native Fr Gerard McNamee was centrally involved in those years. The 1963 team contained men such as Éamonn Cregan, Tony Roche, Bernie Savage, Pat Heffernan and Mickey Graham, all well known in Limerick GAA circles. Éamon Grimes was involved in 1963 and again in '65, joined by Con

The Limerick minor hurling team that won the Munster championship in 1965 and went on to reach the All-Ireland final where they were beaten by Dublin. *Back row (l–r)*: Jimmy Millea (Kilmallock), Éamon Grimes (South Liberties), John Hehir (Dromcollogher/Broadford), Richard O'Connor (St Patrick's), Pat Doherty (St Patrick's), Con Shanahan (Croom), Mattie Grace (Old Christians), Denis Foley (Monaleen), Mike Hennessy (Na Piarsaigh), Bertie Murnane (Caherline), Donal Manning (Old Christians), Edmond Cole O'Kelly (Dromcollogher/Broadford), Peter Fitzgerald (Rathkeale). *Front row (l–r)*: Jimmy Moynihan (Dromin/Athlacca), Michael Keogh (Old Christians), Tony Brennan (Caherline), John Reale (Hospital/ Herbertstown), Ned Boland (Caherline), Mike Flaherty (Kilmallock), Nicholas Hayes (Staker Wallace), Seán Bourke (Garryspillane), Jimmy O'Keeffe (Kilmallock), Séamus Twomey (Dromcollogher/Broadford), Tony Cronin (Mungret), Fr Gerard McNamee (Glenroe).

Shanahan, Bertie Murnane, Mike Flaherty and Nicholas Hayes, along with the noted goal-poacher Seán Bourke, who was highly regarded.

However, the county remained dogged by politics. The skulduggery experienced in the 1950s by John Mulcahy regarding his Railway Cup winners medal didn't stop in the 1960s. Mickey Fitzgibbon had a very able comrade in Seán Cunningham of Doon, as a 1965 minor player explains:

I was togged out and on the panel for all the matches played by the Limerick minors in 1965 and made at least one if not two championship appearances. I didn't receive my Munster championship medal or the All-Ireland runners up medal. I was led to believe that my medal was given to someone who wasn't on the panel at all. In those days there was no medal presentation for our minor team and we didn't hear anything about the medals. Ned Boland and Tony Brennan from Caherline were also on the panel and got their medals through pure fluke. Ned's father met Seán Cunningham by chance one day, enquired about the medals and got them there and then. If he hadn't bumped into Cunningham, they might never have seen their medals either.

I would have no time for Cunningham. He belonged to the old-style GAA dictatorship system. On the night of the 1965 All-Ireland minor final, the Caherconlish lads happened to be in the same car as Seán Cunningham coming from Dublin and wanted to go to the dance in Dromkeen that night. Dromkeen is only a couple of miles from Caherconlish, and the car would have been passing Dromkeen anyway. Cunningham refused to let the driver drop them off, declaring, 'They were collected in Caherconlish village, and will be returned to Caherconlish and nowhere else.'

Both this and the John Mulcahy story should have been highlighted in the media and brought into the public domain as examples of how not to do business. However, to this day there are people in Limerick hurling who tend to be very critical of such revelations coming out into the open. They argue strongly that certain things are tolerable and should remain in the closet. They will always nod the head silently towards the establishment regardless of the severity of any stroke that has been pulled. It happened in the 1960s but Ireland was a different place then, when many undesirable aspects of society were simply swept under the carpet. There is no excuse for strokes being pulled in the modern era. Society in general has moved on but in many ways the GAA has failed to do so, primarily because county board delegates are the product of a former era.

Sweetening delegates with the promise of All-Ireland tickets is believed to be commonplace in Limerick as a way to influence votes and ensure the inner circle retain a strong backing from the floor at county board meetings. It is no coincidence that many of those who voted to save Justin McCarthy as Limerick manager in March 2010 were seated in Croke Park the following September. Justin McCarthy was entitled to any support based on rational discussion and decisions from clubs, but many delegates voted against mandate that night. Limerick GAA is in serious trouble when puppet strings control so many delegates. A staunch Limerick GAA supporter offers the following perspective:

A deceased relative of mine was a delegate to the county board and would have attended on occasions possibly from the early 1940s right up to the 1970s. He often spoke of how delegates at that time went to meetings primed to speak with pre-prepared written speeches from their clubs who were made to suffer in terms of suspensions and fixtures. Even then, prior to mobile phones, the county board had ways and means of finding out these things and always managed to sweeten the delegates. It's a cultural thing, a custom or a tradition if you like, and continues to be very successful for the board.

There was one occasion in the late 1970s when a well-known individual nominated for a position on the county board gave a present of a bottle of whiskey to all delegates prior to the convention. He knew the establishment didn't want him elected and the whiskey gesture was seen as a two-fingered salute to them. There was a rumpus at the convention and the election was postponed, but the whiskey won out in the end when he was eventually elected. Mackey was asked his views on the whiskey episode at the time and said that back in his youth it would have been bottles of poteen rather than whiskey that secured votes!

Our problem in Limerick is the same as it was back in the Mackey era. We will never be in a position to elect the best officers because the schemers and the stroke merchants within the boot room know the internal workings of the county and are experts at procuring votes. Even now all you have to do is examine the idle sub-committees within the county board. Every member on those committees is there for a reason. They are being rewarded with a bit of power for their loyalty to the establishment and will continue to be seen as safe votes. My relative always said that Mick Mackey would not have been associated with the internal workings of the board and the skulduggery that existed. Mackey often viewed his Munster Council delegate position as being somewhat external from the workings of Limerick County Board. However, he felt that Mackey probably distanced himself too much from the goings on and felt that with his profile, he would have had the credibility to expose and fight against things for the good of Limerick GAA. He reckoned that Mackey was guilty of turning a blind eye, which would have been typical of society at the time. Mackey had a profile that would have been similar or greater than the parish priest, the doctor or the guard. If he chose to shout from the rooftops, people would have listened.

My relative often spoke of manoeuvres that took place between members of the farming community where selection on underage teams was concerned. One farmer's son was selected on a county minor team because he paid over the odds for a farm animal. Another promising player was in contention for a place but wasn't selected because his father refused to agree a deal on a purchase. A neighbour of my relative was being taken to a Limerick match one Sunday in the same car as some other players. The car was low in petrol and the driver took a wrong turn claiming that he was taking a shortcut to a petrol station. The car ran out of petrol in the middle of nowhere and the players were stranded. The driver admitted years afterwards that a stunt had been pulled to prevent the players from playing in the game to facilitate other fringe players. Those incidents were commonplace around that time. That winter, Mick Mackey was challenged about the incident at a club function he attended as a guest. It seems that Mackey laughed it off, and suggested that it was nonsense to believe such stories. But that was a true story and Mick Mackey's reaction was not liked.

Another source tells of more strange happenings:

My late uncle told me a story of a child being born to an elderly farming couple. It was secretly known that the true father of the child was a farmhand who had worked on the farm in his youth. Over time, the farmhand moved up in the world, eventually married, had a family and was involved as a selector with a Limerick minor team, possibly in the 1940s. His illegitimate son wasn't showing much hurling promise and struggled to make his local club team, but made the Limerick team. It was said locally that he was chasing his biological father's wealth but agreed to back off in return for being selected by Limerick. He got his place for the full game and a Limerick team carrying a blatant passenger were narrowly beaten in the championship. That was to the detriment of Limerick hurling and needless to say the biological father hadn't seen the end of his son and the whole truth came out in the wash a couple of years later.

We have had a tradition of poor chairmen in Limerick. Prior to his death my uncle always claimed that Donal Fitzgibbon was the best chairman Limerick ever had. He felt he was radical, had vision and any questionable decisions were ultimately backed up with the arrival of four All-Ireland titles to Limerick during his tenure. But my uncle always felt there was a political undercurrent working against Fitzgibbon for the duration of his term. He never understood the logic behind Pat Fitzgerald being voted in as chairman, and felt Fitzgerald undid five years of Trojan work by Fitzgibbon within the space of twelve months. He didn't live long enough to witness

Fitzgerald's appointment as Munster Council CEO, but it would have greatly disappointed him. He was a real old-timer and a supporter of the ban, and always believed that Mick Mackey should have been suspended for attending rugby games rather than, in his own words, being 'anointed' as a vigilante.

He told another story relating to a south Limerick club who played an illegal player in a final. It wasn't any secret and the beaten team objected, and it was only a matter of form that they would be awarded the match and the winners thrown out of the competition. However, late one night word circulated in the pubs that a prominent GAA official was in female company. His car was parked at a remote location on a hill not far from the village and two well-known GAA men went to investigate. They found the car, and certain activities were taking place. One of the men knocked on the window, saying nothing except, 'I take it that the problem with the illegal player is now resolved!' The winning team advanced, and until the truth came out even officers of the board in question couldn't understand how they escaped censure. There are a number of people still alive who can verify that story.

My uncle often claimed that the reason so many people hated Ahane was because opposition teams spent their time trying to timber Mick Mackey instead of minding their own patch. He said the constant targeting of Mackey would rile Ahane and brought an arrogant streak out in them when they scored. That in turn led to frustration boiling over and players from the other clubs, especially Croom, fought among themselves on the field while the games were going on, leaving Ahane players free to score goals. He felt the Ahane players were very down to earth if unprovoked but that humans are bred to react to situations and they only did what came naturally to them.

Current underage board officer Pat O'Dwyer can identify with some of the above, having been a victim in his own playing career:

I played at centre-back against Clare in a challenge game for the Limerick minors in 1968. After the game Tom Boland, the then secretary of the county board, came in and congratulated me on my performance, saying it was the best he ever saw from a minor. Mick Mackey was with him, and he nodded his head in approval and said, 'If you look after yourself, you will play senior hurling for Limerick.' I suppose, looking back, Mackey was a polite individual and wasn't ever going to say anything different. A couple of weeks later I broke my fingers and missed out on the championship game against Cork.

A couple of years later I was contacted about an under-21 challenge game against Galway on a Sunday night. I am still waiting at Carroll's corner in Bruff village to be picked up by a local selector! When he pulled his car onto the main road in Bruff he must have got a temporary loss of direction, and instead of turning left for the village he turned right for Limerick. Limerick only had fifteen players that night and I am led to believe he took a player who wasn't on the panel instead of me, thereby ensuring he would get a full game. I often wondered since what Mick Mackey and Tom Boland might have thought of that. That finished me as a player. I became interested in late-night dancing, and fell out of favour with the local curate who was in charge of the local team at the time.

I would never claim to have made it as a Limerick hurler but I can identify with the many genuine hurlers who were blackguarded like that. The individuals suffered and the county suffered because young players were turned off at a young age and never got to realise their true potential. There were several years when the Limerick senior team had better players sitting outside in the stand than they had on the field. They refused to join the panel as adult players because of the parish pump politics at minor level years earlier. The saddest thing is not that it happened back then because, to be fair, it was a different Ireland and those things were commonplace. The saddest thing of all is that nothing has changed to this very day.

There was controversy for Ahane in 1968 when the club was suspended for twelve months. Willie Keane explains the background:

We played Croom in the county junior football final of 1967 which was played in early 1968. Timmy Woulfe was the referee. A good few players were sent off that day, wrongly in our opinion. He put off players who had never given away a free in their lives, let alone been sent off. At the time we felt we were being victimised, and probably were too. The game wasn't that bad at all. There was nothing between the teams in general play but the referee's interpretation of it was wrong. I remember going into the Croom dressing room to wish them well and congratulate them, etc. and I said that we didn't have any axe to grid with the players. I said the only comment I had to make was that the standard of refereeing was appalling.

There was never as long a referee's report. There was still jealousy and hatred hanging over Ahane from the old days. Timmy's take on that game was that Ahane were a hurling club and knew nothing about football, and as a pure-bred west Limerick football man he was going to lay down the law. We would have pleaded for leniency in the boardroom. You weren't supposed to question referees at the time, and that still seems to hold good to this day. He was the schoolmaster and we weren't to tell him what to do. He was known as a set dancer and I think I told him after the match that he should stick to the set dancing. Donal Brennan was the paperwork man for Ahane and the county board delegate at the time. Mackey was a member of the county board as a Munster Council delegate but it's hard to know if he involved himself in the case. He would probably have had to step aside anyway because of being from the same club.

John Ryan was around:

I don't think Mick Mackey was even at that match. I hit a Croom supporter a belt of a fist the same day. Seán Leonard was playing full-forward, and there was a Croom supporter standing at the corner of the post. He was getting onto Leonard and went in and had a few swipes at him. Then he said to Leonard, 'Hang on one second, I will take off my coat and have a right go at you.' When he took off his coat I stepped in and hit him a belt of a fist which knocked him to the ground. There was fierce fighting going on all over the field. Mick Doyle from Annacotty stayed on the field watching with his hands behind his back. Even though he was playing, he didn't involve himself at all. Next thing someone came up from behind and hit him, breaking his jaw.

P. J. Keane vehemently denies any malice on his part:

The suspension on the club was unfair. The rumour circulated that Timmy Woulfe was in Foynes at one of our earlier games and wasn't impressed. Apparently he saw us playing and said he would sort us out if he ever got the chance. The match wasn't dirty. We were hurlers playing football as opposed to being natural footballers like Kerry. We went out without hurleys and we shouldered. If he deemed it a free it was a free even if there was no foul committed. In the second half we were beginning to establish control a bit at centre field. All I know is that I caught one ball, there was a player on my back and I shrugged him off. I didn't hit anybody but I was sent off. There was a big row about that. I asked the referee what I did wrong. It took a long time for the match to restart. I eventually went off the field protesting that I didn't do anything.

That upped the ante a bit and the next thing there were two more fellows put off. The crowd were getting incensed and the next thing there were two more sent off, and then there was no interest in the match any more, it was just all aggro. All the Ahane supporters in the ground went out onto the field, and everyone on the sideline went on the field with them. In his report the referee mentioned that I went back onto the field after being sent off but I didn't, I was only wandering around the field when the crowd were there the same as everybody else. He wrote a terrible report, and one which wasn't accurate. I was working in Galway and tried to get a hearing but the county board didn't facilitate me. They simply held this meeting and declared that not only were the team suspended but that the whole club was suspended. That was unprecedented and I have never heard of anything like it before or since. We played the match in the spring of 1968 and every team from juvenile up to senior was suspended. I am not familiar with the mechanisms and wasn't privy to them. All I was was a product at the end of a line, a player in his prime who wanted to hurl and play the game he loved. I tried to reason with the county board but there was no going back. I often felt in modern times that if I had the money I would have gone to court and got an injunction. That wasn't the done thing in those days so I was excluded from all games that year. I spoke to Mickey Fitzgibbon and to Jackie Connell particularly and said to them that what was happening wasn't right.

Whether they wanted to make an example of Ahane or whatever it was I don't know, I didn't know the inner workings of it. But I was very sore over that entire situation for a long time. The following year I wasn't even going to play with Ahane and Rory Kiely came to my father two or three times to ask him to persuade me to come back. Then when the weather got fine my appetite came back, I wanted to hurl and I was picked in a challenge game against Cork in Kilmallock and played well. We were going down to play Tipperary in Cork but I wouldn't travel with them any more, there were too many distractions travelling on the day of the match. I travelled on my own to Cork the night before and stayed in the army barracks. I looked after my diet, got up the following morning, went for a walk, and then hurled in the alley for an hour. I visited Seán Warren, an army lad who was dying of cancer. I was relaxed. I went out then and played one of my best matches ever for Limerick but it was a personal thing because I was so sore over what happened with Ahane. I don't know if Mick Mackey did anything to intervene in the suspension of his beloved Ahane. I wouldn't know because I was away from home.

The referee's report, which was printed in the Limerick Leader *on Saturday 20 April 1968, was particularly critical of Ahane. However, it seems an extraordinary thing to suspend an entire club for a year and suggests that Ahane were being put in their box for once and for all by the establishment. The opposition on the day were Croom, and perhaps there were political elements within the county board who retained a deeply held jealousy and hatred for Ahane. The role of Mick Mackey is unclear, and numerous attempts to uncover his views on the entire affair have proven futile. The superb performance of P.J. Keane against Tipperary in 1969 was noted in the* Irish Independent, *but after a year out of hurling he found it tough to get back to full fitness. He drifted from the scene again until a recall in 1970:*

I had been working in Boyle and Rory Kiely rang me to go to Thurles to play the League semi-final against Offaly. They were down by seven points at half time and they put me on. Eventually we won it. They kind of semi-credited me with it but I really only had half an hour in me. The problem was they were playing Cork in the final the following fortnight. In hindsight, I should have said I wasn't fit enough for that level of hurling at that time. They started me and I was on Gerald McCarthy and was OK for the first fifteen minutes. I got a bad dunt from John Horgan when I should have got a free, but the ref gave him a free out instead because I retaliated.

It really finished me because I wasn't fit enough. I went down to Limerick for training one night and didn't get home to Boyle till 2 a.m. It wasn't practical. I would have been better off training on my own. The distance was enormous and you can't do it, it's counter-productive. I had a lot of distractions in my personal life at the time such as moving house, a new baby, etc. and it's hard to hurl at your best with those distractions.

By 1971 Mackey was a dignitary at the Limerick championship and along with a couple of other golden era players he visited the Limerick dressing room at half time in the 1971 Munster final. Jim Hogan was there:

I have a vague recollection of the old-timers coming into the dressing room but can't remember exactly who spoke and what they said. I remember changing my jersey at half time because it was an awful day of wind and rain, but it was a very high-scoring game.

Even back then we had spare jerseys; Tommy Casey the taxi driver was in charge of them and there was always a second suitcase. Tommy idolised Mackey. In later years, I used to visit Tommy in a nursing home in Corbally. He used to talk about Mackey out there, and the nurses told me that sometimes he'd think one of his visitors was Mackey with the McCarthy Cup. He used to taxi Mackey to the Railway Cup games and the Munster Council meetings. Mackey never drove to matches, he was always driven to them.

Joe McGrath is generally recognised as the first of the modern trainers in Limerick hurling, and having played under both Mick Mackey and McGrath when they were trainers, P. J. Keane and Jim Hogan are well qualified to assess the merits of the old school style versus the modern techniques. Keane was impressed by McGrath:

Joe McGrath was a fantastic man manager, and I think that was his downfall, because he was demanding things. He would talk to you about it and what he expected from you. He did it to me and he did it to everyone. Mackey wouldn't have had the same man management approach. He wasn't that sort of communicator, wasn't the type that would have a plan or vision to address us as a group or individuals and work towards that. Many people from his era were out-and-out hurlers and were good at what they did. There's a difference between being an out-and-out hurler and someone with managerial tendencies who can get the best out of people, especially if they come from different backgrounds. You need a man manager who can see potential and knows what he wants from each position and knows how to knit it all together. From a hurling perspective they would have recognised that, but we were short of quality players. You need about eighteen quality players like Kilkenny that can hold their worth with anyone, but we might have had only eight of those players for a lot of my career.

If Joe McGrath was in charge of Limerick in 1973, I would have been on the panel because he would have talked to me and stopped me transferring to Roscommon. I wanted to hurl and he knew that, and I was playing better hurling in 1972 and '73 than I was in 1969 and '70. A new crowd came in, Dick Stokes and Jackie Power, but they

Mick Mackey pictured with Cardinal Cushing in New York in 1970. Also included are Pádraig S. Ó Riain (*third from left*) of Galbally and Paddy Downey, GAA correspondent of *The Irish Times* (*fourth from left*).

were from the same era as Mackey and would have been of a similar mindset. They didn't know me and wouldn't have known my make-up, if I drank or not, if I was intense or not. I don't believe any of the Limerick officials would have known the make-up of the players, what they were working at, whether they were happy or not, and if that was impinging on their training.

Limerick won the All-Ireland in 1973 under the watchful eye of Mick Mackey, who regularly attended training and games. In later years he spoke of his joy at watching the players of '73 emulate his contemporaries by winning the McCarthy Cup. Mackey felt that people needed new success rather than harping back to the old days. As Jim Hogan explains, however, the all-pervasive politics were also rife in 1973:

Joe McGrath has to take an awful lot of credit for winning that All-Ireland title. A lot of the groundwork had been done prior to 1973 and the winning team was laid out for Mickey Cregan. Dick Stokes and Jackie Power came onto the bandwagon for two years when they recognised that there was the makings of a good Limerick team and that was it. Limerick should have won the All-Ireland in '74 as well but they threw it up in the air. The players were out every night celebrating with the cup. At the end of the day it was thirty-three years since Limerick had won an All-Ireland but you have to shout stop at some stage.

As it happened, I eventually retired because of what they did to Joe McGrath. I had a chip on my shoulder as I had lost my place for the All-Ireland final because of the strike in early 1973 [players' strike following Joe McGrath's dismissal as trainer] and Bernie Hartigan was taken off in that game because of his role in the strike. In the League final of 1974, Séamus Horgan was injured with a broken finger but they played him rather than start me. Imagine playing an injured goalkeeper in a national final! Cork beat them out the gate and Ray Cummins scored a few goals. I was sitting beside Phil Bennis on the bench and he was saying we were only wasting our time. Bernie Hartigan only went on as a sub and immediately scored a point from a sideline from about 80 yards out. We were beaten at that stage, and I decided there and then I was retiring. You live to play in an All-Ireland final, and having played in the semi-final the previous year I felt I had a 50:50 chance, but I wasn't picked.

Joe McGrath gave 100 per cent for three years and brought unbelievable spirit back to the team. Politics crept in and they are still there and it's sad. Joe McGrath came to us in 1969 and we got to the League final in 1970 from nowhere, although we got lost in Dublin trying to get to the game and couldn't find Croke Park. In 1971 we won the League and the Oireachtas and were unlucky to be beaten in the Munster final. In 1972 we were beaten in Ennis, and Joe McGrath had nothing to do with the selection of the team but we knew afterwards that they would blame McGrath for losing that match. A lot of people believe that the wrong team was deliberately picked to lose the game and get McGrath out.

We didn't do well prior to McGrath's arrival because training was a joke. There's no point in comparing to nowadays but we would get together a week before the game. Training consisted of three or four rounds of the field and a few sprints across the field and that was it. I was actually giving up hurling completely in 1969 until Joe McGrath came on board. He changed everything; we got sliotars and used to go up to the Shannon Arms and would get some kind of a meal after training. We started to bond then, and the players from different clubs such as South Liberties, Claughaun and Patrickswell were all one unit for Limerick. Previously club rivalries came into it and players would cut each other's heads in club matches. South Liberties and Claughaun used to have murder, and Patrickswell and Claughaun was the same. I will admit that Joe McGrath knew nothing about hurling but he knew how to get players fit and he knew how to manage players. Joe got players to tick but the attitude of the newly appointed Limerick selectors from the Mackey era would have been, 'He's from County Down, what would he know about hurling?' That's basically what happened.

P. J. Keane believes too much credit was taken for the success:

I think Limerick didn't realise the significance of Kilkenny being as weak in 1973 as they were, and should have reasserted themselves to beat the full Kilkenny team the following year. And we haven't won anything since, and we won't until we get cohesion and a structure and the right guy to train them properly. I am strongly of the opinion that the introduction of the school buses has been detrimental to hurling in Limerick. Previously you cycled to school at Limerick CBS, and cycled out to Old Christians for hurling. The school buses came in then and the children had to be ready to get on the bus, because they had no other way home. People weren't going to continue cycling when they had the option of using the bus. As well as missing training, children were no longer improving their fitness through cycling.

Many Limerick people born since 1973 have gone to their graves prematurely without ever seeing the county raise the McCarthy Cup. In the aforementioned 1967 radio interview, Mick Mackey was asked what his wish for the future was. 'To see Limerick win an All-Ireland,' he said. After his wish was finally granted in 1973 he was rarely seen in a Limerick dressing room. He had won All-Irelands, had trained Limerick to win a Munster championship in 1955, and now finally saw Limerick win as a spectator. It hasn't been seen since, and how the county yearns.

ELEVEN

LIFE AFTER HURLING

*M*ick *Mackey earned his crust with the ESB at the power station at Ardnacrusha. Work colleague Johnny Wall spent a lot of time in his company:*

Mackey was a character, and a much-liked character at that. The people loved him, and would have had him for breakfast, dinner and supper if they could. He was also a quiet, withdrawn individual. Perhaps the reason for his quietness was that everyone would want to be talking to Mick Mackey, because he was such a legend and people loved him. Maybe he would have been worn out from talking to everyone, and perhaps he kept to himself because of that. In modern times he would have a pub or something like that to capitalise on his fame, but he never did anything like that. Instead of going into town and making a fortune out of a pub he settled for the quiet life, played a bit of golf and cards and that was it. There's probably more money to be made out of the limelight now, but maybe there wasn't as much to be made out of it that time. He wouldn't ever go to the canteen at work, preferring to keep private, and he always went home for his lunch. He lived in an ESB staff house near the station, which he eventually bought out because the ESB were selling them off. His nickname was 'Feck'. They always called him that at work because he had a saying, 'Ah feck it.' He was a tremendous family man and played cards two or three times a week with Kitty. He was always great to support the local GAA clubs in Clare and he would join any time that there were raffles or any other fundraisers.

Fr Liam Kelly agrees that he was a reserved character:

Mick was a shy enough individual in a lot of ways. When he was with the hurling people of the past he would let his hair down a bit, but in a work environment he would have been very shy and reserved.

He didn't mix in the parish in Clare much at all. He went home to Castleconnell for Mass on a Sunday morning, went out home to meet the family.

Johnny Wall outlines Mackey's responsibilities within the ESB:

He was the senior driver in the transport department of the ESB generating station in Ardnacrusha. The function of the transport department was to make deliveries and collections and transport men to different locations further up the River Shannon to carry out maintenance work. There were about six people working in the transport department and his day-to-day job was to organise the work for them. That time there were a lot of 5-megawatt peat stations in Ireland, including ones in Caherciveen, County Kerry and one in Screeb, County Galway. They were loss-making stations but would be giving employment to the local areas. One unit of power would cost a pound to generate, and we were selling it for thirty pence. But it was creating employment, the farmers were cutting turf and selling it, the ESB were burning it and there were manual labourers employed putting it into furnaces, etc.

You could be sent to one of those plants or to the central ESB stores in Dublin on any given day. Mackey would do a run himself to Dublin, he might have to collect a load of transformers and bring them back to Ardnacrusha or take them elsewhere. He drove on the road four days out of five in any given week, even though he was the senior man. There would have been overnight stays, because he would have gone to places such as the hydro station in Ballyshannon in Donegal.

We used to look after the waterways along the River Shannon from Ardnacrusha up as far as Portumna, and from Portumna on up to Drumshanbo. There are a series of pumps along the bank of the river in Portumna to keep the water off the fields because it's very wet land. There would have been about three miles of pumps up around Meelick/Eyrecourt that needed to be checked about twice a month. Mackey would take me and another guy, but would wait in the vehicle and wouldn't do any manual work. Part of his duty was completing worksheets in the office to account for the work that was done.

In the time I was working with him, he didn't go to too many matches. The nature of the job meant that he was on call and he might get three or four callouts at the weekend. If a problem arose at the station, an electrician or a fitter might need to be collected. Mick would have to collect him and bring him in and take him home again. At that time the ESB wouldn't pay travelling expenses to the men to drive in and out of their own accord when there was a callout. Most of the staff would have been relatively local, from Ardnacrusha and O'Briensbridge, etc. with the furthest away men no further than Killaloe or Newport. The boys wouldn't answer a phone call from the ESB either because the ESB wouldn't pay their home phone bill. So in the event of a callout, Mackey would have to drive to their house, knock on the door and tell them they were needed. When they were on call they needed to be available if the knock came on the door from Mick. In any event Mick knew where to find them if they weren't at home. I took over the same job from Mick a few years after he retired and the same system was still in operation. However, after about five years the system changed. They got money for the phones, and travelling expenses, and that finished the old system of needing to collect people for callouts. That's why Mick would have been tied to home at weekends, because work commitments restricted him going to matches.

He was a very good man at his job, very fair to work under and very helpful. From a work perspective if there was reason to advise you over something, he would always advise you in the right way. He worked a lot of long days, leaving home at 6 a.m. and not returning until 7 p.m. or 8 p.m. If he had to go to Dublin, it meant going through all the towns, because there were no motorways that time but the traffic wasn't as bad. The head office was the heart of Dublin though, Fitzwilliam Street. At that time all the DIY stuff came from Dublin, but now it's sourced locally. On a typical trip to Dublin, he might have had to collect anything from office stationery to transformers related to the running of the station.

My first encounter with him was one Friday morning soon after I started working with the ESB. Every Friday, Mick had to go into Limerick to the bank to collect the suitcase of money to pay wages to the staff in the plant. I was sent with him one Friday, along with the local guard from Ardnacrusha. He had to go in and a suitcase would be handed to him. That was before the days of Securicor, and I would have to stand at one side of him. The guard would stand at the other side, and we walked out into the vehicle, drove to Ardnacrusha again and handed it over to the office staff to make out the wages. Looking back on it, it was high risk, and Mackey could have been in danger of being ambushed. They did away with the cash-based payroll after that.

He was a lovely man and I became very friendly with him. At the same time, he was a very quiet man, and wouldn't initiate much conversation. He would ask you the odd few things but in general he wouldn't make a lot of chat. One day, we were in Portumna and went into a pub/restaurant called Curleys to eat. It was there that I really got to know him. From then on, our times chatting would have been when we were on the road on long journeys. He would talk a lot about hurling and spoke a lot about the 1973 team; he went on the train with them to Dublin for the final. One thing he always said was that if you were playing corner-back or wing-back that you must be out in front and have a good first touch. He often advised me before games. One night we were playing a local seven-a-side tournament and Mackey pulled me to one side before the game. He gave me a good slagging because he knew I didn't talk to the man I was marking because we had been sent off together a few times. Mackey more or less told me that he was expecting a right good old-style clash that night!

Seán Duggan also knew Mackey through work:

I worked with the ESB and Mackey would come to Galway on work-related business so I would meet him occasionally. He was a good conversationalist, and was a good ambassador for the game off the field as well as on it. If he was in Galway he would go to club matches while he was here and we would discuss the matches from times gone by. It didn't worry me if the opposition had several Mick Mackeys because I still had my own job to do. We would have approached Limerick as a team, each man had his own man to look after, and it was up to him to hold him for the hour. I can say from my experience of fourteen years as a hurling goalie that I never came across anyone who came into the goalmouth to do me, most especially Mick Mackey. It was an honest effort on the part of the forwards, and stories to the contrary are greatly exaggerated.

John Ryan recalls him playing inter-firm hurling:

The last time I saw Mick Mackey hurling was in Highfield, off the Ennis Road, where the houses are built now. They often played inter-firm games there. Someone I knew was playing with the ESB and he asked me would I go with him. When I got there, Mick was playing in goals. He had boots and the socks, and a normal trousers and a jersey. It was the last time I saw him standing on a field with a team. It was one of his last games of hurling and he had completed the circle and was back in goals, where many great outfield players eventually finish up.

Johnny Wall participated in Mick Mackey's final game in 1971:

I played with him in his final game. He stood into an inter-firm game because we were stuck for players. He was almost sixty at the time, and the game was played down in the old field in Blackwater. There was a tournament between the married men and the single men within the ESB. The married team were short a couple of players and Mackey stood in at corner-forward. Whenever the ball came near him he hit it immediately and he was well able to hit it, especially along the ground. The old magic was still in the wrists. He only played for twenty or twenty-five minutes and he had enough of it. I was sorry afterwards that there weren't photographs taken.

That time they had their own fire station at the plant in Ardnacrusha. Mackey was in charge of it. They only had one fire engine and the hoses weren't in great condition. We all had to do a fire drill every so often, bring out the hoses and have a dummy fire. Nothing big ever happened in Ardnacrusha, but Todds in Limerick city took fire one day and every fire brigade they could get their hands on was called in to assist. They said afterwards that Ardnacrusha fire brigade played a major role in quenching the fire. The major role was that when they connected the hose to the hydrant it was all holes and the water sprayed everywhere and helped to keep back the crowd! Mackey got huge mileage out of that one afterwards.

He finished up working with us early after getting a stroke. I remember well the day he got it. His son Mike came down to us in the ESB to give them a hand, because he refused to get into the ambulance. We went up to give a hand and one of the men was a guy of 16 or 17 stone called Jim Seymour. It took six of us to put him into the ambulance because he was such a strong man and offered such resistance. Mackey had the biggest hands I ever saw on any man. My own hands are a decent size but it would take two of my hands to fill one of his.

In later years he also spent time with Jimmy Smyth:

I travelled with Mackey a lot and spent a lot of time in a car with him, but we never spoke much about hurling. We spoke about other things that interested him and interested me. We could be talking about politics, his homeplace, my homeplace, we would be talking about cars, which I was very interested in. We spoke hurling when it was necessary but not in general. We would not have been talking about the previous year's All-Ireland for instance. Not talking about hurling would have been my way as much as his. I'd say if there was someone who was more willing to talk about hurling he might have engaged in such conversation. He might have been known as a gallery man off the pitch but he was a withdrawn person when I knew him. Perhaps Mackey was also a quiet man off the field in his playing days, and as far as I know he was. It was only on the pitch that he was a showman. He played a lot of cards and was a great man to mix with the ordinary people.

Funnily enough, I never heard him talking about Ring. He never once mentioned his name in my company. There was only one day he referred to Ring, and didn't even mention his name, and that was in a dressing room. Ring was a very tidy man and would have his togs folded, his boots prepared and would test them out three or four times. He was also very meticulous about his socks. Mackey said something like, 'He is very meticulous, isn't he, like a butt of a pony.' Mackey would always stand behind a player on the field and would have been sizing up a man regarding his weight and his body and his strength, etc. Mackey didn't talk about any hurler to me, so it was not unusual that he wouldn't mention Ring.

Mackey had his own views on Christy Ring:

Ring wasn't a centre-forward, he was only a wing man. He didn't make much of a hand of the centre-forward position the few times that he played there. I think he played in 1947 on Peter Prendergast and he hadn't a very good game, if I remember. But he was a dangerous wing man. He wanted to be on the wing, he wanted the room to turn and come inside and all that. (Mick Mackey interviewd by Val Dorgan, RTÉ Television, 1969)

He discussed his own hurling heroes with Johnny Wall:

I often asked him about the great hurlers that he played against. He never expressed anything about having a grudge against any player. He mentioned Jim Langton, Lory Meagher, Batt Thornhill, Jack Lynch, Tull Considine and Tommy Doyle as being the best. He spoke a lot about Jack Lynch. He thought Jack was the bees knees and always maintained that Lynch was a classy hurler. Jack used to visit him at the house and Micheál O'Hehir used to visit him as well.

Séamus Power attended many meetings with Mackey:

I would have got on very well with Mackey. We used to hold our Munster Council meetings mainly in Limerick until they changed it to Tipperary Town because they realised it was more equidistant to all six counties. We used to have the meetings in the Gaelic League hall in Thomas Street, a dilapidated place. You would be perished from the cold there in the wintertime. We would have a cup of tea or a meal. It would be nothing ornate or anything like that, and that's where Mackey and myself used to have a pint. You couldn't say that Mackey was vocal at meetings and he didn't really contribute to administrative issues because it wouldn't really bother him. Of course, if something pertained to a Limerick domestic issue he would be briefed but in that case they would have sent the county board secretary or expert into the meeting to state the case. If Limerick were fighting for a Munster final that would be a straightforward thing and he would be fighting for that.

Donie Nealon feels that Mackey was effective in putting Limerick's case:

He was good at fighting his corner for Limerick in the boardroom. A big development took place in Limerick in the 1950s and he would have been pushing to get the top games played there. He would have been influential in the development of the Gaelic Grounds, which was heavily financed by the Munster Council in the 1950s. You didn't have a lot of home and away fixtures at that time, of course. When Mick Mackey was on the Munster Council, especially in my playing days, the majority of Tipperary versus Cork Munster hurling championship clashes were played in Limerick. Mackey would have had a huge say in securing those lucrative games for the Gaelic Grounds.

In later years, I got to know him really well when I was on the Munster Council. On that council he didn't speak that often, but when he spoke people tended to listen. He was a long-term member there, and people appreciated what he had to say on different matters.

I was fortunate enough to be on Railway Cup teams and grateful to him that I was chosen a number of times when he was a selector.

We looked at him for quiet but sound advice on the day we were playing. He'd have a word in your ear and he was never negative or critical, always positive and helpful and would advise you about the person you were marking. He was a very nice person in that respect, and players had huge admiration for him. Players were conscious of his stature in the game a couple of decades earlier; we knew he came with a tremendous record in terms of achievement from his own playing days. He was so well known that he was almost a father figure – somebody to look up to when we looked in the dressing room.

My father and others would have seen him play throughout his career. Burgess is not far from Limerick, and obviously we were aware of the fame of Ahane who were on the border with Tipperary at Newport/Birdhill. Everyone was conscious of the threat of Mackey and if you couldn't hold Mackey, or at least contain him to some degree, your chances of winning were seriously diminished. Limerick were a powerful team at the time, but naturally you had to contain Mackey; he was the lynchpin of that forward line. I always felt that, given his closeness to the border, he had a soft spot for Tipperary if Limerick weren't playing. I remember we were getting off the bus for

Man of steel: Mick Mackey lives up to his reputation during this tug of war contest.

The Parteen panel that won the East Clare junior hurling championship in 1970 that included Greg Mackey. *Back row (l–r):* John McNamara (selector), Willie Dooley O'Brien (selector), Willie Sherlock, Tom Shinnors, Cyril Prenderville, John Wall, Greg Mackey, Johnny Prenderville, Johnny Hickey, Mike Flynn, Matt Larkin, Séamus 'Dagger' McMahon, Tom O'Connor (selector). *Front row (l–r):* Eoin Conway, Paddy Corkery, Brendan Ryan, Tom O'Connor Jnr (mascot), Kevin Spring, Pat O'Connor, Billy Ryan.

an All-Ireland final in Croke Park and over he came to wish us the best of luck and you knew he was genuine and being sincere.

It seems amazing that Mackey mellowed so much, and didn't appear to have any border anxiety in later years. The provocative gesture in the 1936 Munster final and the humiliating defeat to Newport in the church tournament of 1931 must have slipped from his memory. As for his offspring, it seems Mackey wasn't too keen on them following in his footsteps, as Johnny Wall recalls:

Mick was a great family man, but he never pushed his children into hurling. I don't think Mick wanted his children to hurl; the talk at the time was that he was wary of the dangers of the game following belts he got himself as a player. Consequently, Mick's sons never hurled much. I played with Greg, who was well able to hurl and was well regarded as a player. Greg played a bit with Parteen, but didn't seem to have a lot of interest in training. I was a long time in Parteen, and

Mick would come to watch Parteen hurling but I can't ever recall him bringing the lads to training.

Fr Liam Kelly offers a different perspective:

I often spoke to Mick about it, and it wasn't so much the belts he was in fear of, even though that was the perception out there at the time. What he would have said to me was that he didn't want his sons compared with him. He was very conscious of the potential talk, for instance comments such as, 'You weren't half the man your father was, etc.' He was very conscious of that. He left his children go their own way and find their own niche and they chose not to hurl. I often felt that Greg would have been the best of them as a hurler, while Pat was playing soccer. Greg was carefree in his approach to hurling initially but gained interest later. He was the complete opposite to his father, who was very focussed whether at work, playing or training a team. There was no messing when Mick was around; even when he was training us he didn't suffer fools gladly.

Greg Mackey offers his own perspective:

My father never took me to training or watched me playing. He never really discussed hurling with us much at home, except to give an odd laugh if one of us brought home a GAA-related story from the locality. Other than that, the GAA wasn't really discussed unless visitors came to the house. I was very involved in Ahane for a while in later years but I have drifted away from it now. My son Michael won an under-21 championship with Ahane in 1998 alongside well-known players such as Seánie O'Connor and John Meskell. I would have been involved with underage teams in Ahane around that time, and was also a county board delegate for the club. As a player I wouldn't have had the interest in training that I needed to have, and I was away from home a lot through work. That said, I won a county junior championship with Parteen. I also played illegally for Young Irelands in Limerick city at one stage when we won an underage championship. I played a bit of rugby too, and made the Shannon senior team, and even represented Munster for a while.

Mackey took his famed focus onto the pitch and putt course, as Gerry Piggott explains:

The Ahane under-21 panel that won the Limerick under-21 championship in 1998 and included Michael Mackey, son of Greg Mackey and grandson of Mick Mackey. *Back row (l–r):* Declan Fitzgerald, Seánie O'Connor, Billy O'Keeffe, Tadhg Clifford, William Hayes, Brian Meskell, Alan Doherty, John O'Connell, Conor Cremin, Martin Hough, Darragh Kennedy, John Paul O'Malley. *Front row (l–r):* John Meskell, Donal O'Sullivan, Brian Healy, Adrian Collins, Michael Mackey, Kieran Hurley, David Laing, Pat Culhane.

I used to play pitch and putt in Ardnacrusha at one time, and Mackey would see me coming out so we'd have a few bob on a game. He'd start these antics, coughing or dropping the club when you would be taking a shot for a putt. He'd try anything to put you off your game. He was like a big child! If children were playing haws there on the road, he would nearly go down to try and beat them. He had a competitive instinct and he couldn't be beaten.

Fr Liam Kelly speaks of the many tales associated with Mackey:

He used to say that they were bad times in the 1930s and '40s and people hadn't a penny, the only thing they had to look forward to were the matches. They turned up in their droves because it was the only outing they had. And he used to say that if they weren't playing well or if it was a bad match, 'we had to provide a bit of entertainment for them, give them an auld laugh anyway.' That was the role of the players, and while Mackey was known as being a showman he used to say, 'I was forced into it, I wouldn't like that sort of stuff at all.' They had to turn it on for the crowd, and the crowd loved it, and that's why Mackey became such a hero. He said to me several times, 'We had great times but I suppose we overdid it.' Between Limerick and Ahane they played on something like sixty-eight Sundays in a little over a year and went the length and breadth of the country playing tournaments. He used to say, 'We built churches and we built halls' and when he was sick in hospital he asked me, 'Will that stand to me now when I go upstairs?'

There was a famous story about playing against Cork in the final of the Thomond Feis at the Gaelic Grounds. It was a close game and Cork hit the ball wide. Scanlan pucked it out fast to Mick who was outside on his own in the middle of the field. He stuck it in under his jersey and took off running. The ref was still below at the other goals, and with the crowd going wild Mackey struck the ball to the net and it was allowed. He got away with it, the umpires had no say in those days.

Paddy Tuohy is not convinced by this particular tale, however:

I personally believe that all the stories about Mackey putting the ball into his jersey and running without the ball are only a myth. They are designed to add to the legend of Mackey, but there were no television cameras in those days. I think it's one of those stories that carried legs and added to his name as a superstar.

Some locals believed Mackey had genuine challengers for his throne, as Fr Liam Kelly explains:

There was always a local issue in that there was a rivalry between Power and Mackey. Power was Monaleen, and Mackey was Ahane. The Monaleen crowd beat the Ahane people to the punch when they put up the statue to Power in Annacotty. There was always a rivalry there, although Jackie would never admit it. Jackie was a terrific fellow, there would be none of that stuff about him at all. The supporters would be worse about it because they felt that Power didn't get enough credit. The thing about Jackie Power was that he played in every position for Ahane. He even played in goals. Mick never really fancied himself as a defender, although he did go back as a full-back in his last game against Treaty Sarsfields.

Timmy Ryan started out before the era of Mackey and Power. Timmy was the kind of a player that stood out on his own in that he was solely a midfielder and the greatest of his era and wouldn't have been seen as a player who would play in any other position. So Mick Mackey and Jackie Power couldn't really be compared with him because they never figured prominently at midfield, although they would have played there occasionally. I saw Timmy playing for Ahane towards the end of his reign and he scored two points from centre field by doubling on puckouts. It was incredible to see him doubling on the ball overhead and putting it over the bar at the other end of the field. They were absolutely outstanding scores. He would never miss an overhead ball.

Mackey had a completely different style to Timmy Ryan. I always remember the television interview Mick gave to Val Dorgan in 1969. Dorgan asked him about inventing the solo run. Mick had a habit of sniffling his nose at that time [when he was talking] and replied, 'I don't know really.' Dorgan asked him what kind of science did he bring to the game. 'Ara sure,' sniffled Mick, 'we weren't too particular, if we couldn't go around them, we went through them.' He used to love using that statement in later years. Mackey was very knowledgeable and always had an innate sense of what to do on the field. He had been through the mill so much himself he knew what worked and what didn't. Obviously, the route one approach worked for him where he could knock about three opponents on the ground on his way through. His strength wasn't developed from doing manual work. He inherited that physique from his grandfather.

Michael Hynes commented on the rivalry:

There might have been local rivalry, but I have to say that Timmy Ryan, the Mackey brothers and Jackie Power were all friendly people. John Mackey was shy but was very honourable and decent and wasn't as flamboyant as Mick. He was very modest in comparison. Mick Mackey was a great hurler, but Timmy Ryan was also a great hurler, a big, strong, tall man. Jackie Power came in and won his first All-Ireland at a very young age so that showed he was a quality player. He was working away from Limerick later in his career and was always coming back for club and county games. The travelling was hard but he still played well any time he put on a jersey. That time you had to go because you would lose your job. Mackey got all the credit when he was playing and for years afterwards. However, it was always felt locally that the other hurlers didn't get the credit they deserved.

Ahane dinner dance photo from 1969. *Back row (l–r):* Tony Herbert, Tom Conway, Fr Liam Kelly, Tom Hayes, Mick Herbert, Mick Hickey, Seán Herbert, John Mackey, Paddy Kelly, Liam Cummins, Michael Minihan, Fr White. *Middle row (l–r):* Arthur Graham, Jimmy Close, Mick Kennedy, Timmy Ryan, Pat Fanning, Jack Keane, Jimmy Hassett, Paddy Byrnes. *Front row (l–r):* Jackie Power, John Doyle, Mick Mackey, Pat O'Connor, Mick McGrath.

Paddy Tuohy believes in the team ethos:

While Mackey got the credit, Limerick – and Ahane particularly – won every honour and won them as a team. John Doyle once said, 'I was lucky to be on a team that won eight All-Irelands whereas Christy Ring won eight All-Irelands for Cork. Tipp won eight for me, but Ring won eight for Cork.' Relating that to Mackey, from listening to older people speaking, Mackey was able to activate a team and they do credit him with being able to carry and drive the team. But it was about a team rather than an individual.

I worked with an O'Riordan from Abbeydorney and he once told me how he often came from Abbeydorney to Limerick by train in the 1940s to see Mackey in club games for Ahane. They had heard so much about the superstar that they wanted to see him in the flesh. It was a big adventure that time, and they would go home that evening to the pub, and the lads would gather around them. 'Well, did you see him?' 'Was he as good as they say?' 'How would Slasher from Kilmoyley [the unbeatable hurling legend from a neighbouring club and a powerfully built man] compare with Mackey?' 'I will tell you, Mick Mackey would drive the ball further with one hand than Slasher would with two,' O'Riordan's father replied.

Timmy Ryan and Mick Mackey had what could be called an awkward relationship over the free-taking incident at the end of the 1935 All-Ireland final. It is widely said that they got on well at times and that Mackey would visit Timmy Ryan's pub but that on other occasions there could be awkwardness. Local party politics also entered the equation, as Tony Herbert explains:

Timmy Ryan was a lot more popular than Mackey in the locality. But politics also came into that, and Timmy Ryan was Fine Gael whereas Mackey was Labour. 'Tyler' Mackey was a Labour councillor and always headed the poll at that side of the country. Timmy Ryan was Fine Gael. Pat Reilly, the chairman of the county board at the time, was also a strong Fine Gael man and Reilly controlled Timmy Ryan.

When Mackey finished with Ahane he was living in Ardnacrusha and did very little work with Ahane afterwards, certainly in my time, and when I was gone to Dublin afterwards I didn't ever hear that he did much work for the club. He would go to the Ahane matches alright but other than that I don't think he had any major input. He was always on the Munster Council, representing Limerick. He had a big say in the council. He liked to have his own way and he got away with it. He was a man who liked a bit of publicity and he wouldn't accept second place behind anyone else. He wanted to be top of the class.

He wasn't top of the class against John Keane, as Fr Liam Kelly explains:

Mackey admitted that his toughest opponent was always John Keane. He used to say, 'They said Keane always bate me, but they were only exaggerating. I played well in matches against him too!' But Keane was the only man that could hold him consistently. Mackey could get scores at vital stages in games, however, even against Keane. He was incredibly determined and didn't ever like to be written off. Once he told me a great story about going down to play Mallow in some tournament final. They were travelling by train and they stopped at some other station along the way. Mick overheard these two men talking. One of them said, 'That auld Ahane crowd are going down

Mick Mackey in jovial mood at a dance. *(L–r):* Brian Connors, Maureen Shanahan (nee Scanlan, a sister to Paddy Scanlan), Mick Mackey, Peggy Duffy, Bill Shanahan.

to play Mallow.' 'Ah yes,' said the other man, 'Mallow will ate them.' 'But they didn't,' said Mick with gritted teeth, 'Mallow didn't ate us.'

John Mackey was a completely different player. He was a complete background man and shied away from the limelight, almost to the extreme of Mick. John never went to a Limerick match after he retired. I often meant to delve deeper but I never did. Perhaps he had the interest lost or else he felt he had given all he could to the game of hurling. John was a great family man though.

Vera Mulcahy recalls life as John Mackey's daughter:

In our youth, we were encouraged to play all sports. Dad was coming from an era back in the 1920s and '30s when the ban existed and was at its most severe. I know that he did give an interview to Arthur Quinlan in the old *Cork Examiner* many years ago and said the ban was alright back in the troubled times but that it possibly should have gone by the 1950s, twenty years before it did. He was a definite believer that once we got our independence and were ruled by our own Irish government, the ban had outlived its usefulness. I often got a little inkling from Dad that maybe he'd have liked to try his hand

Mick Mackey photographed with his grandchildren, Gerry Doyle (*left*) and Catherine Doyle.

at rugby. He would certainly be proud to see his grandson Johnny Moroney play in the AIL [All Ireland League] for Young Munster today. He had a great passion for rugby and also liked soccer. When we were teenagers back in the 1970s you really only had the domestic soccer shown on television and that game was played at a very slow pace. I wonder how he would have enjoyed it now when you have the Premiership and Sky Sports. He never lived to see my own daughter Niamh represent Ireland in soccer but I can only imagine that it would have thrilled him. When we were growing up we were encouraged to play and enjoy whatever sport we liked.

Catherine Doyle is Mick Mackey's granddaughter:

To us [grandchildren] he was a grandad rather than a famous hurling name, but we would have been very young when he died. We wouldn't have been as conscious of his name at that age, and that probably comes with the innocence of youth. I remember him as being a bit of a rogue. He was very lighthearted and was always joking with us and in general would have been a humorous person.

Vera Mulcahy recalls her father's reflections on the game:

The game is very fast today and is a different game. He would always have said that the training in his day wasn't as hard as it was in later years because they cycled everywhere. There was no such thing as hamstring injuries because they were cycling a lot and their legs were strong as a result. He always said that they could eat what they wanted, because everyone was doing manual work. Even if you worked in an office you came home in the evenings and worked. Most people had their own cows and hens, and everyone tilled gardens and cycled or walked to training. They could eat loads of home-cured bacon and cabbage and usually left nothing on the table because they were working it off. He spoke very little about his own hurling days until after Mick's funeral when a lot of the old players from Cork were gathered and he was able to reminisce and tell us how good players like Jim Regan and Jim Young of Cork were. He had great admiration for Jimmy Langton of Kilkenny and really rated him very highly. When Limerick and Kilkenny played in that era the player who often marked my father was Paddy Phelan, a granduncle of D. J. Carey. Apart from that, he spoke very little about his own hurling days. The one thing he always said was that Éamonn Cregan was by far the greatest player of the modern era. In the 1970s my father's team-mates from the golden era always agreed that Cregan would have made their great team both as a defender and as a forward, and always compared his versatility to that of Jackie Power.

Maurice Regan concurs:

Johnny Flavin, who used to hurl with Fedamore against the great Ahane teams, always claimed that Cregan was the best hurler in modern times to wear a Limerick jersey. He used to say that he was the only hurler as good as the players from the golden era. Flavin would have played with the Clohessy brothers and Tom McCarthy from Kilfinane in club games for Fedamore and would have seen all the Limerick greats first hand so he would have known what he was talking about.

Mick Rainsford acknowledges the versatility of both Cregan and Power:

You could put Éamonn Cregan and Jackie Power in any position from one to fifteen in any team and they would star. Both players proved it countless times at the highest level that they could perform both in defence and attack.

Vera says John Mackey did his talking on the field:

My father was the quieter of the two brothers. Whatever you had to do it was done on the field of play and different stories were told to us by people who played club hurling with him that he did his talking on the field. Maybe his marker and himself would end up walking down to Barrington's to be stitched but it was left on the field of play. Off the field, to us growing up he was a real gentleman. And when you hear stories about how tough he was – seemingly he was a very fast player on the field of play – it was hard to believe that he was the type of player who would pull first and ask questions later.

As regards his own team-mates, he would never have spoken of Mick to us, but he spoke highly of Timmy Ryan, Paddy Scanlon and Jimmy Close. They were all great men in those days. It actually reminds me a bit of the Kilkenny camogie team of the 1970s and '80s for whom Angela Downey was outstanding. Yet when you go to a function and you see the Kilkenny team of that era being honoured, it's very apparent that while she was extremely talented in her own right, she had wonderful players around her. It's very similar with the Kilkenny hurlers of today with Henry Shefflin, because there's also Eoin Larkin, Eddie Brennan, etc. Back then Limerick and Ahane had the players and it must have been very easy to play well if you got the right ball into you. I remember Tom Conway a neighbour used to say to me one time, 'The ball your father used to love was that height [a foot high] off the sod in Thurles, coming flying in to him, he would double on it then or let it come up.' I would say he rated nearly all his team-mates highly and had huge respect for all the teams they played. The great John Keane of Waterford died in Limerick and I remember my father going to the funeral and acknowledging that he was an outstanding centre-back.

Mick was more flamboyant and seemed to like the limelight. He was always very interested in Ahane camogie, and when I was starting off with them they had been beaten in two or three All-Ireland club finals by the great St Paul's team in Kilkenny. Mick always went to those matches and had a great interest in any Limerick person being involved in any Gaelic code. He was different to my father in terms of the limelight. When the match was over my father would go away

Mick and John Mackey pictured with well-known ballad singer Ann Mulqueen during a traditional session at An Chistin in Limerick.

and find a quiet corner, sit down and enjoy his pint. Mick on the other hand liked to talk and be the centre of attention and meet people. My father certainly didn't have the same physique as Mick, but I believe he was very very fast off the mark. I remember a neighbour who played club hurling with them said that my father would die to win the match, whereas Mick's main priority was his personal performance regardless of the outcome.

I'd imagine they played with injuries in those days and just put on the bandage and played away. Because they played a lot of first-time hurling, the ball came to your area of the pitch and you just pulled first time. Therefore an injury back then wouldn't restrict a player as much because he wasn't as reliant on movement. Nowadays players may be covering more ground, but the game was just as fast then because the ball was moving.

John Ryan comments on the brothers:

When John Mackey retired he was never seen, though some people have said that he'd arrive late and unnoticed to games and would slip away early so that he wouldn't be seen. John was into keeping a few greyhounds and he never got involved with the hurling afterwards. John played on longer than Mick for Limerick though. He never got the same credit that Mick got. Willie Keane once told me that his father always maintained that you could rely on John to win the match.

A lot of the older people around the club locally had better time for John because they felt he would win a match for the club quicker than Mick. I remember seeing Mick going on as a sub in his last game for Limerick and he looked very heavy in comparison with the year before. He seemed to put on weight easily as he got older. Someone like Éamonn Cregan lasted a long time, but he was a different build of a man to Mackey. Ciarán Carey would be similar to Cregan in that he could stay going forever because he is probably a similar weight now to when he was minor. I knew Mick Mackey's grandfather, also called Mick. My earliest memory of him is of a big heavy man with a hat and a moustache. Mick seemed to inherit that build, though his father 'Tyler' was a bony man and never put on weight. John Mackey never put up much weight but he was built more like 'Tyler' and never got heavy even in later years.

Paddy Tuohy compares Mackey to a soccer legend:

At peak fitness, Mick Mackey wasn't a very slight individual. He was strongly built and had short legs and a long body. He would have been of similar build to Maradona. Maradona has gained a lot of weight in later life and Mick was very similar in that regard. Mackey was strong, though. I met someone in Waterford once and he had an old scar having received eighteen stitches years earlier. He said Mackey was running by him and hit him a ferocious belt without realising it, such was his strength.

Mackey had his own legendary status, as Séamus Ó Ceallaigh explained:

Mackey was the real playboy, the real playboy of Munster hurling. He drew the crowds, he was an artist. A different man from Ring altogether; Ring used the brain more, they were different types of men. They were both great hurlers but Mackey was more colourful, he was a real playboy. ('A Celebration of Munster Hurling', RTÉ Television, 1976)

In 1979, Mick Mackey's great rival Christy Ring passed to his eternal reward. Fr Liam Kelly was the chauffeur for the outing to Cork:

I got a phone call from Mick one Friday. 'Liam, Ringy is dead,' he said. 'We will have to go to that. Are you driving?' On the Saturday morning, Dermot Kelly, Liam Moloney, Vivian Cobbe and myself set off early, with Mick perched on the throne [front seat of the car]. We went to the funeral mass at the cathedral in Cork which was packed. The cathedral was probably the best place for it, because the church in Cloyne was small and wouldn't have held the crowd. From there we entered the funeral cortege. There were three hearses, and the hearse would stop at the border of every parish on the road to Cloyne. The local team would come out, take the coffin out of the hearse, shoulder it across the border and put it back into the hearse again, so it took a long time to get to Cloyne. In the meantime we had driven on and got to Cloyne earlier than the rest. The funeral wasn't due for another hour so Mrs Ring, who would have known Mick, came out and brought us into the house. Ring was back living in his native Cloyne at the time of his death. We went in and one room in the house was covered with pictures and souvenirs. It was like a museum. At the funeral afterwards, Jack Lynch gave a magnificent oration and got quite emotional. He then spread some clay over the coffin and all the old hurlers from the past went up and did the same.

We went back into the hotel in Cork city for the meal, which may have been in the Metropole. I always remember at one stage, Mick Mackey was standing at one side of me and Mick O'Connell the Kerry footballer was standing at the other. I said to myself, 'I hope someone takes a picture of this!' After the meal we were invited down to Blackpool to the Glen Rovers club. Dr Jim Young was chairman of Glen Rovers at the time and there was another big event with speeches, while the women were making tea for the visitors. Our group were brought up to the stage one by one, Mackey of course being number one, and each of us were presented with a copy of the book *The Spirit of the Glen*. The crowd were milking this. Then another Glen Rovers man thought of a great idea to get Mick Mackey up in front of the crowd again, so we were all presented with a tie.

This was a Saturday evening, and while there was no evening Mass in those days, I was on duty for 9 a.m. mass at St Joseph's church on the Sunday morning. The boys were drinking away to their hearts' content and it continued through the night. Eventually I was starting to get bothered about it. Time was passing, it got to 3 a.m., and 4 a.m., and I was wondering when I would get out of there. I eventually got Dermot Kelly out of there and had Kelly outside in the car and tucked him in. I went back in for Mick, and while I was bringing Mick out, there was Kelly coming back in against me. We got out eventually, and started the long drive back. As we were approaching Buttevant we got a puncture but I couldn't get any of them out of the car to help because they were plastered. A farmer came up the road on a tractor with lights and stopped. He saw Mackey in the car and took over from me, jacked up the car as quickly as he could and changed the wheel. His day was made when he jacked Mick Mackey up in the car that morning. Eventually we arrived at 8.15 a.m. at St Joseph's church in Limerick. I went in to wash myself and get everything prepared for Mass. The boys came into the back seat of the church and were almost falling on top of each other. I said to them afterwards, 'It was surprising that ye were able to stay awake.' I brought Mick home after Mass and he said to me, 'We gave Ringy a great send off.' 'You can say that Mick,' I replied. 'Not only a full day but a full night as well.' Mick would have thoroughly enjoyed that day when the funeral took place. He was meeting all the old hurling people from earlier years. Of course, he was back as the king again, now that his great rival was dead.

Fr Liam Ryan recalls Mackey as a golfer:

Mackey was a great character socially when he was in the hurlers' association. He was very prominent and turned up to most golf outings. The Mick Mackey trophy is still there in his honour. We played for it in the Charleville golf outing in 2010. There's also a Christy Ring trophy and that was played for in Castletroy in 2010. I spent two years in St Louis, Missouri from 1962 to '64 and used to go up and hurl with the Limerick team in Chicago. They brought Mackey out one summer for three weeks. It was great craic. He was the life and soul of the place and would have come in contact with a lot of people from home, especially from Tipperary and Cork. He had a great dislike of Cork but was very close to the Tipperary people, Johnny Leahy and Paddy Leahy and the like. In later years he became great friends with those but not with the Cork people. Cork beat them so often, I suppose, whereas they had the upper hand on Tipperary for most of his career apart from 1937 and 1945. Not every Limerick person of his time would be the same though!

Jim Hogan recalls an amusing story:

Mackey went into the bar of the Imperial hotel in Cork after a game with a friend of his, and there was a ne'er-do-well sitting at the bar. This guy never did a day's work in his life and was always going

Mick Mackey and his wife, Kitty, at an awards function where Mick presented Ger McMahon (St Patrick's) with an award upon Ger's selection for the Limerick senior hurling team.

around bumming pints here and there. 'Paddy, can we have two pints there,' says Mackey to the barman. The guy at the counter, sensing an opportunity, added, 'Make that a goal, make that a goal!'

Arthur Graham remembers Mackey's humility:

Even though I played hurling with Mick Mackey, I really only got to know him well afterwards. I played cards with him regularly at The Hurlers pub and he was a very good card player. He would always want to win playing cards and his competitive streak was there all the time. I knew him as a neighbour rather than as a celebrity and there was nothing pretentious about him, he was very down to earth. It was years afterwards when it dawned on me that I actually played with a legend, when people would say, 'You played with Mick Mackey.' At the time, he was only another one of the lads on the team.

Willie Keane can recall him playing cards:

Mick used to come to Hickey's for cards, and McCabe's [in earlier times] across from the hall in Castleconnell. They had a regular nine players on a Sunday night. He was very fond of cards. From a hurling perspective, he had no real involvement in team affairs. He had achieved everything he could achieve.

The Mackey family in 1961 *(l–r)*: Greg, Ruth, Audrey, Mick, Michael, Kitty.

Greg Mackey recalls why he wasn't involved with the club:

Despite being a driver for the ESB, my father never drove anywhere and had no car of his own until 1965. That more than anything was the reason he drifted from Ahane GAA club. When he was involved with Limerick and Munster there was a car sent for him and it was usually Tommy Casey who collected him from the house. Ger Doyle [Mackey's son-in-law, married to Ruth Mackey] and myself got together and got him sorted with a car. Prior to that, he used to cycle from Ardnacrusha on a Sunday night to McCabe's house in Castleconnell to play cards. Matt Whelan used to play with him. Jackie Mac's thatched pub was beside McCabe's. They used to bring drink out the back door of the pub and in the back door of McCabe's where the cards were being played.

When he started working for the ESB in Ardnacrusha he was still living in Castleconnell. Along with a few others in the area, he used to cycle to work. First they would cycle down to the river in the village of Castleconnell to a location called 'the ferry' near where the footbridge is located now. They got a boat across the Shannon to County Clare and cycled the rest of the way to Ardnacrusha.

Willie Keane recalls that Mackey didn't need fancy gear:

I saw Mick playing in his underpants one year because he had no togs. He just took off the pants and started hurling away. He wasn't worried about gear with sponsors' logos on it! He had slowed up quite a bit in later years and depended a lot on his ball control and his weight. He might knock over three or four but he was carrying too much weight and wasn't able to finish as he was in his early years. You still wouldn't knock him, though. He never spoke to me much about his playing career and I knew him well.

John Mackey never became involved and preferred to have a few pints than go to a match. When John was playing for Limerick he always went drinking after the game with Jimmy Maher [Tipperary goalie], yet in the match he would always have clattered him. I remember in Reilly's field one Sunday they had to tog out on the field. John came on and gave his watch and a ten-shilling note to me to mind and told me that whatever about the watch, I was to make sure and guard the ten-shilling note, that he needed it for later on in the night.

Arthur Graham recalls a minor issue:

I was secretary of the club from the early 1970s to the early '80s and I think I only heard from Mick two or three times, over issues that weren't very contentious. He wrote to me once when Jimmy Close died. I don't think Jimmy's wife was in great financial circumstances after his death, and I remember Mick writing to me to ask the club to do something to help her out financially. We did hold a fundraiser after that. I went to see Mick with Mick Hickey two or three times when he wasn't well. Himself and Mick Hickey were great talkers, and told great stories. Mick was ill for several months before he died.

We had a good team in the 1970s but our hoodoo team was South Liberties and they would beat us by a point or two and then go on to win the county, so we weren't far away. I remember Mick Mackey coming into the dressing room a few times to talk to the lads and gizz

GAA Convention: Mackey opts out

Rory Kiely is back in power

The *Limerick Leader* stirs things up and hints at GAA politics with a headline bearing the news that Rory Kiely had replaced Mick Mackey as Limerick delegate to the Munster council.

them up. Outside of that he didn't have a whole lot of contact with the club in that decade. John drifted from the club too. I used to meet him at Hickey's and he would prefer to be talking about his greyhounds or his garden of spuds than hurling. A lot of people who played with him claimed he was a better hurler than Mick. Mick Hickey would tell you if he was alive that Mick Mackey hogged the limelight far more perhaps than he was entitled to. He would also say that Jackie Power was a better all-round hurler because you could play Power anywhere.

The only thing contentious Ahane ever had with Mick, and it wasn't really contentious, related to his Munster Council position. Mick was the delegate for years, and when he left the position he never informed the club. It wasn't taken very well at the time. I was secretary of the club and the Munster Council position was more or less handed over to Rory Kiely. Mick wasn't well at the time so I'm sure nobody said a word to him. We would have felt that, with a club delegate having held the position for so long, we should have been afforded the opportunity to nominate someone for the contest to replace him. Both Rory and Mick were nominated but Mick pulled out, meaning that Rory had the position unopposed. We assumed Mick was staying on but he resigned before we even knew it.

When Mick Mackey opted out it caused a surprise among the Limerick GAA following. Although he was in bad health at the time and the move couldn't have been totally unexpected, generally such a hero would announce his departure well in advance. As long as he was standing for election he would not be opposed. If someone did oppose him, the commonplace thing was for the lesser name to withdraw prior to the election. To this day, many believe the situation with Rory Kiely to be a little too convenient and are suspicious that Mackey and Kiely struck up an agreement. Rory Kiely's club, Feenagh/Kilmeedy, nominated Mick Mackey for the position. A neighbouring club, Castletown/Ballyagran, in turn nominated Rory, which was originally interpreted as a throwaway nomination – a means to an end. Perhaps there was more to it than that, but Rory was always standing on high moral ground by virtue of Mackey being nominated by his own club. Brendan Fullam recalls meeting his hero:

I met Mick for the first time in Killorglin, staying in a place called Stephens and Champs, a guesthouse. They served lunches every day. I came in one day and sat down as usual. There was a man sitting to my left and across the table was his friend. The fellow across the table said to me, 'Did you ever hear of the Mackeys?' I answered, 'Of course I did, who didn't!' And he said, 'What did you think of them?' and I answered, 'They were great, will we ever see their likes again?'

I can't explain why, but the man on my left had said nothing, and remained very quiet. Then suddenly something hit me that it was Mick Mackey, and so I introduced myself. I asked him to autograph something I had upstairs. I had cuttings of newspapers in a book, went up and got it and asked him to sign it under his photograph. Afterwards he stood up by the fireplace and I was amazed at the girth of the man. Donal Flynn, a Cork man who hurled with Galway and Connacht in 1947, described Mackey as being like the pier of a gate. He said Mackey was so solid and strong that you couldn't knock him. What struck me about him was that he was so open. I can still hear him saying that it was very hard to get on the Munster team. It was a big thing at the time to play for Munster. To get on the team wasn't easy back then.

We went our separate ways, and then I started writing, and I knocked on his door years later. He was recovering from the stroke at the time. He was the first to write in my journal. I have never forgotten him sitting there, and the size of him when the journal was open. I said to him, 'Mick, recall a special memory,' and he paused for a few seconds and said, 'It's all memories now.' I often ask myself what was going through his mind when he said that. Maybe he felt that his days on earth wouldn't be for long more. I never forgot his answer that day. I went back again for a photo, and he chatted away, and he never had a bad word for anyone. I gather he had great admiration for John Maher and Mick Kennedy. The first day I was there, he told me to be sure to call to Garett Howard, because he was a mine of information.

Mick Mackey receives the Bank of Ireland All-Time All-Star award in 1980. *(L–r):* Gerry O'Donnell (Assistant General Manager, Bank of Ireland Limerick Region), Charles J. Haughey (Taoiseach), Mick Mackey, Frank O'Rourke (Chief General Manager, Bank of Ireland), Dermot Kelly (Manager, Bank of Ireland Caherdavin).

He spoke about 1936, and the time they had over in the States. I felt if you asked a question you would get an answer but I wasn't going to ask unfair questions, such as whether he was better than Ring or not. He told me that in the GAA season the rugby supporters were the biggest supporters of the GAA in Limerick and that in the rugby season the GAA supporters were the biggest supporters of rugby. I had been at the All-Ireland in 1980 when Limerick conceded two early goals. Mackey made a comment to me, 'If Mick Kennedy was there, he would be wrapped around his man and the ball would be driven out over the sideline.' That's why he liked Kennedy, the ball was gone from the danger area without lifting it.

Mick Mackey was the first recipient of the Bank of Ireland All-Time All-Star award in 1980. Dermot Kelly brought him home from Dublin:

We were coming down to Limerick from Jury's in Ballsbridge at around 5.30 pm and my wife's sister had a pub in Coolrain, County

Mick Mackey returns to Herbert's bar with the Bank Of Ireland All-Stars Hall of Fame award in 1980. *Back row (l–r):* Dermot Kelly, Willie Keane, Mick Herbert, Brendan Jones, Bernie Hartigan (partially hidden), Jimmy Hassett, Seán Herbert, Paddy Kelly, Éamonn Herbert, John Doyle, Arthur Graham, Dan Mescall, Jerry O'Riordan. *Front row (l–r):* Rody Nealon, Mick Mackey, Paddy McMahon, John Mackey.

Laois, so we dropped in. Mick was like the pied piper up there, and the people just flocked around him in the pub. My sister-in-law rang the locals to tell them he was there, and they came down the mountains from Camross to meet him. There was nothing official planned for him that night on his return to Limerick so I rang ahead. Socially, if you didn't know him well, I would say he was a bit shy and might have come across as being a bit dour. He knew he was the best and he liked to be respected as the best. I was secretary of the hurlers' association from 1973 to 1988 and Jim Young, Mutt Ryan, Tommy Doyle, etc. were in it. I asked the majority of them who was the best, and they said Mackey would go through you and Ring would go around you.

I played against him when he was finishing and I was starting. I was playing with the City Gaels divisional team against Ahane in 1950. When I was a youngster Mackey called to our house one morning to see my father and that was my first time meeting him. Having been in awe of him as a ten-year-old, I was now playing against him. I probably thought, 'He won't hit me a belt because he knows my father.'

Whatever happened there was a melee in the square and players were hammering one another and then there was a 21-yard free. The

The grave at Castleconnell cemetery where Mick Mackey and his wife, Kitty, are buried.

referee sent them all back to the line and I was nominated to take the free. I was only seventeen and a half at the time. Mick Mackey was over on my right and I was just about to go for the ball. He walked across in front of me and said, 'Kelly, you have a lot to learn about this game yet.' I missed the 21-yard free. He psyched me out of it, and I believe he did that type of thing a lot as a player. It came naturally. That time opposition players were continuously trying to half kill him. I would echo what others have said about his competitive instinct; he was definitely the most competitive 45 player in Ireland. I used to call to Mackey's house sometimes and unfortunately he fell ill. He told me that he was standing by the fire ready to go out playing cards one night and he just fell down. He was getting strokes. Eventually he passed away, but he had been weak for a long time before he died.

On 13 September 1982, Mick Mackey passed to his eternal reward. Fr Liam Kelly spent a considerable amount of time with him during his final hours:

I was the parish priest in Parteen at the time and he was living in Ardnacrusha. I used to go up twice a week all the time he was in hospital. He used to insist, 'I want to see you tomorrow.' The famous one about the wet day in 1935 was a story he decided to keep to himself. Whenever he was asked, he wouldn't answer. This became a real joke with everybody. They often had a hop off him but he would

The *Limerick Leader* of Monday 13 September 1982 breaks the devastating news that the iconic legend Mick Mackey had passed to his eternal reward.

DEATH OF MICK MACKEY

Mick Mackey, one of the greatest hurlers of all time, died at 1.50 p.m. this Monday. Members of his family were present at his bedside. The late Mr. Mackey entered hospital two weks ago. He was acknowledged as the greatest hurler ever to have graced the playing fields.

LIMERICK LOSES ITS HURLING MONARCH

By CAMAN

Former comrades: Timmy Ryan, Jackie Power, Paddy McMahon and Mick Hickey at the removal of Mick Mackey's remains to Castleconnell.

never divulge what happened. The day before he died, I visited him in the Regional hospital. 'Come here Liam, come here,' he said, calling me over to the bed. 'I missed it!' he said. He didn't say any more but he wanted to get it off his chest before he was gone. He was telling me that he went for goal from the free in 1935. It was like the famous secret of Fatima, it was out at long last.

Ralph Prendergast was one of the last to see him:

I visited him in the hospital on the night he died but he was close to the end so all I did was hold his hand. He passed away a couple of hours later. I will always cherish a memory of a small presentation that was made to me on my return from America. Mick Mackey and John Madden of Canal Banks, a great Claughaun man, made it to me. We had a great chat when I came home from America. Madden had been in America with Mackey in the 1930s. In later years, my step-brother was dying and he asked me if Mackey was the greatest of them all. Without having seen him, I said that Mackey was. My opinion is that Ring was manufactured but Mackey was born.

Michael Hynes remembered the death of another Ahane legend:

Paddy Kelly died three weeks after Mick Mackey, so we lost two great Ahane hurlers in quick succession. Pat Reale looked after Mackey very well in the Regional hospital. Reale was a nurse there, and afterwards Kitty Mackey gave him one of the medals.

Ned Wheeler remembers a benefit night after Mackey's death:

I used to work for Texaco in Carlow delivering oil and used to meet Mick in Mullinahone when he was delivering ESB poles to the area. After he died, there was a dog benefit night for the Mackey Stand in Limerick. I sponsored a greyhound. Paddy Buggy was there and was GAA president at the time and I met Mick's wife and daughter. It was a great evening.

Tony Herbert outlines the respect the Tipperary greats had for him:

When I was at my brother Seán Herbert's funeral at Castleconnell, the Tipperary players Johnny Ryan, Mutt Ryan and the Sweeper Ryan all went down to see Mick Mackey's grave. Johnny Ryan said, 'Whatever you say about Mackey, he was the greatest of them all.' He said that when there were a lot of people around and they all agreed. That's what the Tipperary players maintained.

Willie Keane feels he should have a major trophy in his name:

Mackey achieved everything in the game, and arguably more than anyone else, even those who came after him. It's amazing that there is no major competition called after Mick Mackey when you consider the Christy Ring Cup, the Nicky Rackard Cup and the Lory Meagher Cup are all presented for high-profile competitions.

A competition in his memory may follow, or given that the Munster senior hurling championship trophy doesn't bear a name, perhaps that's the logical choice. Munster Council CEO Pat Fitzgerald might well make representations of that nature. The Mackey Stand in the Gaelic Grounds carries the family name, along with the Ahane GAA grounds, known as Mackey Park. Both the stand and the park are attributed to the Mackey family rather than specifically to Mick Mackey. Greg Mackey was involved in Ahane GAA club at the time the grounds were named and openly acknowledges that there was strong opposition to the grounds being called after his father. Some of that opposition came from those who are connected to the Mackey family through marriage. Former Ahane chairman Séamus Walsh outlines the difficulties:

It was proposed originally that the GAA grounds be called after Mick Mackey. The feeling in the parish at the time was that some people didn't want the GAA field called after Mick himself or the Mackey family. Some of the former greats were still alive at the time and while they didn't want it called after Mick, they wouldn't have wanted it to be called after themselves either. The preference was for a general name rather than specifically naming any individual or family. Unquestionably there were people who didn't want it called after Mick, feeling that too much centred around him to the detriment of the other great players. Another angle was that there would have been much higher regard locally for John Mackey than there was for Mick. Some high-profile Ahane people were very vociferous in their opposition to the proposal and eventually a compromise was reached. It was agreed to call it Mackey Park in memory of the contribution of 'Tyler', Mick, John and Paddy Mackey. I remember discussing the Mackey Stand with Seán Murphy at some point and for similar reasons it was called after the Mackey family rather than specifically Mick Mackey.

Mackey wasn't short of recognition for his achievements on the field and that does create jealousy within a small area. We saw that more recently when the Limerick under-21 team won the three in a row and at least one club was damaged by the jealousy of older players who should have known better. A fine underage prospect left his club because some of the older boys within the club

Kitty Mackey, Helen Mackey, Greg Mackey and Dick Leonard with some former Ahane players at the club's press conference at Hickey's Bar, Castleconnell, where details of the club's plans for their new field were announced.

couldn't lose the 'big fish in a small pond' mentality. They were jealous of his growing profile and undermined him in every way possible, leaving him no option but to depart so that he could once again enjoy the game he loved. It seems to have been the same among Mackey's former team-mates.

In 1961 Mick Mackey was presented with the Caltex Hall of Fame award at the Gresham hotel for being the outstanding personality in hurling circles since the GAA was formed. In 1979 at the Limerick Sports Personalities Gala Ball he was presented with the Limerick Hall of Fame award. The next honour bestowed upon him was the aforementioned Bank of Ireland All-Time All-Star award. For a period in the 1980s a greyhound stake was run in his memory. A Mick Mackey Cup was the prize for tournament games between Limerick and Clare at one stage in the 1980s but like most tournaments it came to an end. Nowadays another trophy, the Mackey Cup, is presented to the winning captain of the Limerick primary schools interdivisional hurling competition. This is a prestigious competition in which the cream of talent from the primary schools represent their division and play a straight knockout four-team competition. It has proven to be the breeding ground for future senior inter-county hurlers.

To finish it's appropriate to read some quotations from the great man himself, taken from his 1969 interview with Val Dorgan on RTÉ Television:

In '36 against Tipperary in the final I scored 5-3 but I don't know if it was a great final really. I think 1940 was the final that I enjoyed most. I was lucky to be captain.

Johnny [Jackie] Power was a great hurler, he was a man you could play anywhere. And then we had Mick Kennedy left-full-back; I always rated him and I think my Cork friends agree with me that Kennedy was the best left-full-back that played in that position. All our team were better than anyone else in their own position on their day. If one of us had a bad day, someone else pulled up. Timmy Ryan was a wonderful midfielder, he could range the whole side of the field, he was going all day. He would be hitting it on the centre-half-back and he would be down helping you.

I think what made our team was the great spirit that was among them. They had great heart and they never accepted defeat, we could have been bate to the ropes but still they would come back.

'Twas hardly as good [the 1960s] as the time we were playing. I don't believe it. 'Twas harder in our time anyway, there was more shoulder to shoulder, the tackling I'd say was closer, and possibly harder. But of course it would be very hard to judge that.

I wouldn't like to say our team was the best of all time but it was a pretty good team all the same. Of course it was a great time for hurling. All the Munster counties were capable of coming out of Munster that time, and then you had Kilkenny in Leinster and Dublin in Leinster; you had Leix at that time who were no joke. It would be hard to judge, and of course the 1920s to the 1930s were a great period in hurling too. I suppose the mid '20s and from '30 to '40 were the great periods.

Kilkenny were a great team and I liked playing against them, liked hurling against them. Of course Tipperary and Cork, there was always great rivalry between us. They were teams I enjoyed playing against.

The Wexford team of the 1950s were a big, strong team, good hurlers and good ground hurlers but they did a lot of handling of the ball, I don't know if it would be allowed in our time. You might let him handle one but you would hardly let him handle it a second time.

The Tipperary team of the 1960s were a handy team and I suppose they got the value out of them with what they did win. They kept them together well and they were a good team.

The ideal hurling forward wouldn't want to be too small but he wouldn't want to be too big either. I suppose around 5'8' or 5'9' is the right height. It isn't easy shift a fellow that height.

I played in a couple of football matches, in fact we were in a Munster semi-final I think in 1945 against Kerry, but we had a lot of strange fellows at that time, the army were around and we had fellows from Kerry with us, we had a nice team. I enjoyed football too. Mick O'Connell is about the best player that's around at the moment, a wonderful player. I think Paddy Kennedy was my man, that was in the old Kerry team, he was a great midfield man. And Bill Delaney of Leix, and Tommy Murphy of Leix was a master footballer.

There is more publicity now, but I am not sure if it has affected [Mick] O'Connell's game, maybe it has. There is a share of publicity. But still in our time there was a lot of publicity too. There was good writers at that time, Green Flag and all those fellows, there was a certain amount of publicity. I didn't mind critical publicity, I had to take it as it came, it never bothered me.

Hurling is a very skilful game, if you take the injuries, especially in county games, there are very few. A fellow might get a cut finger or a thing, but it's terrible skilful. I mean two fellows standing under a ball there and if people are playing the game properly there will be nobody ever injured.

I was always strong and I knew I was strong from hitting against older fellows, I felt I could take that sort of thing, but you weren't bould enough, you were staying in the background, you were in dread to come out and do it. It was as the years went on that I was sorry that I didn't do this or do that. If you were to go back a second time, you would always play it different really and you would do different things, but you won't ever get a second chance.

I don't know what made people call me great. I loved hurling which was only natural because my father was hurling and my grandfather. I liked hurling really, I found it very easy, it came very easy to me.

There is one goal that I scored in Thurles against Cork in the Munster final [1944 replay] but it wasn't given. The whistle was blown. It cost us that match and possibly an All-Ireland because Cork went on and won that All-Ireland, one of the four that they won. That's one I won't forget really.

We got a trip to the States in 1936 and they still say we were the best team that ever went into America. They still say that in New York; it was very enjoyable really.

It is unlikely that Limerick will ever see another like Mick Mackey. In his time, he was not only a hurling hero but a national celebrity, with few rivals. There isn't a powerful running player with a similar style in the modern game and it remains a great pity that video footage of Mackey in his prime is so rare. One thing that can never be denied though is that he was Limerick's – and arguably Ireland's – greatest ever hurler.

☙

TWELVE

MODERN HEROES

V*era Mulcahy is a daughter to John Mackey. She was widely recognised as one of the best camogie players of her generation and served Limerick well from the mid-1970s to the mid-1980s. She first came to prominence as a fifteen-year-old in September 1973 when the Limerick senior hurling team returned to Castleconnell with the McCarthy Cup. Dressed in the green and white of her beloved Limerick, she presented some Waterford glass to the victorious team on behalf of the Ahane GAA and camogie clubs. As a player she was part of the Limerick team that won the All-Ireland junior camogie title at Croke Park in*

A Limerick camogie panel from the early 1980s. *Back row (l–r):* Helen Clifford (Bruff), Martina O'Donoghue (Croagh/Kilfinny), Helen Sheehy (Croagh/Kilfinny), Joan O'Brien (Ballyagran), Geraldine O'Brien (Ballyagran), Betty Conway (Ahane), Vera Mackey (Ahane), Bernadette O'Brien (Ballyagran), Bridget Darcy (Ahane). *Front row (l–r):* Helen Mulcair (Croagh/Kilfinny), Pauline McCarthy (Ballyagran), Ann O'Sullivan (Ballinvreena), Helen Butler (Ballyagran), Bríd Stokes (Croagh Kilfinny), Elizabeth Moloney (Bruff), Ann Sheehy (Croagh/Kilfinny).

The Limerick camogie panel that were beaten narrowly by a Fiona Rochford-inspired Wexford in the All-Ireland intermediate semi-final played at Ardfinnan in August 2010. The starting Limerick team included John Mackey's three granddaughters, captain Claire Mulcahy, interprovincial star and former Young Player of the Year Niamh Mulcahy, and the youngest sister Judith Mulcahy. The photograph also includes Sarah Carey, daughter of the legendary Ciarán Carey and granddaughter of 1973 All-Ireland medal winner Phil Bennis. Another player, Dymphna O'Brien, is a well-known ladies football All-Star. *Back row (l–r):* Katie Campbell (Na Piarsaigh), Catherine De Bhal (Feenagh/Kilmeedy), Catriona Davis (Killeedy), Orla Curtin (Kinvara), Joanne O'Gorman (Feenagh/Kilmeedy), Janette Garvey (Tournafulla), Eileen O'Brien-Costello (Granagh/Ballingarry), Niamh Mulcahy (Ahane), Sarah Carey (Granagh/Ballingarry & Patrickswell), Judith Mulcahy (Ahane), Sarah Collins (Ballyagran), Aideen McNamara (Na Piarsaigh), Joanne Clifford (Granagh/Ballingarry), Mairéad Ryan (Galbally), Claire Casey (Na Piarsaigh), Caroline Scanlon (Killeedy), Niamh Richardson (Murroe/Boher). *Front row (l–r):* Dymphna O'Brien (Killeedy), Aisling Enright (Bruff), Kerrie Brosnan (Ballyagran), Aoifa Sheehan (Granagh/Ballingarry), Claire Mulcahy (Ahane), Síle Moynihan (Ahane), Vera Sheehan (Granagh/Ballingarry), Deirdre Fitzpatrick (Killeedy), Michelle Casey (Killeedy), Fiona Hickey (Granagh/Ballingarry), Mairéad Fitzgerald (Granagh/Ballingarry), Kristie Carroll (Galbally), Moira Dooley (Ahane).

1977. However, luck was not on her side in 1980 when the Limerick senior camogie team lost to Cork after a replay, again at Croke Park. She has been a loyal servant to camogie as an administrator, referee and selector, not only within Limerick camogie circles but also at Munster and national level.

The Mulcahy sisters, Claire, Niamh and Judith are granddaughters of John Mackey, and daughters of Vera. Niamh is the most decorated of the trio and was voted National Camogie Young Player of the Year in 2007 along with Munster Young Player of the Year. She first came to prominence in June 2001 at Páirc

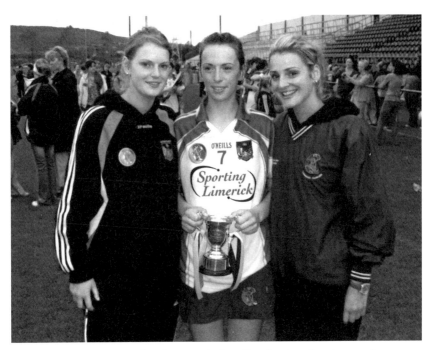

John Mackey's three grandaughters with the All-Ireland Under-18 B trophy won at Mallow, County Cork, in 2009. (*L–r*): Niamh, Judith (captain) and Claire.

Uí Chaoimh on the day that Brian Begley scored two goals for the Limerick senior team against Waterford in the Munster championship. Mulcahy, who was playing in the primary schools game at half time, soloed the length of the field and crashed a superb shot to the back of the net, to rapturous applause from the Limerick faithful. She has also represented the Irish ladies' soccer team at various underage grades and delivered many inspirational performances. For good measure she captained the Mary Immaculate College camogie team in the 2011 Purcell Cup. In addition, she represented both the Ahane hurling and camogie teams at the 2004 Féile na nGael, starring for the hurlers in the final where they beat Shelmaliers of Wexford.

The leadership qualities don't just extend to Niamh, as her older sister Claire captained the Limerick camogie team in 2010 when they narrowly missed out on qualification for the All-Ireland intermediate final. She also captained the Limerick under-18 team to Munster and All-Ireland success in 2004. Not to be left out, the youngest sister, Judith, captained the Limerick under-18 camogie team to the All-Ireland under-18 B title in 2009 after a thrilling late comeback against Waterford. All three sisters were on the panel that won the All-Ireland senior B camogie championship after a replay against Cork in 2007. In the drawn game, Niamh demonstrated her ice-cool temperament by slotting over an 80-yard free in injury time to secure a second bite of the cherry. For good measure, she was presented with the 'player of the match' award in the replay. Their father Ger Mulcahy, a native of Dromin/Athlacca, won two Munster championship medals in 1980 and '81 and was dual underage star with Limerick in the mid-1970s. He also won a National Hurling League medal in 1985.

Johnny Moroney is a grandson of John Mackey and is part of the Young Munster squad that participates in Division 1A of the AIL. He had the unusual distinction of being replaced in the 2010/11 AIL fixture with Shannon at Thomond Park to facilitate the comeback of Paul O'Connell after a lengthy injury. He is a son of Cora Moroney (nee Mackey) who was an outstanding camogie player in her time.

David Doyle is a great-grandson of Mick Mackey, and a grandson to Ruth Doyle (nee Mackey). He plays his club hurling with St Patrick's and was part of the Limerick under-16 squad in 2010. He is highly regarded in Limerick hurling circles as he strives to emulate the achievements of his great-grandfather.

Turlough Herbert is a son of Mick Herbert and had a distinguished career as a hurler. He was part of a star-studded Limerick team that won the Tony Forrestal tournament in 1984 which included stars of the future such as Frankie Carroll, Ciarán Carey and Pat Heffernan. He won both a Harty Cup and All-Ireland Colleges title in 1987 on a team that also included Pat Heffernan and future Clare captain Anthony Daly. He appeared destined for greatness but suffered a horrific knee injury in 1990 which kept him out of the game for two years. Tom Ryan brought him onto the Limerick senior hurling panel from 1994 to '96 when he won two Munster championship medals. He started at wing-back in the 1995 Munster final against Clare and was introduced as a substitute in the 1996 All-Ireland final defeat to Wexford.

Seán Óg Herbert is a son of Seán Herbert, and is widely known in Limerick GAA circles for his work as a full-time coach with Limerick County Board. He played for the Limerick minor hurling team in 1976 when they were beaten by Tipperary in the Munster final. He won a National League medal with Limerick in 1985. Soon after, work commitments took him to Dublin and he represented them against Offaly in the 1987 Leinster senior hurling championship. His brother Kevin is widely known as the man who led Ahane

The Limerick team that lined out in the 1989 Munster Under-21 hurling final. *Back row (l–r):* Anthony Fitzgerald (Claughaun), Michael Hickey (Murroe/Boher), Conor Shiels (Na Piarsaigh), Aidan Fitzgerald (Blackrock), Tom Hennessy (Kilmallock), Paul Foley (Patrickswell), Ciarán Carey (Patrickswell), Richard Walsh (Doon). *Front row (l–r):* Mike Houlihan (Kilmallock), James O'Donovan (Doon), Turlough Herbert (Ahane), Mike Galligan (Claughaun), Kevin Herbert (Ahane), Anthony Kirby (Knockainey), Aidan Collins (Dromcollogher/Broadford)

The Dublin senior hurling team were beaten 1-18 to 1-13 by Offaly in the 1987 Leinster semi-final. *Back row (l–r):* Joe Morris, Paul Pringle, Ger Hogarty, Declan Feeney, John Murphy, John Treacy, John Thompson, John Twomey. *Front row (l–r):* Niall Howard, Paudie O'Neill, Canice Henebry, Brian McMahon, Dessie Byrne, M. J. Ryan, Seán Herbert.

to victory when they ended a 43-year famine by winning the 1998 Limerick senior hurling championship. He also represented Limerick in hurling and along with his first cousin Turlough played on the Limerick under-21 team beaten by Tipperary in the 1989 Munster final. Another brother, Pat, had a distinguished career for Limerick and played in the National League final back in 1974 but wasn't part of the panel that won the Munster championship that year. He won two Munster championship medals in 1980 and '81, and two National League titles in 1984 and '85. Another brother, Kieran, played minor hurling for Limerick in the 1970s, a fifth brother, Fr Tadhg, played Harty Cup and club hurling, and their sister Maeve represented Ahane in camogie. The Herbert family are connected to the Mackey family through the marriage of John Mackey and Helen Herbert (sister of Mick and Seán Herbert).

The Kerry connection comes in the form of Ger Power who captained the Kerry senior footballers to the 1979 All-Ireland football title. He had a distinguished career and won every honour in Gaelic football. His father Jackie, a noted footballer himself, was known to be immensely proud of his son's achievements.

The Clare connection comes in the form of Stephen McNamara (grandson of Jackie Power) and Mark Lennon (Mick Mackey's grandson and son of Audrey Lennon (nee Mackey)). McNamara was part of the Clare team that broke the hoodoo by winning the 1995 All-Ireland senior hurling title. He was involved as a substitute in 1997 and won his second All-Ireland medal on the day that Mark Lennon inspired the Clare minors to victory in the curtain raiser.

Don Givens was a distinguished soccer player for the Republic of Ireland and is the son of Dan Givens who represented Limerick in the Mackey era. Prior to becoming a professional soccer player, he played hurling for his father's native Ahane as a youngster. He also held the position of under-21 manager for Ireland for a number of years.

Kate Herbert is the daughter of Kevin Herbert and in 2010 had the distinction of playing in two major grounds in half-time primary schools camogie games, Páirc Uí Chaoimh and Croke Park. She is destined for a bright future in the game.

Jimmy Ryan is a son of Timmy Ryan 'Good Boy' who lined out for the Tipperary senior hurlers in the 1970s alongside established stars such as Babs Keating, and won a National League title in 1975.

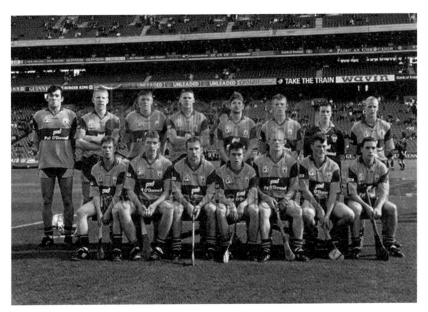

The Clare team, featuring Mark Lennon, that beat Galway in the 1997 All-Ireland minor final. Mark is a grandson of Mick Mackey. *Back row (l–r)*: Stiofán Fitzpatrick, Kenneth Kennedy, Mark Lennon, John Reddan, Gordon Malone, Donal Madden, Ger O'Connell, Gearóid Considine. *Front row (l–r)*: Brian 'Beano' McMahon, Danny Duggan, Paddy Moroney, Brian McMahon, Colm Mullen, Conor Earlie, Wayne Kennedy.

Richard McCarthy represented the Limerick minor hurling team that played in the 2005 All-Ireland minor hurling final. He won an All-Ireland junior club hurling medal with Blackrock in 2010 and is part of the Limerick senior hurling panel. Richard's grand uncle, Tom McCarthy, represented Limerick in the 1930s.

John Stokes is a son of Neddy Stokes and a nephew of Dr Dick Stokes. He was dual player for Limerick at both underage and adult level and is widely recognised as an innovative hurling coach and the driving force behind a nursery at Thurles CBS that has led to a revival of hurling in the town.

Niall, Peter, Keith and Marcus Cregan from Croom have represented their county at underage level and have given sterling service to hurling in Croom over the past decade. Peter Cregan was part of the Limerick senior hurling panel in recent years and is considered unlucky not to have had a greater involvement. They are relatives of the Cregans who represented Limerick in the 1940s.

Tommy Clohessy, a son of Paddy Clohessy, represented the Limerick senior team in the defeat to Clare in the 1967 Munster championship.

Famous Limerick hurler Éamonn Cregan and his brother Mickey Cregan, who trained the 1973 All-Ireland-winning team, are sons of Ned Cregan, who played for Limerick in the golden era of the 1930s.

THE HOMILY AT THE FUNERAL MASS OF MICK MACKEY, BY REV. FR LIAM KELLY

Mick has come home to his native and beloved Castleconnell to find his resting place. He was always a Castleconnell man and proud of his long association with the Ahane club.

When we were youngsters over the road in Monaleen, Mick was our idol. We had that sense of reverence and awe for the name Mackey. A legend in our time, W. B. Yeats has it, 'The names that stopped our childhood play'. We had hurleys in our hands before we could walk, and our sole ambition was to emulate the feats of Mick and his men. Then the thrill of pulling on the green and gold jersey of Ahane for the first time. Then meeting the great man himself, to come under his direction and coaching, his inspirational talks before a game and at half time. Something reminiscent of the war-cry, 'Cuimhnigh ar Luimneach'. I remember Mick being full of admiration for a rising star and his ultimate accolade, 'He'd put his head where another wouldn't put his hurley.'

If as scripture says 'we are all here on earth to help others', Mick surely deserves a high place in Heaven. His influence was felt throughout the length and breadth of Ireland and beyond. The turnout last night at the removal and today was evidence of his popularity and the impact he made on the social life of the people. He meant an awful lot to a lot of people. There are so many anecdotes and stories told about Mick – people were swapping them until the late hours last night, most of the time some maybe a bit exaggerated or even apocryphal.

What was it that Mick had? Something we all know in our hearts but difficult to articulate. His dynamism, the sheer force of his personality, his leadership, courage, spirit of abandonment. All these and something more. Someone described it last night as 'the old Dúchas'. Something that is at the heart of our nation and at the heart of our faith. Mick cherished the things that we all hold dear – his faith, his county and his national pastimes.

256

His team-mates and his varying opponents can tell you that even in the heat of battle, in the midst of all the turmoil there was always a twinge of humour. He loved the bit of fun. He always gave of his best and led by example. He liked to win but it wasn't everything. He didn't mind whether he lost or was held scoreless.

One important aspect of Mick's career which can be easily overlooked today was the impact he and his team had on the social life of the people in depressed times, and not just locally but countrywide. Everywhere people spoke of his exploits, relived the great moments and looked forward eagerly to the next big occasion. Mick was very conscious of this, he loved the supporters and often played to them, giving them a tremendous lift, benefiting them in a deeply spiritual way. It gave the people not only enjoyment but hope and encouragement, and helped them to rise above their anxieties and problems.

Off the field he was a quiet, gentle man, bringing to his house the same noble qualities he exhibited on the playing fields of Ireland. He was a great family man and loved young people, especially small children. Those who knew him in the army and his workmates in the ESB, privileged to have known him personally, can all testify to his kindness, consideration and generosity. After his retirement Mick devoted many years to administration and coaching. He loved the gatherings of old hurlers and valued their friendships, where one could always sense that special atmosphere which makes hurlers a breed apart – fraternity. A man who shared so much with so many. Apart from his passion for the game he was a man of simple tastes – a game of 45 and an odd half pint.

As the nation mourns one of its greatest sons we pray for Kitty and his family who will miss him most. There is a legitimate place for grief when we mourn our dead. Jesus wept when He was told that His friend Lazarus was dead. St Paul in our second reading says, 'we must not grieve like those who have no life'. Our faith in the resurrection of Jesus Christ must sustain us. In our Mass today Mick's death is united with the death of Our Saviour and by sharing in His death he also shares in His resurrection. This is the sure hope our faith holds out for us. This was the faith and hope expressed by men like Mick Mackey which sustained the people of his time. Mick always had close links with the church and was proud of the fact that he travelled all over the country playing in tournament games for the local churches. Many will recall some of the great games organised for the Retreat House. He said to me once, 'I suppose we should have a fair chance of getting into Heaven after playing all those matches. We never turned down any request.'

Mick has played the game of life and attained his glory. Now he makes a new beginning, he enters the new and even more glorious half where the Lord has selected a special position for him to occupy in his eternal home. ('*If we die with him we will live with him; if we endure with him, we will live with him*' – St Paul.)

We recall the words of the journalist Grantland Rice: '*And when the last great scorer comes to mark against your name, He'll ask not whether you won or lost, but how you played the game.*'

In times of change Mick is saying something to us all. Are we going to continue pursuing a comfortable and easy life? When we are in doubt do we just do nothing? Do we ask what everyone else is doing before committing ourselves? The dedication and self-sacrifice of Mick Mackey and his men is now folklore and can still serve as an inspiration to us all. He is saying especially to our young people: If you are inclined to settle for a colourless, selfish consumerism, remember Mick. He tells us what human beings are made for, what they are capable of. Mick and his men showed us that there is glory in life, the glory of God is man fully alive and fully responsive to God's power working in and through Him. These men nourished and inspired so many thousands of people not only in their own day but down through the years. It is fitting that today we should recognise the glory in life that was Mick Mackey and thank God for it.

Ta Dia buíoc dó. Go ndéanaid Dia trócaire ar a anam dhílis.

BIBLIOGRAPHY

ᨄ

Newspapers*:*

Irish Independent
Irish Examiner (previously *The Examiner, Cork Examiner*)
The Irish Press
Limerick Leader
Nenagh Guardian

Books:

Cronin, Mike, Duncan, Mark and Rouse, Paul, *The GAA: A People's History* (Cork, 2009)

Dorgan, Val, *Christy Ring* (Dublin, 1980)

Fullam, Brendan, *Captains of the Ash* (Dublin, 2002)

Fullam, Brendan, *Lest We Forget* (Cork, 2009)

Horgan, Tim, *Christy Ring: Hurling's Greatest* (Cork, 2007)

Horgan, Tim, *Cork's Hurling Story* (Cork, 2010)

Keane, Colm, *Hurling's Top 20* (Edinburgh, 2003)

Limerick GAA Yearbook (various years)

Martin, Henry, *Unlimited Heartbreak: The Inside Story of Limerick Hurling* (Cork, 2009)

Martin, Henry and Lundon, James A., *From the Great Depression to NAMA: Limerick Senior Intercounty Hurling Championship Records (1929–2009)* (Limerick, 2009)

Murphy, Seán, *The Life and Times of Jackie Power* (Limerick, 1996)

Murphy, Seán, *Come on Ahane, the Spuds are Boiling* (Limerick, 2002)

Murphy, Seán and Ó Ceallaigh, Séamus, *The Mackey Story* (Limerick, 1982)

Ó Ceallaigh, Séamus, *History of Limerick GAA from Earliest Times to the Present Day. Part 1: 1884–1908* (Limerick, 1937)

Ó Ceallaigh, Séamus and Murphy, Seán, *A History of Limerick GAA: 100 Years of Glory, 1884–1984* (Limerick, 1987)

Power, Conor, *My Father: A Hurling Revolutionary* (Waterford, 2009)

Smith, David, *The Unconquerable Keane* (Dublin, 2010)

Audiovisual Material:

All-Ireland Hurling Final 1940, Irish Film Institute
Mick Mackey interviewed by Val Dorgan, RTÉ Television, 1969
'A Celebration of Munster Hurling', RTÉ Television, presented by Paddy
    Downey and Niall Tobin, 1976
Mick Mackey interviewed by Liam Campbell, RTÉ Radio, 1967

Picture Credits:

Seamus Walsh: pages xiv, xv, 240.
Greg Mackey: pages xvi, 3, 7, 8, 47, 77, 90, 100, 175, 218, 220, 225, 233,
    234.
Ahane GAA Club: pages 13, 16, 99, 207, 229, 241, 244.
Irish Examiner: pages 18, 31, 53, 59, 87, 89.
Gerry Piggott: pages 20, 21, 57.
Cora Moroney nee Mackey: page 22.
James Lundon: page 27.
Jim Ryan: pages 28, 58.
Johnny Wall: page 29.
Patsy Coffey: pages 38, 42, 147.
Christy Murphy: page 41.
Catherine Doyle: pages 65, 217.
Andy Fleming: page 70.
John Mulcahy: pages 93, 96.
Dermot Kelly: pages 135, 169, 239
Arthur Graham: pages 136, 223, 243.
Fr Liam Ryan: pages 155, 160.
P. J. Keane: pages 165, 183, 194.
Limerick Yearbook 1982: page 167.
Justin Nelson: page 178.
John Reale: page 197.
Harry Greensmyth: page 248.
Limerick Camogie Board: page 249.
Vera Mulcahy nee Mackey: page 250.
Kevin Herbert: page 251.
John Power: page 252.
Sportsfile: page 253.

INDEX

ca

Page numbers in *italics* refer to pages with photographs